Contents

PERFORMERS AT A TRIBAL
DANCE FESTIVAL, P9

Welcome to PNG & Solomon Islands

True adventure awaits in this enigmatic corner of Melanesia. Smouldering volcanoes, forest-cloaked mountains and coral-ringed islands set the stage for one of the world's most flamboyant cultures.

A Land Apart

Are you up for an adventure? Here in PNG you can trek through steaming jungles and ford rushing rivers with expert guides. Your goal may be a remote village, a magnificently plumed bird of paradise or a kangaroo that has elected the life arboreal. Why not test your mettle on a multiday trek following the steps of Australian diggers along the Kokoda Track, or summit a 4000m-plus Highland peak for a panoramic, coast-to-coast vista.

Aquatic Adventures

The Solomon Islands and PNG are both world-famous diving destinations, with excellent conditions most months of the year. The biodiversity beneath is astounding, with a colourful array of hard and soft corals and teeming fish life, along with a jaw-dropping collection of WWII plane and ship wrecks. Live-aboard boats and first-rate dive resorts provide access to sites far from the hordes. The waves are equally uncrowded for surf lovers, with fantastic reef, point and beach breaks scattered around the region's northern shores. There's also fantastic fishing in these pristine waters, with yellowfin tuna, mackerel, sailfish and the legendary Papuan black bass in abundance.

Cultural Wonderland

Home to more than 800 distinct languages, PNG and the Solomons provide incomparable opportunities to be immersed in a variety of fascinating traditional cultures. It's well worth planning your trip around one or two of the major annual festivals: see colourfully painted and feathered Highland warriors, fearless snake-wielding fire dancers and brilliantly attired island oarsmen chanting to the backdrop of pounding drums. Festivals aside, there are myriad paradigm-altering experiences to be had: an impromptu *singsing* (celebratory dance or festival) on the Trobriand Islands, learning about the legends of an eerie skull cave or sharing fruit with new-found friends on a bumpy PMV ride.

Island Idyll

Travel is rarely easy in Melanesia, but rewards are bountiful. After a few weeks of hard travel, find your way to a palm-fringed, sun-drenched coast and unwind. Opt for a luxury ecofriendly resort with activities or a rustic village guesthouse footsteps from the sea. Spend your days snorkelling coral reefs, combing sandy beaches, paddling placid rivers or lounging beneath a palm tree. By night, watch the sunset, feast on fresh seafood and watch the sky slowly fill with stars.

Why I Love PNG & Solomon Islands

By Lindsay Brown, Writer

Papua New Guinea is blessed with an astounding mix of traditional cultures and natural splendour, making it a personal favourite. From the Highlands to the islands there's a myriad of cultural riches, best witnessed during spectacular festivals where body decoration simply defies the imagination. Bunking down in a sleepy beachside village is the perfect antidote to modern city-living ailments, and something I highly recommend to independent travellers. Adventurers will find coral gardens the equal of anywhere else, while jungle trails provide the opportunity to see weird and wonderful wildlife: tree kangaroos, cuscuses and scene-stealing birds of paradise.

For more about our writers, see p260

Above: A Southern Highlands Huli wigman (p122)

PNG & Solomon Islands

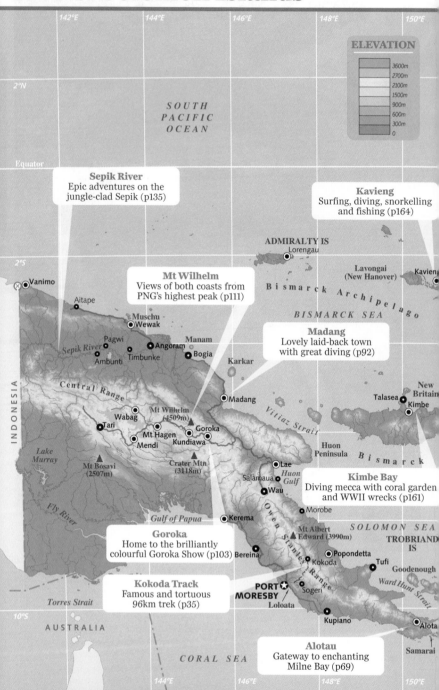

ELEVATION

3600m
2700m
2100m
1500m
900m
600m
300m
0

SOUTH PACIFIC OCEAN

Sepik River
Epic adventures on the jungle-clad Sepik (p135)

Kavieng
Surfing, diving, snorkelling and fishing (p164)

ADMIRALTY IS
Lorengau

Lavongai (New Hanover)
Kavieng

Mt Wilhelm
Views of both coasts from PNG's highest peak (p111)

Bismarck Archipelago

BISMARCK SEA

Vanimo

Aitape

Muschu
Wewak

Manam

Pagwi
Angoram
Bogia
Karkar

Sepik River
Timbunke
Ambunti

Madang
Lovely laid-back town with great diving (p92)

INDONESIA

Central Range

Madang

New Britain
Talasea
Kimbe

Vitiaz Strait

Wabag
Mt Wilhelm (4509m)
Goroka

Tari
Mt Hagen
Kundiawa

Mendi

Lake Murray

Mt Bosavi (2507m)

Crater Mtn (3118m)

Huon Peninsula

Bismarck

Lae
Salamaua
Huon Gulf
Wau

Kimbe Bay
Diving mecca with coral garden and WWII wrecks (p161)

Fly River

Gulf of Papua

Kerema

Morobe

Owen Stanley Range

Mt Albert Edward (3990m)

SOLOMON SEA

TROBRIAND IS

Goroka
Home to the brilliantly colourful Goroka Show (p103)

Bereina

Kokoda
Popondetta
Tufi

Goodenough

Kokoda Track
Famous and tortuous 96km trek (p35)

Torres Strait

PORT MORESBY
Sogeri
Loloata

Ward Hunt Strait

AUSTRALIA

Kupiano

Alota

CORAL SEA

Samarai

Alotau
Gateway to enchanting Milne Bay (p69)

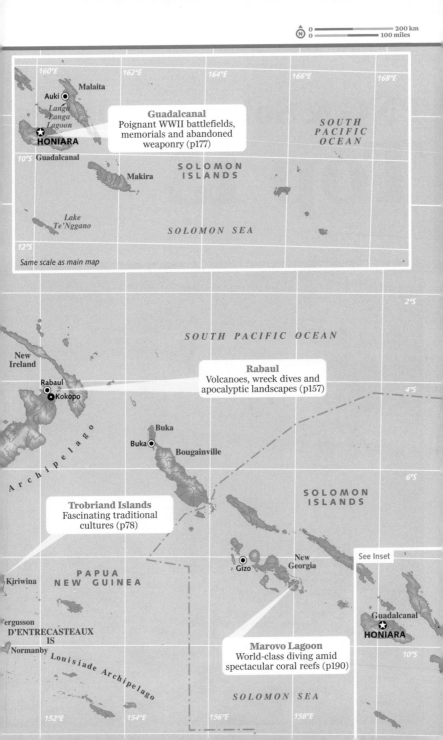

0   200 km
0   100 miles

160°E   162°E   164°E   166°E   168°E

Malaita
Auki ⊙
Langa
Langa
Lagoon
HONIARA

Guadalcanal
Poignant WWII battlefields,
memorials and abandoned
weaponry (p177)

SOUTH
PACIFIC
OCEAN

10°S Guadalcanal   SOLOMON
                         ISLANDS
              Makira

Lake
Te'Nggano

SOLOMON SEA

12°S
Same scale as main map

2°S

SOUTH PACIFIC OCEAN

New
Ireland
Rabaul ⊙
⊙ Kokopo

Rabaul
Volcanoes, wreck dives and
apocalyptic landscapes (p157)

4°S

Buka
Buka ⊙   Bougainville

Archipelago

SOLOMON
ISLANDS

6°S

Trobriand Islands
Fascinating traditional
cultures (p78)

Kiriwina

PAPUA
NEW GUINEA

New
Gizo ⊙   Georgia

See Inset

Guadalcanal
⭑
HONIARA

ergusson
D'ENTRECASTEAUX
IS
Normanby   Louisiade Archipelago

Marovo Lagoon
World-class diving amid
spectacular coral reefs (p190)

10°S

SOLOMON SEA

152°E   154°E   156°E   158°E

PNG & Solomon Islands'
Top 15

Diving & Snorkelling

1 PNG and the Solomons rank among the best of destinations to don a mask and fins, with an irresistible menu of underwater treasures: luminous coral reefs festooned with huge sea fans; warm waters teeming with rainbow-coloured fish; canyons and drop-offs that tumble into the abyss; and a host of eerie WWII wrecks – not to mention the thrill of diving uncrowded sites. A handful of idyllic dive resorts such as Kimbe Bay (p161) provide the perfect gateway to your undersea adventure. To reach even more remote and pristine environments, sign on to a live-aboard vessel. A snorkeller in Kimbe Bay

Fabulous Festivals

2 Rio's Carnaval has nothing on the magnificent pageantry of a Highland festival. PNG's biggest fests, such as the Mt Hagen (p114) and Goroka Shows (p107), are pure sensory overload, with massive feather headdresses, rustling grass skirts and evocative face and body paint adorning enormous numbers of participants – more than 100 different tribal groups – from all across the Highlands and further afield. *Singsing* (celebratory dance or festival) groups perform traditional songs and dances in this pride-filled extravaganza. The thrill of coming face to face with such uplifting traditional cultures is indescribable – and well worth planning a trip around. A tribal man at the Goroka Show

FRANCO BANFI/GETTY IMAGES ©

RICHARD KENDALL/GETTY IMAGES ©

Milne Bay

3 At the eastern edge of the mainland, Milne Bay (p68) is a landscape of remarkable beauty. You'll find scattered islands, coral reefs, lovely palm-fringed beaches, hidden waterfalls, meandering rivers and steep-sided, rainforest-covered mountains plunging to the sea. The opportunity for adventure is staggering, with great birdwatching, bushwalking and island-hopping. Alotau is the gateway, and host of the colourful Canoe Festival, with gyrating *singsing* groups, string bands and longboats racing across the waterfront.

Marovo Lagoon (SI)

4 A visual feast awaits you at Marovo Lagoon (p190). A profusion of dive sites at South and North Marovo offer excellent fish action, suitable for all levels of proficiency. The reefs are blanketed with sea fans and act as a magnet for marine species, from tiny critters to marauding pelagics, including manta rays and sharks. The lagoon is dotted with hundreds of small idyllic islands, while beneath the surface there's a vibrant assemblage of dramatic walls, exhilarating passages and uncomplicated reef dives.

Sepik River

5 Besieged on all sides by thick jungle and shrouded in mist, the mighty Sepik (p135) wanders across northwestern PNG like a lazy brown snake full of food. The river is the region's lifeblood, home to a string of villages rich in artistic tradition, and the cultural treasure chest of the Pacific. Here you can hire a crocodile-headed canoe and thread the seasonal waterways from one village to the next, sleeping in stilt homes and exploring the towering *haus tambarans* (spirit houses).
Children canoeing on the Sepik River

Highland Highs

6 The craggy ridges of the Bismarck Range culminate with the wind-scoured peak of Mt Wilhelm (p111), the tallest mountain in Oceania. A predawn start has trekkers clambering up its rocky slopes to see the mainland's north and south coasts before the clouds roll in. Other popular trekking peaks include Mt Gulwe and Mt Hagen. In the vicinity of the latter and in the jungles near Tari the goal is to spot as many species as possible of the magnificent birds of paradise – the most emblematic of PNG's fascinating wildlife. Bird of paradise

Tribal Art

7 Treasure hunters will be spoilt for choice with woodcarvings, bark paintings, masks and other tribal art from across PNG. One of the best areas for crafts is the Middle Sepik (p141), where master carvers carry on age-old traditions creating shields, masks, figures, canoe prows and story boards. Artistic traditions also flourish in the Trobriands, such as carved ebony walking sticks, bowls and sculptures inlaid with mother of pearl.

Mask from the Middle Sepik

Kokoda Track

8 It's muddy and gruelling, with maddeningly steep uphill scrambles followed by slippery, bone-jarring descents. Treacherous river crossings ensure feet don't stay dry for long, while the humidity wreaks havoc on even the best-prepared trekkers. Why walk the 96km Kokoda Track (p35)? To follow in the footsteps of giants, recalling those who fought and died on this hellish, mountainous stretch. As you pass through remote villages and pause beside evocative war memorials you'll find the rewards far outweigh the physical challenges.

TRAVELGAME/GETTY IMAGES ©

KEITH-J-SMITH/ALAMY STOCK PHOTO ©

Mataniko & Tenaru Falls (SI)

9 Magnificent scenery lies within a half-day's travel of Honiara, including Mataniko Falls and Tenaru Waterfalls (p188) – both with lovely natural pools perfect for a refreshing dip. A guide is required for both. If you're fit, opt for the two-hour hike to Mataniko Falls, which are in fact little cascades that tumble into a small canyon. The stunning Tenaru Waterfalls – an easy four-hour walk (return) – rewards visitors with a dreamy tropical ambience and the offer of a refreshing swim in its snug natural pool. Tenaru Waterfalls

Melanesian Markets (SI)

10 Honiara's expansive Central Market (p177) is a wonderful and largely hassle-free place to experience a typical Melanesian city market. Fruit and vegetable stalls are watched over by colourfully clad women and surrounded by the pungent odours of the fish section at the back. Gizo boasts another intriguing market on the waterfront. Villagers from neighbouring islands arrive each morning by boat to occupy stands under the shade of tall trees. Soak up the atmosphere, feast on sweet bananas, chat with the locals and quench your thirst with coconut water.

Rabaul

11 One of the prettiest towns in the South Pacific was devastated by Mt Tavurvur, which erupted in 1994 and buried much of Rabaul (p157) under volcanic ash. Today you can wander the abandoned, post-apocalyptic streets of this once-thriving community, and take in adventures further afield. You can visit Matupit Island, with its village of megapode egghunters, go diving in wreck-strewn Simpson Harbour and peer back in time at eerie WWII bunkers hidden in the hillsides. There are great views to be had, particularly from atop the volcanoes that loom over the town.

Idyllic Island Getaways

12 There are some places where you arrive, put down your pack and think: this is it! This is why I travel. White-sand beaches, swaying palms, the day's freshly caught seafood served by moonlight. Offshore from New Ireland's Kavieng (p164), a handful of thatch-roof guesthouses scattered on tiny islands near Lavongai provide the type of getaway that would make Robinson Crusoe proud. Days are spent snorkelling coral reefs, surfing virgin waves, visiting welcoming villages and soaking up the pristine island ambience.

Trobriand Islands

13 Anthropologists have long been fascinated with the Trobriand Islands (p78). You'll find a remarkably intact Polynesian culture, with unique traditions – based on a strict matrilineal society – and a distinct cosmology. It's well known for its colourfully painted yam houses, wild harvest festival and celebratory cricket matches (complete with singing and dancing). Visitors here are still a rarity, and have a fantastic opportunity to stay in local villages, visit skull caves and coral megaliths, and take in the pretty island scenery.

Watching a woodcarver at work, Trobriand Islands

WWII Relics (SI)

14 The Solomon Islands has everything in spades. WWII relics scattered in the jungle will captivate history buffs. Outside Honiara (p188), you can visit poignant battlefields and memorials, as well as abandoned amtracks, a Sherman tank, Japanese field guns and the remains of several US aircraft. West New Georgia also has a fantastic collection of WWII relics, including a sunken Japanese freighter, several large Japanese anti-aircraft guns and numerous museums featuring WWII debris and memorabilia.
WWII relic, Betikama SDA Mission (p188)

Madang

15 One of the most attractive towns in PNG, Madang (p92) straddles a small peninsula surrounded by a deep-water harbour littered with WWII wreckage. It's one of the more tourist-oriented towns, but the vibe is positively low-key. Huge, bat-filled casuarina trees tower over streets, the market buzzes with good-natured laughter and a smattering of offshore islands boast sandy stretches for your beach towel. Relaxing waterfront guesthouses provide a fine tropical ambience, and there is excellent diving and snorkelling just outside of town.

Need to Know

For more information, see Survival Guide (p229)

Currency
Papua New Guinea
kina (K)

Language
Tok Pisin (English
creole), English, Hiri
Motu and 800-plus
other languages

Visas
Nationals of most Western countries can obtain
a free 60-day tourist
visa on arrival. Visas can
also be obtained in
advance at PNG diplomatic missions.

Money
There are ATMs in large
towns. Credit cards are
accepted at midrange
and top-end lodging,
restaurants and shops.

Mobile Phones
Local SIM cards can
be used in Australian
and European phones.
Digicel has the most
extensive network.

Time
Papua New Guinea Time
(PGT) is GMT/UTC plus
10 hours. Autonomous
Region of Bougainville is
GMT/UTC plus 11 hours.

When to Go

Tropical climate, wet & dry seasons

Tropical climate, rain year round

Rabaul
GO May–Nov

Madang
GO Jun–Sep

Goroka
GO May–Nov

Port Moresby
GO Mar–Nov

Alotau
GO Nov–Jan

High Season
(May–Oct)

➡ Slightly busier
season, with larger
crowds at big-name
festivals and higher
accommodation
prices.

➡ Generally cooler,
drier weather, but
rainier in Milne Bay.

➡ Best time to hike
the Kokoda Track.

Shoulder
(Apr & Nov)

➡ Generally
hot and humid,
with increasingly
unpredictable rain
patterns.

➡ Surfing season
starts in November.

Low Season
(Dec–Mar)

➡ The wet season
for much of PNG.

➡ Mild weather, less
rain in Milne Bay.

➡ Heavy rains,
washed-out roads in
the Highlands.

➡ Best surfing on
the north coast and
islands.

Useful Websites

Lonely Planet (www.lonely planet.com/papua-new-guinea) Destination information, travel forum and photos.

PNG Tourism Promotion Authority (www.papuanew guinea.travel) Official website of PNG's peak tourism body. Has good links.

The Garamut (garamut. wordpress.com) Blog covering current events in PNG.

National (www.thenational. com.pg) PNG's main newspaper.

PNG Business Directory (www. pngbd.com) Business and tourism website.

Important Numbers

PNG has different police emergency numbers for each city.

Papua New Guinea country code	☏675
International access code	☏05
Directory assistance (local)	☏013
Directory assistance (international)	☏0178
Ambulance	☏111

Exchange Rates

Australia	A$1	K2.35
Canada	C$1	K2.36
Euro	€1	K3.50
Japan	¥100	K2.74
NZ	NZ$1	K2.12
Solomon Islands	S$1	K0.38
UK	UK£	K4.41
USA	US$1	K3.07

For current exchange rates see www.xe.com.

Daily Costs

Budget: Less than K400

➡ Stay in a village guesthouse: K50–150

➡ Meal from a *kai* (fast-food) bar: K5–10

➡ PMV trip between towns: K10–50

Midrange: K400–800

➡ Double room in a midrange hotel: K300–450

➡ Lunch and dinner in hotel restaurants: K50–100

➡ Flying between regions: K300–600

➡ Hire a local guide for a day: K40–60

Top End: More than K800

➡ Lodging in a resort: from K500

➡ Fine dining: K100–150

➡ Eight-day Kokoda Track adventure: from A$3000

Opening Hours

Opening and closing times can be erratic, but you can rely on most businesses closing at noon on Saturday and remaining closed all day Sunday.

Banks 8.45am–3pm Monday to Thursday, 8.45am–4pm Friday

Government offices 7.45am–12.30pm and 1.45–4pm Monday to Friday

Post offices 8am–4pm Monday to Friday, 8am–11.30am Saturday

Restaurants 11.30am–2.30pm and 6pm or 7pm–10pm, or whenever the last diner leaves

Shops 9am–5pm or 6pm Monday to Friday, 9am–noon Saturday

Arriving in PNG

Port Moresby's Jackson International Airport (p239) There's free transport from most midrange and top-end lodging by advance notice; make a free call from the tourism office at International Arrivals if your hotel van doesn't show up. Taxis (some have meters, but most don't, so negotiate) cost around K30 to Waigani or Boroko; and K40 to Town.

Getting Around

Air Travel between regions is mostly by flight (often via Port Moresby).

Car Very few roads and expensive rental rates means self-driving is not a very useful option.

Taxi Available in the major towns; may or may not have working meters.

PMV Public motor vehicles generally run (when full) wherever there are roads. PMV is the generic term for minibuses and dilapidated pick-ups. Even small boats plying the coast can be PMVs.

Boat Banana boats are ubiquitous; there are also inter-island transfer and trade boats and large passenger ferries.

For much more on **getting around PNG**, see p241

If You Like...

Festivals & Celebrations

Pounding drums, magnificently masked and painted warriors and mesmerising dances constitute the traditional *singsings* (celebratory dances or festivals); and the colour and hype is further amplified during PNG'ss large regional festivals.

Milne Bay Kundu & Canoe Festival Giant, brightly painted ocean-going canoes, costumed dancers and traditional song transform sleepy Alotau into a riotously colourful stage. (p70)

Goroka Show One of PNG's biggest festivals and an alluring mash of feathered headdresses, face paint and *kundu* drums. (p107)

Crocodile Festival An up-and-coming fest in the tiny settlement of Ambunti on the Sepik. (p140)

Warwagira & Mask Festival New Britain's big bash features string bands, forest spirits and the surreal Baining fire dancers. (p152)

Kalam Cultural Festival Get an up-close look at important customs, including initiation rites, at this little-touristed traditional celebration. (p101)

Wildlife Watching

Spotting magnificent birds of paradise in misty mountain forests and snorkelling with graceful manta rays through crystal-clear seas – it's all part of the great Melanesian wildlife-watching experience.

Tari Basin This world-famous birding site has a staggering array of feathered beauties, including the celebrated birds of paradise. (p122)

Tetepare Island Pygmy parrots, leatherback turtles, dugongs and crocs: one of the best places to see wildlife in the Solomons. (p194)

Kumul Lodge A lodge with a singular purpose – to put you in touch with PNG's magnificent birdlife. (p116)

Loloata Island Resort A top place to see well-camouflaged rock wallabies just outside of Port Moresby. (p60)

Normanby Island Head to this island in Milne Bay for a chance to see the remarkable Goldie's bird of paradise. (p76)

Dramatic Scenery

With rainforest-covered mountains, misty waterfalls, lush river valleys and sparkling cobalt coastlines, PNG and the Solomons have countless places to stop and savour the scenery.

Highlands (Okuk) Hwy Weave through a stunning backdrop of towering mountains and verdant valleys from Goroka to Tari. (p103)

Lake Kutubu A beautiful highland lake amid countryside of peaceful traditional settlements. (p120)

Rabaul The active volcano-strewn terrain of Rabaul makes a fantastic setting for a walk on the wild side. (p157)

Tufi Steep, fjord-like *rias* showcase welcoming villages set between topaz waters and the vast untouched interior. (p67)

Marovo Lagoon In a word: jaw-dropping. Hundreds of lovely islands covered with palm trees and ringed by coral. (p190)

Kolombangara A volcanic island well worth exploring for its Jurassic Park–like scenery. (p200)

Walks & Treks

For an unforgettable taste of PNG, grab your kit, lace up your boots and head into the bush. You'll pass through remote villages, spy wildlife and perhaps see hulking WWII relics slowly being reclaimed by the jungle.

Kokoda Track PNG's most famous overland adventure is 96km of ups and downs, traversing rushing rivers and walking slippery narrow ridges while retracing the diggers' footsteps. (p35)

Mt Wilhelm The three- to four-day climb is hard going, but the rewards are great: views of both coasts from the 4509m summit. (p112)

Mt Gulwe PNG's second-highest peak and a volcanic-peak-bagger's goal. (p117)

North Coast If you want to get well off the beaten path, hire a guide in Alotau and walk your way between villages on Milne Bay's scenic north coast. (p74)

Epic Journeys

Often it's the journey that is more memorable than the destination, whether you're mingling with locals in timeless villages on the Sepik or discovering unimaginable beauty on an island-hopping adventure off the PNG coast.

Sepik River Take a journey along one of the world's mighty waterways to discover fascinating cultures. (p135)

D'Entrecasteaux Islands Load up on provisions, hire a boatman and head out for a village-hopping adventure around Milne Bay. (p76)

Boluminski Highway Cycle the 263km journey from Kavieng down New Ireland's east coast, overnighting in beachfront guesthouses. (p170)

Vanimo to Wewak Leave the aeroplane behind and hop on a boat and/or a rugged 4WD between Vanimo and Wewak. (p133)

Top: Woman with feather headdress at the Goroka Show (p107)
Bottom: Mt Tavurvur volcano, near Rabaul (p157), East New Britain Province

Village Life

One of the great ways to see PNG is to stay in a village, share meals with villagers and sleep in traditional dwellings. By day, be led to the sights by local guides.

Abelam Villages Maprik, near the Sepik River, has striking *haus tambarans*. Apangai has three of these carved wooden beauties. (p132)

Simbai Stay in this Madang Province village to see the Kalam Culture Festival, then head off on a five-day trek to the Ramu River. (p101)

Trobriand Archipelago To experience some of the most traditional cultures of PNG, arrange a village stay on Kiriwina Island. (p78)

Tufi Villages There are many beautifully set villages near Tufi, such as Kofure, with white-sand beaches, swaying palms and local seafood. (p68)

Boluminski Highway Cycle from one postcard seaside village to the next along the picturesque New Ireland coast. (p170)

Surfing

There's great surf in PNG and the Solomons, and you won't have to contend with crowded waves. On the north coast and the islands, the best waves coincide with monsoon season from November to April.

Nusa Island Retreat Run by a knowledgeable surfing expat, this Kavieng gem is a great spot for a surf getaway. Boats take you to the best breaks. (p167)

Boluminski Highway You'll find great breaks all along New Ireland's east coast; you can stay in a sweet village guesthouse at Malom or Dalom or in the surfer-run Rubio Guesthouse. (p171)

Vanimo A tiny outpost across the border from Indonesia with legendary breaks. (p132)

Wewak A pretty town with golden-sand beaches and reputable breaks on the north coast. (p125)

Ulingan Bay Home of the Tupira Surf Club with a great break right at the back door. (p99)

Ghizo Island Great surf, with practically virgin waves (and good diving, too) in the Solomons' Western Province. (p1)

Diving & Snorkelling

The diving and snorkelling in the region is staggering: you'll find a fantastic array of marine life, WWII wrecks, coral gardens and muck diving. Take a banana boat for a day or a live aboard for a week.

Madang Lovely Madang has loads of great dive spots and a top-notch operator to get you there. (p92)

Kimbe Bay World-renowned Kimbe Bay, in West New Britain, also boasts a top diving resort, Walindi Plantation Resort. (p161)

Tawali First-rate diving and live-aboards in Milne Bay's North Coast. (p74)

Rabaul Go wreck-diving in Simpson Harbour, then head to the reefs on the peninsula's western side for coral and coral life. (p157)

Marovo Lagoon World-class diving with coral gardens, caves, drop-offs and astounding marine life. (p190)

Tulagi Wrecks Diving among a series of impressive WWII vessels lying just offshore. (p189)

Island Getaways

With hundreds of islands in these parts, you'll find both resort-style pampering and rustic, Robinson Crusoe–type getaways. Both offer magical settings of palm-fringed beaches, coral reefs and bird-filled rainforests.

Sibonai Guesthouse This peaceful village guesthouse is a great for birdwatching and snorkelling and seeing Normanby Island. (p77)

Lavongai Hop a boat from Kavieng to the islands near Lavongai for empty beaches, good surf and home-cooked seafood. (p168)

Muschu Island Swaying palms, coral gardens, a jungle interior and rustic lodging near Wewak. (p128)

Tetepare Island A rainforest-covered Solomons island with eco-friendly accommodation that makes a great base for wildlife watching. (p194)

Mbabanga Island Another Solomons gem with idyllic beaches and a pretty lagoon that's perfect for snorkelling. (p198)

Samarai Island With decaying remains of the former colonial capital and hospitable villagers. (p75)

Savo A rough diamond that's easily accessed from Honiara with hot springs and dolphin-watching. (p189)

Month by Month

June

The dry season, which runs through to September in most parts, is in full swing, with cooler temperatures and fewer showers. Weather can be less predictable in Milne Bay and Lae.

🏃 Spear Fighting Festival

Held on the remote island of Santa Catalina in the Solomons, this three-day event, known locally as Wogasia, takes place in late May or early June and features men from the island's two tribes squaring off and throwing spears at one another. Keep your distance!

🎭 Whit Monday

This religious fest happens on the eighth Monday after Easter and is celebrated with fervour all over the Solomons. Expect processions with singing and dancing.

July

July is a generally cool and dry time to visit PNG and the Solomons. The cultural calendar picks up, with some of the best festivals and shows.

🎭 Warwagira & Mask Festival

During the first two weeks of July in either Kokopo or Rabaul, this is a combined event showcasing the mask cultures of PNG before the Warwagira highlights local customs: *dukduks* and *tumbuans* (masked forest spirits) come out of the sea from canoes at dawn to dance. At night, Baining fire dancers perform. (p152)

🎭 Malagan Festival

Held in Kavieng or Namatanai towards the end of July, this festival features unique Malagan art, traditionally made as totems to honour ancestors and the recently deceased. Malagan carvings are rare outside New Ireland and highly prized among collectors. (p166)

August

In most of PNG and the Solomons, August is hot and humid, though heavy rain showers are thankfully infrequent. In Lae, however, it's rainy season (May to October).

🎭 Ambunti Crocodile Festival

This small four-day event features cultural groups from the Sepik region performing to promote tourism and crocodile conservation. In addition to colourfully garbed dancing, village crafts and food stalls, there's 'the triathlon' – a 1km run, followed by canoe race, then swimming in crocodile-infested waters! (p29)

🍴 Milamala Festival

Usually held on Kiriwina Island in the Trobriands, this energetic and sensuous yam festival may take place in July, though August is most likely. (p79)

🎭 International Orchid Show

In early August, the grounds of Port Moresby's Parliament Haus come alive with thousands of orchids, including rare and unusual species from both coastal and mountain regions.

Sepik River Festival

This festival takes place in mid-August in the mid-Sepik's Kanganaman village with *singsings* (celebratory dance or festival). Participants come from seven villages in the area. (p143)

Enga Cultural Show

In mid-August, sleepy Wabag comes alive during its colourful Highlands fest. With *singsing* groups, live music and arts and crafts stalls, it's not unlike the larger, better-known Goroka and Mt Hagen Shows. (p118)

Tufi Cultural Show

Tufi's big shindig lights up the region in mid-August, when you can see a two-day *singsing*. In addition to brilliantly costumed singing and dancing groups, there are traditional demonstrations of craft-making.

Mt Hagen Show

Held in late August, this Highlands fest is a two-day spectacular. It features elaborate headdresses, colourful make-up and over-the-top costumes, with performing *singsing* groups from all across the country. (p114)

September

Still firmly rooted in the dry season, September is the festival season, and usually a cool(er) and pleasant time to visit.

Garamut & Mamba Festival

In early September, Wewak keeps the dance-loving spirits alive with colourful traditional music and dance. In addition to *singsing* groups, there's the all-important yam-planting ceremonies. (p128)

Goroka Show

If you can only make one Highlands fest, the famed Goroka Show in mid-September features big numbers of outrageously feathered and costumed clans staging unforgettable performances. Accommodation should be booked early. (p107)

Frangipani Festival

The brave folks of Rabaul celebrate their tenacity with floats, dancing and music under the watchful gaze of smouldering Tavurvur. (p159)

Hiri Moale

On Ela Beach in Port Moresby, this long-running fest is on Independence Day (16 September) and features canoe racing by native Motu groups as well as *singsings* and live music. (p48)

Kalam Culture Festival

This traditional festival at Simbai, a tiny Highlands outpost, features male initiation rites, nose piercing and bride-price payments. Held the Wednesday and Thursday after the Goroka Show. (p101)

October

The last official month of the dry season, with increasingly erratic weather patterns. The festival calendar is winding down.

Kundiawa Simbu Show

In early October, tiny Kundiawa sees a flurry of activity around its colourful show. Expect a fine assortment of *singsings* with dancers in traditional dress and *bilas* (finery).

Morobe Show

One of the last big *singsings* of the year happens in Lae in late October. Agricultural displays and fiery *singsing* groups are the big draw – perhaps the best reason to come to this rugged coastal city. (p85)

November

Temperatures are climbing in most of PNG. Milne Bay, with its own unique weather patterns, offers cooler weather through to January.

Milne Bay Canoe & Kundu Festival

In early November, Alotau, the gateway to the enchanting islands of Milne Bay, hosts a magnificent festival. Brilliantly painted canoes packed with costumed warriors race in the bay, while elaborately garbed *singsing* groups perform on stages. (p70)

Itineraries

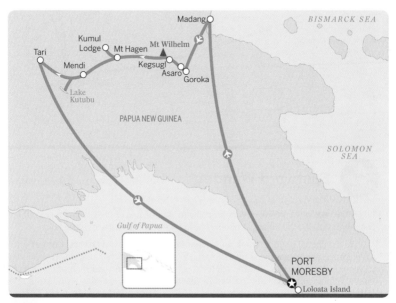

 **Highlands Fling**

Take in the highlights of the Highlands and the coast on this two-week tour.

Spend a day taking in the highlights of **Port Moresby** before flying up to pretty **Madang**. Spend a couple days diving or snorkelling and exploring nearby islands before taking a short flight or a PMV bus up the Highlands (Okuk) Hwy to **Goroka** and see the Goroka Show – and don't forget to visit the mudmen of **Asaro** just outside of Goroka.

Continue through Kundiawa up to **Kegsugl** for the amazing three- or four-day trek up **Mt Wilhelm**. After enjoying the view of both coasts, make the descent for travel onward to **Mt Hagen**, enjoying the spectacular scenery and a game of Highlands darts. For birds of paradise spend a couple of days at **Kumul Lodge** on the road up to Wabag. If there's no clan warfare, continue along the highway to **Mendi** and stunning **Lake Kutubu** and then **Tari**, but if the feisty Southern Highlanders are fighting you'd better do this leg by aeroplane – the beautiful Tari Basin, however, is worth the expense. Don't miss the Huli wigmen in all their feathered glory.

From Tari fly back to Port Moresby and, if time allows, spend a final day relaxing on **Loloata Island**.

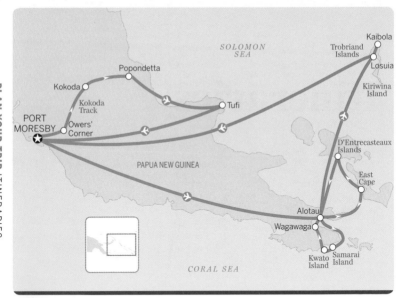

4 WEEKS **Eastward Wander**

Leave the relative comforts of Port Moresby to take on one of PNG's most memorable and challenging treks, the famous Kokoda Track, then recover on an idyllic beach.

Take the classic Kokoda Track route from **Port Moresby** and **Owers' Corner** and get a feel for the challenges faced by the troops by walking for days along this rugged path, traversing chilly streams, visiting old bunker installations and war memorials and stopping at remote villages along the way. At the end of the trek, spend a day relaxing in the settlement of **Kokoda**. From there catch a PMV to **Popondetta** and fly on to **Tufi**, an area of stunning coastline with steep fjord-like *rias,* and a lush, mountainous interior. Go diving or snorkelling, fish for your dinner, explore the area by boat and kayak, and spend a few nights in one or more of the village guesthouses in the area. Accommodation is rustic, but the setting is fantastic – white-sand beaches, swaying palms and coral reefs at your doorstep.

Fly from Tufi back to Port Moresby and on to **Alotau**, gateway to the idyllic beauty of Milne Bay. Spend a day experiencing the market, the harbour and fine views from Top Town. Then catch an afternoon boat out to the colonial-era capital of **Samarai Island** and nearby **Kwato Island**. The bungalows of Nuli Sapi make a fine base for exploring the area before heading back to Alotau and over to **Wagawaga**. Visit waterfalls, go for a dugout canoe trip on the Dawadawa River and enjoy serene views from Ulumani Treetops Lodge. Afterwards, cross back to Alotau, load up on provisions and fuel and head up to **East Cape** by boat for an adventure exploring the **D'Entrecasteaux Islands**. Birdwatching, rainforest walks, postcard beaches, coral reefs and peaceful villages are all part of the allure of this little-visited region.

For the final leg of the journey, fly from Alotau up to **Losuia** on Kiriwina, the largest of the Trobriand Islands. Spend three days visiting traditional villages, learning about yam power and magic and perhaps catching a *singsing* (celebratory dance or festival) or a festive cricket match. Stay at least one night in a village; **Kaibola**, perched near a picturesque beach, is a good option. From Kiriwina it's an easy flight back to Moresby.

Top: Kaibola Beach (p80), Trobriand Islands

Bottom: Bomana War Cemetery (p59) near Port Moresby

Solomons Sojourn

Island Odyssey

World-class diving, virgin waves and idyllic island retreats: the Solomon Islands is a place for adventurers.

Start your journey in **Honiara**. Take in the market, the wharf and national museum, then tack on a tour of the battlefields and pretty beaches outside the capital. Next take a boat to **Savo**, a volcanic island with boiling hot springs, a massive megapode field and pretty, tropical scenery. Spend a few days unwinding here before boating back to Honiara and catching a boat to **Marovo Lagoon**, a great setting for snorkelling, swimming and simply soaking up the tropical beauty. Catch a boat up to the north end of the lagoon for a stay in one of the pristine ecolodges, then continue by plane from Seghe airstrip to **Munda**, a fine base for diving, surfing and bushwalking in New Georgia. From here continue west by boat to **Gizo**, a first-rate diving and up-and-coming surfing spot. Fly back to Honiara, then catch a boat to **Langa Langa Lagoon** for a blissfully relaxing night or two on scenic Malaita Island.

A world away from the Highlands, the island provinces are a mecca for surfers, divers, bushwalkers and those wanting an idyllic Robinson Crusoe–type getaway far from the crowds of modern cities.

From Moresby fly up to Hoskins to spend a couple of days based at Walindi diving, snorkelling, birdwatching and bushwalking around **Kimbe Bay**. Afterwards, fly on to **Rabaul**. There, visit Matupit Island and check out steaming Tavurvur, the volcano that buried the Pacific's prettiest city, before getting under the water at the WWII-era Submarine Base. Fly on to **Kavieng**, where you can get your fill of surfing or diving, before heading towards **Lavongai** for a remote tropical-island getaway. Work your way slowly down the **Boluminski Highway**, stopping at rustic village guesthouses. Continue to the end of the road at Namatanai and consider taking a banana boat back to Kokopo, near Rabaul. Hop on a plane to tiny **Buka** before crossing the Buka Passage to **Bougainville** for a ramble through this mysterious mountainous island with enormous DIY ecotourism potential.

Plan Your Trip

First Time in PNG

Remote and exotic, Papua New Guinea is a challenging destination where it's difficult to just wing it. Careful pre-trip planning, from deciding which part of the country to focus on, to booking accommodation and weighing up transport options, will make travel in PNG more rewarding.

Tours to PNG

If you have a specialist interest (birdwatching, military history, diving, surfing, indigenous culture…), arranging an all-inclusive trip to PNG with a specialist tour agency led by experts is the easiest way to get what you came for. It's the most expensive way to 'do' PNG, but it removes logistical hassle and ensures that you make the most of your time on the ground.

To name but a few, recommended companies include:

Battlefield Tours (www.battlefields.com.au) Caters to travellers with a particular interest in military history.

Intrepid Travel (www.intrepidtravel.com) Varied itineraries that incorporate a whole range of activities.

Solomon Islands Dive Expeditions (www.solomonsdiving.com) Arranges live-aboard boat trips for serious divers.

Sol Surfing (www.surfingsolomonislands.com) Targets surfers on a tight schedule in search of empty waves.

Trans Niugini Tours (p114) Offers high-end cultural and birding excursions along the Sepik, in the Highlands and the Western Province, along with accommodation in its own luxury lodges.

Etiquette

Greetings

'Westernised' handshakes are common, but so is the clasping of hands. If meeting a chief or *bigman,* it's customary to bow and keep your head below theirs. Smiling and nodding at people you meet goes down well; standoffishness and refusing to engage with locals does not.

Photos

Never take photos of a *haus tambaran* (spirit house), sacred objects or people without getting permission first.

Public Behaviour

While holding hands between friends of the same gender is common and acceptable, public displays of affection between couples are seen as vulgar.

Dining Out

Top restaurants in Moresby enforce a dress code. If staying in a village community, sharing your food is the appropriate thing to do and it will be gratefully received.

Women

Gender equality is not a fact of PNG life; solo female travellers may not always be treated with a desired level of respect.

Local Tours Within PNG

Whether you want to climb Mt Wilhelm and meet the Asaro mudmen in the Highlands, go diving in the Solomons, organise a river expedition up the Sepik or hike the Kokoda Track, it's entirely possible to arrange tours on the ground with local operators. However, finding a guide when you're already in PNG can be fairly time-consuming.

You'll find local guides for individual destinations listed under Tours in our On the Road chapters, and here are some handy tips:

➡ Forums such as LP's Thorn Tree (www. lonelyplanet.com/thorntree) and Tripadvisor are not a bad place to start.

➡ Ask expats and other travellers for recommendations. Asking locals is likely to trigger the *wantok* system and see you directed to a cousin.

➡ Even one-man operations usually have a contact number and email address; some have websites.

➡ Phoning is the quickest and most reliable way of getting hold of an independent guide; emails are usually answered but replies can take awhile.

Activities

Travel to PNG is all about being outdoors in the elements and there's an incredible wealth of activities to choose from.

GETTING YOUR VISA

➡ Visitors from Western Europe, the Americas, New Zealand and all Pacific countries are eligible for a free visa on arrival.

➡ Visas are valid for up to 60 days.

➡ Citizens of Australia and all other countries must apply for visas well in advance.

➡ Visas on arrival may be obtained at the airport in Port Moresby. Gurney Airport in Alotau is due to start offering visas on arrival in late 2016.

➡ For more information on visas, see p237.

Birdwatching

PNG is home to thousands of species of flora and fauna and seeing some of it, especially the rich bird life, is becoming easier with the existence of specialised birding lodges and knowledgable local guides.

Birders report that in a three-week trip you'll see about 300 species. A small number of local guides are well worth seeking out. You can plan and execute your trip with these guys for a fraction of the cost of a tour.

Samuel Kepuknai from Kiunga Nature Tours (p144) is *the* man in remote Western Province, while former hunter Daniel Wakra of New Guinea Natural Tours (p47) knows the sites around Port Moresby very well. Kumul Lodge (p116) in Enga Province and Ambua Lodge (p123) in Tari have programs specifically for birdwatchers and excellent guides.

Boating

Few roads. Lots of rivers. More islands. It's a combination that makes boating in one form or another almost inevitable in PNG.

PNG has some of the world's largest and most spectacular rivers, with the Sepik often compared to the Amazon and Congo Rivers and used by local people as a highway. A Sepik cruise is a languid way of taking in the indigenous culture and rich birdlife along the river.

If you don't own a cruising yacht, for island-hopping there are four alternatives: use the regular coastal shipping; take a tour; charter a boat; or make friends with someone who owns a yacht. The dense scattering of islands along PNG's coastline lends itself beautifully to sea kayaking. Tufi Resort (p68) is due to commence guided sea kayaking trips in late 2016, but generally it's BYO everything.

Diving & Snorkelling

PNG offers some of the most interesting, exciting and challenging underwater activities on earth. Those who like diving on wrecks will find dozens of sunken ships – either as a result of WWII or the maze of spectacular coral reefs. And the reefs are not only for divers – excellent visibility and an abundance of fish make them perfect for snorkellers. Milne Bay, New Britain, New Ireland and the Solomons are stellar diving destinations. For more on diving, see p31.

Fishing

In PNG there are dozens of rivers brimming with fish, including species such as barramundi, mangrove jack and the legendary Papuan black bass. And off the coasts there's no shortage of big fish either. Yellowfin tuna, mackerel, sailfish, and blue, black and striped marlin are just some of monster fish hooked by die-hard anglers that come here from all over the world.

The **Game Fishing Association of Papua New Guinea** (www.gfa.com.pg) has an excellent website with lots of information on events and competitions, and the contact details of fishing charters and fishermen-friendly lodges throughout PNG.

Surfing

The southern coast of the PNG mainland gets swell from June to September. However, the best waves are during the monsoon season from late October to April along the north coast and in the islands.

The best places to head are Kavieng, the western end of New Ireland, Wewak and Ulingan Bay, both on the northern coast of the PNG mainland and, the pick of the lot, Vanimo, on the north coast near the border with Indonesian Papua.

The **Surf Association of Papua New Guinea** (320 0211; www.sapng.com) has a decent website with links to surfing tours. Besides the surf camps, it's also worth looking at the World Surfaris (www.worldsurfaris.com), PNG Surfaris (www.pngsurfaris.com) and No Limit Adventures (www.nolimitadventures.com.au) websites for their all-inclusive surfing charters and packages.

Trekking

PNG is a trekking paradise. The country is crisscrossed with tracks, many of which have been used for centuries by the local population, and it is rarely more than a day's walk between villages.

Your major costs will be paying for guides. Expect to pay a guide around K200 per day and a porter anything between K100 and K150 per day. You'll also have to provide or pay for their food. The best way to find a reliable guide is to ask around the local expat population – they will usually be able to put you in touch with someone who knows someone. All of the tour companies can provide guides or at least information on where you might procure one.

PRE-DEPARTURE CHECKLIST

- ☐ Apply for visa
- ☐ Book accommodation and flights
- ☐ Arrange cruises and tours in advance if travelling in remote areas
- ☐ Arrange any necessary vaccinations and pick up anti-malaria tablets

Don't Forget

- ☐ All-purpose electrical plug adaptor
- ☐ Torch (flashlight) for destinations without electricity
- ☐ Spare batteries for your camera
- ☐ Powerful insect repellent
- ☐ Prescription medicines
- ☐ Sturdy boots if hiking, sandals if hitting the beach

The Kokoda Track is the most popular trek in PNG. Mt Wilhelm is climbed fairly often, and some people then walk from there down to Madang. The Bulldog Track will appeal to those with a military or historical bent...and a wide masochistic streak.

Cultural

PNG is second to none when it comes to sheer wealth of indigenous culture and many visitors arrange their trip around a cultural festival, be it the Goroka Show (p107), Mt Hagen Show (p114), Ambunti Crocodile Festival or the Sepik River Festival (p143). Others make visiting a culturally rich area the focal point of their trip, from expeditions up the Sepik River in order to visit ornate *haus tambarans* (spirit houses) and get a glimpse of the crocodile skin-cutting ceremony to trips to the Highlands to spend time with Asaro mudmen in Goroka and with the Huli wigmen in Tari.

Day One

Flying into Papua New Guinea for the first time is a culture shock, and spending a night in the capital is largely unavoidable, since it's the main travel hub. Don't panic.

TOP TIPS FOR YOUR TRIP

➡ Be prepared for your trip to be expensive.

➡ Do your research to figure out the best time of year to visit, depending on your interests.

➡ If you have your heart set on attending a particular event, such as the Goroka Show, make arrangements months in advance as lodgings and flights can book up.

➡ Travel light. Baggage allowance for internal flights tends to be 16kg.

➡ Be respectful of local customs. Since every bit of land belongs to someone, ask permission before wandering across gardens, beaches and bush.

➡ Bone up on some Tok Pisin if you're planning to spend time in the Highlands.

➡ Expect travel delays. Don't expect everything to run like clockwork.

➡ Take sensible precautions regarding personal safety and never go trekking without a guide.

➡ Invest in a waterproof canoe bag for your belongings and a pop-up Sansbug mosquito net tent.

➡ Most PNG hotels have a poor track record of responding to emails, so make a reservation by phone in advance.

➡ Pick the part of town depending on how long you're planning on staying and what you're after: Town and Boroko for easy dining options; Waigani for proximity to the National Museum and Parliament Haus; and lodgings near the airport if you wish to avoid Moresby altogether.

➡ You probably don't have to worry about running the gauntlet of taxi drivers outside the airport; most Moresby hotels offer free pick-up and their shuttles loiter outside the international terminal.

➡ Worried about communication while in PNG? Don't be. In the international arrival terminal you can pick up a local Digicel SIM card for your digital device; it offers the best coverage country-wide.

➡ It's always good to have back-up cash, since credit cards are not widely accepted in

PNG. There are ATMs at the airport, in Boroko and Town, and you can take advantage of the money-changing agency inside the international terminal and change your foreign cash into kina.

➡ Getting around town in the evenings can be tricky; get your lodgings to call a taxi and hold on to the driver's number.

Getting Around PNG

PNG is a country with few roads, an extensive coastline, and difficult-to-get-to destinations only reachable by plane. Travel around PNG is expensive and can be time-consuming, so it's best to pick a part of the country that you're particularly interested in, or else risk drifting into insolvency.

For detailed information on transport to and around PNG, see p239.

Plan Your Trip

Diving in PNG & Solomon Islands

Both PNG and the Solomons are famous for their strong visual appeal below the surface. Imagine a resplendent tapestry of hard and soft corals, colourful fish life, dizzying drop-offs, a wealth of WWII ship and plane wrecks and warm waters year-round. Rounding off the picture is the almost complete lack of over-development.

PNG

Papua New Guinea offers truly world-class diving. The marine biodiversity is exceptional, incredibly healthy reefs look like a Garden of Eden and the absence of crowds is a prime draw. Another clincher is the mind-boggling array of WWII wrecks – ships, aircraft and even submarines.

Madang

Abundant marine life, superb reefs and atmospheric wrecks – Madang (p92) has it all.

Magic Passage (Map p97) A charismatic site off Madang's outer reefs. You'll likely come across aggregations of barracuda, trevally and sweetlips, as well as photogenic barrel sponges and a variety of soft and hard corals.

Planet Rock (Map p97) A submerged seamount around which barracuda, tuna, snapper, jacks and whitetip reef sharks whirl.

B25 Mitchell (Map p97) Off Wongat Island, this coral-encrusted aircraft lies in less than 15m. This is an atmospheric wreck with abundant fish life. Most of the guns are still visible.

Henry Leith (Map p97) This tugboat sits upright in 20m off Wongat Island and makes for an easy, attractive dive. It's covered with gorgonians, sponges and soft corals.

Practicalities

Conditions

PNG and the Solomons are diveable year-round. Milne Bay's best seasons are September to January and April to June. Tufi's best season is September to May.

Average surface sea temperatures are 25°C to 30°C; don't bring more than a 3mm wetsuit.

Visibility varies greatly, from 10m to 40m.

Dive Centres

Outfitters are highly professional, with well-trained instructors offering introductory dives, exploratory dives and certification programs.

Most dive centres are PADI- or SSI-affiliated, and accept credit cards.

Prices generally don't include equipment rental; consider bringing your own gear.

Live-Aboards

Live-aboard dive boats operate out of PNG and the Solomon Islands. Check the websites for itineraries. Some boats and their base ports:

MV Bilikiki (p207) Honiara, Solomon Islands.

Solomon Islands Dive Expeditions (p207) Honiara, Solomon Islands.

Chertan (p75) Alotau, Milne Bay.

FeBrina (p162) Walindi, New Britain.

Golden (www.mvgoldendawn.com) Port Moresby.

Diving in PNG & Solomon Islands

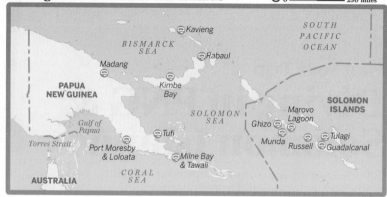

Port Moresby & Loloata Island

Port Moresby has probably the best diving of any capital city worldwide, with a variety of dive sites easily accessible from the dive shop on Loloata Island (p60), though visibility sometimes doesn't exceed 10m.

Loloata Island Jetty (Map p48) Loloata is noted for its superb 'muck diving' potential, and Loloata Island Resort's jetty is no exception, with lots of tiny critters and bizarre fish, from mantis shrimp to dwarf lionfish.

Boston A20 Havoc (Map p48) A few minutes' boat ride from Loloata Island, this WWII aircraft wreck rests in 18m on a silty bottom. The nose gunner's section was dislodged from the aircraft when it crashed, but overall it's in good condition.

Pacific Gas This 65m-long vessel, formerly a liquid gas carrier, was scuttled in 1986 for recreational diving. The bow rests at about 15m, while the propeller is at 43m. Fish life thrives on and around the wreck.

Suzie's Bommie This big pinnacle rising from the sandy floor to about 12m below the surface is an oasis of life. Look for unusual, tiny pygmy seahorses that can be found on gorgonians.

Tufi

Tufi (p67) offers a mix of muck dives, WWII wreck dives and reef dives. The offshore reefs, including Stewart, Cyclone and Veale, are pristine and offer an eye-catching combination of hard and soft corals, as well as prolific marine life.

Tufi Wharf Offers superb muck diving. The scattered remains of two PT boats can be seen at 40m directly down the wharf.

B17 Bomber Black Jack Off Cape Vogel, this is one of the best aircraft wreck dives in the South Pacific. The *Black Jack* rests almost intact in about 45m on a sandy floor.

Milne Bay & Tawali

Muck diving, great sheer walls, coral seamounts and lots of pelagic action: it's impossible to get bored in Milne Bay (p68). Visibility is variable and currents might be tricky. Most of the best diving is at the mouth of Milne Bay (the bay itself doesn't have much to offer divers), so your best bet is to base yourself at Tawali Resort (p74) or sign up for a live-aboard dive cruise.

Cobb's Cliff A vertigo-inducing drop-off where hammerheads and manta rays are commonly spotted. The reef also hosts a huge variety of colourful invertebrates and small critters.

Barracuda Point Get a buzz drifting along a steep drop-off and keep your eyes peeled for sharks and other biggies.

Nuakata Island Pristine reefs and abundant fish life, including marauding pelagics, such as grey sharks, tuna and Spanish mackerel.

Rabaul

This is one of PNG's finest areas for wreck dives, with a collection of shipwrecks lying in Rabaul Harbour (p157), and reefs along the north coast of the Gazelle Peninsula.

Submarine Base (Map p152) A steep wall at the edge of a vast submerged caldera, wreathed with soft corals, gorgonians and barrel sponges (p160).

George's Wreck (Map p152) This coral-encased wreck lies outside Rabaul Harbour. The bow rests on a steep slope in 15m; the stern deck in about 55m.

Manko Maru (Map p158) Sunk in 1943, this wreck sits in 35m in Rabaul Harbour. The cargo hull can be penetrated.

Reimers Reef Famous for its contoured topography, with overhangs, swim-throughs and canyons; astoundingly dense fish life; and a fabulous mixture of hard and soft corals.

Tom, Dick & Harry Reefs (Map p152) Features a string of seamounts that plummet to 50m.

Midway Reef (Map p152) This long narrow reef is brilliantly coloured, with an array of hard corals and gorgonians. It's mostly sheltered and visibility usually exceeds 40m.

Kimbe Bay (West New Britain)

Kimbe Bay (p161) is famous for towering seamounts crowned by coral formations that project from the continental shelf. The bay is home to more than 413 types of hard coral and 860 species of fish, from cute pygmy horses to massive hammerhead sharks. The tapestry of colours and textures is equally fascinating: soft and hard corals, sea fans, giant sea whips and huge barrel and elephant-ear sponges compete for space on the reef. Strong currents and variable visibility can disappoint, though. Most sites are a lengthy boat ride away (average 45 minutes).

Kavieng (New Ireland)

The large reef system stretching between Kavieng (p164) and New Hanover offers thrilling dives, especially in the passages. Myriad marine life includes rays, turtles, barracuda, tuna, jacks and grey sharks.

Solomon Islands

Diving in the Solomons and PNG is similar, though most dive operations are land-based, whereas PNG is famous for its live-aboards. But what sets the Solomons apart is a unique sense of 'forgotten paradise'.

Guadalcanal

Guadalcanal (p177) is the obvious place to start your diving adventures: world-class sunken WWII vessels lie close to shore. Most sites can be reached by car from Honiara.

Bonegi I (Map p180) Close to shore about 12km west of Honiara, this giant-sized Japanese merchant transport ship, also known as the *Hirokawa Maru*, lies in 3m descending to 55m.

Bonegi II (Map p180) Also known as *Kinugawa Maru*, the upper works of this WWII wreck break the surface a towel's throw from Bonegi Beach. Its stern reaches down to 27m.

USS John Penn (Map p180) This large US-troop ship was bombed and sunk about 4km offshore, east of Honiara. Experienced divers only.

US B-17 Flying Fortress bomber (Map p180) At Ndoma, this excellent aircraft wreck lies 100m offshore in less than 18m. A chance for novices to explore a famous WWII plane.

Tulagi

Easily accessed from Honiara, Tulagi (p189) is a must for wreck enthusiasts, and has a few awesome reef dives as well. Many wrecks are deep dives, in the 30m to 60m range. Visibility averages from 5m to 15m.

Kawanashi This Japanese seaplane in about 30m is easily one of the most photogenic sites off Tulagi. The port wing, the cockpit and the propellers are heavily encrusted with marine invertebrates.

Moa This NZ minesweeper rests in less than 40m in Tulagi Harbour. Look for the massive rudder and a huge coral-encrusted gun on deck. Often shrouded in misty water layers, giving a ghostly aura.

USS Aaron Ward This 106m-long US Navy destroyer is noted for its extensive arsenal of big guns. It rests between 35m and 65m.

USS Kanawha Not far from Tulagi Harbour, this monster-sized oil tanker sits upright in 45m.

RUSSELL ISLANDS

The Russell Islands are the Solomons' best-kept secret, with pristine sites, a dramatic topography and stellar visibility due to regular currents. The only way to dive this sensational world is to sign up for a live-aboard cruise with the MV *Bilikiki* (p207) or Solomon Islands Dive Expeditions (p207).

Catalina A short boat ride from Tulagi, this WWII seaplane sits on a coral seabed between 25m and 35m. It's overgrown with soft and hard coral. Lionfish, anthias and angelfish add colour and activity.

Twin Tunnels This awesome reef dive features two chimneys (lava tubes) that start on top of a reef. Strong currents usually mean pelagic action.

Munda

The Munda area (p194) is a diver's treat, with a good balance of scenic seascapes, elaborate reef structures, dense marine life and atmospheric wrecks.

Shark Point A 25-minute boat ride from Munda, this sloping reef is ideal for grey reef sharks, silvertips, devil rays, snapper, batfish and turtles. You'll have to go deep (around 40m) to spy the sharks.

Corsair This WWII US fighter rests undamaged close to the shore on a sandy bottom in 50m.

P-39 Airacobra This well-preserved WWII American fighter was found in April 2011 in 28m.

Susu Hite A relaxing dive on a lively reef in less than 20m – perfect for novices.

Top Shelf This site features top-notch coral gardens and varied fish life.

SBD Douglas Dauntless Bomber A US plane resting on a sandy bottom in 12m in Rendova Harbour. It's fun to sit in the cockpit.

North Marovo Lagoon

This exceptional dive area (p190) has dramatic walls, exhilarating passages and simple reef dives.

Uepi Point (Map p192) This iconic dive site sizzles with electric fish action against a backdrop of corals, sea fans and sponges.

Cotton Candy Wall (Map p192) This lagoon dive off Mbaleva Island is full of surprises. Picture yourself drift down a drop-off lavishly blanketed in pink soft corals of varying hues.

Charapoana Point (Map p192) An impressive drop-off, lavishly draped with sea fans. Likely place to spot pelagics. Seasoned divers can do the Point to Point across Charapoana Passage to Uepi Point.

Lumalihe Passage (Map p192) This passage between the ocean and the lagoon acts as a magnet for a host of small species and predators.

General Store (Map p192) 'A bit of everything' on the outer reef. Lots of swim-throughs and small canyons carved into the reef. A photographer's delight with twists, turns and light plays.

Elbow Caves (Map p192) A network of gutters carved into the reef wall. Sunbeams play through skylights in the caves – magical.

BOTCH (Map p192) Stands for 'Bottom of the Channel'. Drift dive on the sandy bottom of Charapoana Passage.

Ghizo

Not-to-be-missed Ghizo Island (p196) is noted for its stunning mix of WWII wrecks and superb offshore reefs.

Toa Maru This well-preserved 140m Japanese freighter 15 minutes north of Gizo still has crockery, sake bottles, ammunition, gas masks, medical supplies, anti-aircraft guns, a motorcycle and two small tanks. It rests from about 18m down at the bow to around 37m at the stern. Perfect for novices.

Secret Spot A first-class dive site famous for its schooling fish and atmospheric seascape, with a mix of sandy valleys and a sheer wall.

Hellcat A small aircraft on a sandy floor in 10m, to the southeast of Kennedy Island. It's an easy dive that's usually offered after a deeper reef dive.

Joe's Wall This precipitous wall sports healthy coral formations and invertebrates.

Yellow Corner This reef dive will make your spine tingle, with a profusion of yellow-tinged soft corals that enhance the visual appeal of the site.

RESPONSIBLE DIVING

➡ Avoid touching living marine organisms with your body or equipment; practise and maintain proper buoyancy control.

➡ Take great care in underwater caves; air bubbles can damage fragile organisms.

➡ Minimise your disturbance of marine animals.

➡ Take home all your rubbish and any you find as well.

➡ Never stand on corals, even if they look solid and robust.

➡ Do not collect seashells or buy any seashell or turtleshell products.

➡ Use professional dive operators who maintain high safety and ethical standards.

Plan Your Trip
Kokoda Track

Crossing the Owen Stanley Range has become a pilgrimage for many Australians. Through experiencing the rugged terrain and sharing just some of the trials of the men who fought and died here, it is a chance to pay respect to those who defended Australia from the advancing Japanese in WWII. For the Kokoda story, see p224.

Why Do It?

Halfway through you may wonder why you decided to walk the Kokoda Track. Your blistered feet will hurt, your clothes will be wet with sweat and by day's end you'll undoubtedly be tired and hungry. But what your pictures won't show (assuming you muster the energy to take a few) is your growing sense of awe. For with every steep, slippery step on this 96km natural rollercoaster, Australians, Americans and Japanese fought for their lives, against each other and against the terrain. In 1942 there were no guesthouses, no porters, no relief from dysentery, and there was the constant fear of ambush.

Crossing the Owen Stanley Range has become a pilgrimage for many Australians, a chance to pay their respects by sharing some of the trials of the men who fought and died here. And what started as a trickle is turning into a tide. In recent years, there has been an average of some 4000 trekkers (95% of them Australian) every year who have gritted their teeth and tackled the mountains. The majority walk as part of an organised group; only the most experienced trekkers could consider walking this track independently.

Apart from the wartime history, relationships built with today's residents of the track, and particularly the guides and carriers who trek with you, are mutually rewarding. They serve as a reminder that the Kokoda Track is about people; not just a distant, heroic military campaign.

Need to Know

When to Go

May to September are the coolest, driest and best months to trek, although most companies operate from March to October. Always prepare for rain.

What to Pack

Total pack weight should not exceed 15kg:

☐ comprehensive trail guide: Clive Baker's *The Kokoda Trek* or Bill James' *Kokoda Field Guide*

☐ comfortable, well-made boots (already broken in)

☐ tent

☐ lightweight sleeping bag

☐ poncho or other wet-weather gear

☐ pack bladder and water bottle

☐ water purifier

☐ medical kit

☐ head torch (flashlight)

☐ zip-lock bags to keep papers/maps dry

Websites

Kokoda Track Authority (www.kokodatrack authority.org) List of licensed tour operators.

Kokoda Trekkers Forum (www.kokodatrail.com. au/forums) Training tips, advice and testimonials.

Kokoda Commemoration (kokoda.commemora tion.gov.au) Snapshot history of WWII events.

Kokoda Track Foundation (www.ktf.org) Opportunities to give back.

Kokoda Track – South

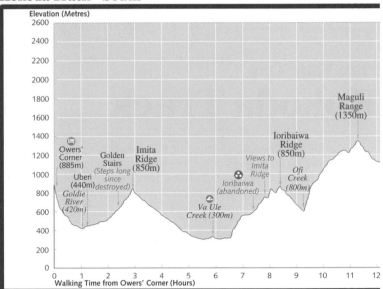

Elevation (Metres)

Owers' Corner (885m)

Uberi (440m)

Goldie River (420m)

Golden Stairs *(Steps long since destroyed)*

Imita Ridge (850m)

Va Ule Creek (300m)

Ioribaiwa (abandoned)

Views to Imita Ridge

Ofi Creek (800m)

Ioribaiwa Ridge (850m)

Maguli Range (1350m)

Walking Time from Owers' Corner (Hours)

Planning Your Trek

Most people walk the track with a company specialising in organised treks and all the logistical arrangements will be dealt with by them. The first decision when considering walking the Kokoda Track is whether you prefer a hassle-free, albeit more expensive, guided trek or a cheaper, locally arranged walk. The following advice is a starting point for all walkers.

All trekkers (but not porters or guides) must pay a K300 trekking fee and obtain a permit from the Kokoda Track Authority (KTA; p234) before starting the trip. The KTA is also a great place to 'bump' into guides and porters who sometimes hang around here.

There are basic 'resthouses' in most villages plus various shelters and campsites along the track. Some of the resthouses and camp sites are small, so if you meet another party you might have to camp in the village or move on to the next village.

Most porters are very resourceful and able to find accommodation with *wantoks* (kinfolk). However, it is your responsibility to bring all the equipment, including tents and utensils, that your party will need. The same is also true for food; your guide will take only the clothes they are wearing.

Organised treks supply the bulk of your food, which accompanies you on the backs of local carriers. It's replenished about halfway along via a chartered flight; there are no trade stores on the track (only at Sogeri and Kokoda). Bring any comfort food yourself and keep it light.

Whether you're on an organised trek or walking with locals, ensure that you have comprehensive individual medical insurance.

Training

Train for at least three months. Do stair-training and running, and practise hiking with a heavy load. As one LP reader put it, 'Practise by climbing the stairs in an office tower at home. For realism, cover yourself in mud, carry a sack of onions on your back and wear slippery shoes.'

Guides & Carriers

If you're trekking independently, don't do it without a good guide. A personal recommendation is best – the KTA is a good place to start. You could also try asking other trekkers on the www.kokodatrail

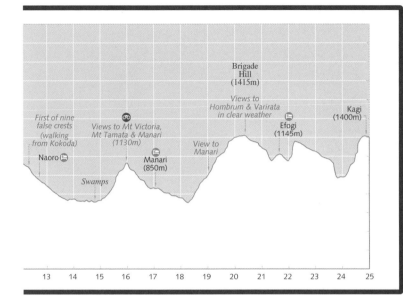

.com.au/forums. There are dozens of guides and carriers working on the track and most of them are freelancers.

It is also possible to hire carriers at Kokoda, although you can't just expect them to be able to drop everything at a moment's notice and head off. The maximum that a carrier can carry (and is permitted to do so under KTA rules) is 18kg.

Having a carrier might mean the difference between finishing the trek or giving up. One carrier between two or three is a good idea. If the weight becomes too much, you can employ a carrier in most villages along the track, but they are getting busier as the route becomes more popular. Pay guides about K100 per day and carriers about K80 per day, plus K20 per day for food and lodgings; you'll also need to pay their airfares back home.

Organised Treks

You can choose to walk the track with one of dozens of companies, which takes most of the hassle out of the preparation, leaving you to focus on getting fit. Costs depend on the length of the trek, whether it includes airfares from Australia, what equipment is provided and whether you employ a carrier. Check operator websites for full de-

tails and make sure you are comparing like with like. Most prices include transport out of Port Moresby.

Price is not the only consideration when selecting a trekking company. It's worth asking a few questions before handing over a fistful of kina.

HEALTH & SAFETY

The Kokoda Track is not PNG's most difficult trek, but it's no walk in the park either. Aim to do it in nine days, not six. Take advantage of the services of local carriers and never walk with fewer than four people. If there is an accident, two can get help and one can stay with the injured. Remember to protect yourself from the sun and heat. Keep hydrated, and don't forget rehydration salts – maintaining your fluid and carbohydrate levels is absolutely critical.

Robberies and conflicts among traditional landowners have led to the track's closure in the past, but in recent years the situation has been fairly calm. Still, it's worth keeping an ear open.

Kokoda Track – North

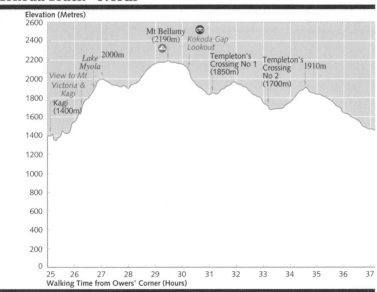

Elevation (Metres)

Mt Bellamy (2190m)
Kokoda Gap Lookout
Lake Myola 2000m
View to Mt Victoria & Kagi
Kagi (1400m)
Templeton's Crossing No 1 (1850m)
Templeton's Crossing No 2 (1700m) 1910m

Walking Time from Owers' Corner (Hours)

PLAN YOUR TRIP KOKODA TRACK

➡ If you are particularly keen on the military history, a knowledgeable guide is a must. What sites will you be shown? What level of information can you expect from your guide?

➡ Most trekking companies carry a satellite phone or a two-way radio; if they don't have one and there's a problem, no one can hear your screams.

➡ How is their safety record? Besides your own insurance – which is essential – what additional insurance do they carry and what does it cover?

➡ Ask about equipment; if they supply tents it may be possible to inspect them.

➡ While agony loves company, it's a trail, not a highway. How many people in a group?

➡ What is their code of ethics? Do they carry out accumulated rubbish? Do they pay guides and porters reasonable wages? Do they contribute to local communities?

Trekking Companies

Adventure Kokoda (in Australia ☑1300 783 303; www.kokodatreks.com; treks from A$3795) A high-profile company led by Charlie Lynn, son of a WWII Kokoda digger. One of the best operators.

Ecotourism Melanesia (Map p56; ☑7076 7277; www.em.com.pg; treks from A$3220) Perhaps the largest locally owned inbound tour

operator in PNG. Not cheap, but has an excellent reputation.

Executive Excellence (www.executiveexcel lence.com.au; ex Brisbane from A$6350) Known by some as the 'men in tights', this Brisbane-based operation employs ex-soldiers and includes a pre-departure training program.

Kokoda Trekking (www.kokodatrekking.com. au; without/with porter A$2895/3475) This PNG-owned company sponsors the Kokoda Challenge. Their trips are cheaper and encourage greater interaction with local guides and carriers.

Kokoda Treks & Tours (www.kokoda.com. au; treks A$3575) When it comes to war history, Frank Taylor is hard to beat. His Milne Bay, Buna, Gona & Kokoda tour concentrates on the beach heads of the Kokoda campaign and is perfect for those interested in the battles but not physically ready to tackle the 'Track'.

PNG Trekking Adventures (www.pngtrek kingadventures.com; treks from A$2495) Highly regarded company operated by long-time Australian expats based in Port Moresby.

Local Operators

For local Kokoda trekking operators, contact the Kokoda Track Authority (p234) for recommendations.

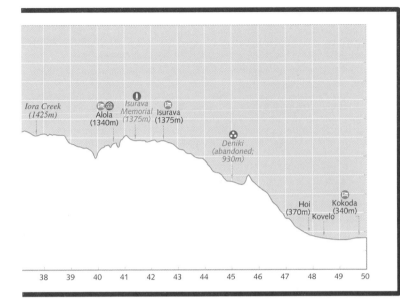

Iora Creek
(1425m)

Alola
(1340m)

Isurava
Memorial
(1375m)

Isurava
(1375m)

Deniki
(abandoned;
930m)

Hoi
(370m)

Kovelo

Kokoda
(340m)

38 39 40 41 42 43 44 45 46 47 48 49 50

Fuzzy Wuzzy Expeditions (☑7127 2458, 629 7469; defol@fuzzywuzzy.com.pg) Defol Orere is an experienced tour leader who also works with the Kokoda Track Authority.

Kokoda Holidays (☑7164 3221, 340 4294; kokodaholidays@daltron.com.pg) This small operation is run by David Soru.

Getting To & From the Trek

The Kokoda Track runs between Owers' Corner in Central Province and Kokoda in Oro Province. At the southern end you'll need a 4WD to reach Owers' Corner, taking the turn-off just before Sogeri – look for a white-painted stone war memorial. At McDonald's Corner there is a strange metal sculpture of a soldier; this is where the road once ended and the track started, but the actual track now starts further on at Owers' Corner. PMVs run from Gordons Market in Port Moresby to Sogeri early in the morning. From there, you'll need to wait and hope for a lift to Owers' Corner or start walking the 16km. The KTA can help arrange transport. Note: the road is often impassable, so be prepared to walk at least part of it if required.

The Trek

Depending on how fit you are, it takes between six and 11 days to traverse the track (walking for about 50 hours from beginning to end). The itinerary shown here is indicative only. It starts at Owers' Corner, but just as many people walk the other way, which involves about 550m more climbing. By making it a longer trip you have more time for side-trips, exploring the battlefields and experiencing village life.

Day 1: Owers' Corner–Va Ule Creek (10km, six hours) The Va Ule Creek campsites are about one to three hours past Imita Ridge. Watch for the extensive weapon pits on the northern face of Imita Ridge, where the Australians made their last stand in 1942.

Day 2: Va Ule Creek–Naoro (17km, seven hours) The track follows the original wartime route over Ioribaiwa Ridge. There's a memorial on the ridge and there are many interesting weapon pits, bunkers and relics strewn across the slopes. Naoro has spectacular 270-degree views over the valley and there is a large resthouse.

Day 3: Naoro–Efogi (19km, seven hours) About halfway between these points there are three

KOKODA CHALLENGE

If you find walking the Kokoda Track challenging, imagine taking it at full speed, running through sweltering humidity, rain showers and darkness, while taking only short breaks in hopes of completing the route not in days but in hours.

The Kokoda Challenge (www.kokodatrekking.com.au/kokodachallenge.html) was first held in 2005, and although it hadn't been run for a few years at the time of writing, it is expected to soon reappear back on the calendar of PNG sporting events. The race is usually a small, intimate affair with some 70 runners – with 20 spots reserved for international athletes – competing for top honours. Although some high-ranking ultra-marathoners and international trail runners have entered, the long-running champion is Brendan Buka, a porter from Kokoda, who has set the course record for races in both directions. The fastest run ever was in 2008, when Buka raced from Owers' Corner to Kokoda in a thigh- and knee-defying 16 hours and 34 minutes.

If the race hasn't been reinstated, or you can't make it, Australia also hosts its own 96km Kokoda Challenge, held in the Gold Coast hinterlands each year (see http://kokodachallenge.com).

resthouses in Manari village. After the long climb up Brigade Hill you suddenly come into the open and have a wide panorama down the 1942 battlefield, across to Kagi and Mt Bellamy in the distance and Efogi, just below you. On a clear day you can see all the way back to Hombrum and Varirata, near Sogeri. There are about three resthouses in Efogi, the biggest village on the track.

Day 4: Efogi–Kagi–Mt Bellamy (12km, eight hours) Three hours of climbing and descending past Efogi is Kagi, another spectacular village site. From here, the track climbs to its highest point at Mt Bellamy. You can side-trip from the track to Lake Myola in three to four hours return. Along the way, and just off the track, is the huge crater where a WWII bomber blew up and scattered aircraft parts in all directions. Your guide/carrier should know the place.

Day 5: Mt Bellamy–Alola (17km, 11 hours) After a long down and up section, the track passes Templeton's Crossings, followed by another up, down and up to Alola – quite a tiring section.

Day 6: Alola–Kokoda (19km, 10 hours) When you reach the Isurava Memorial, allow yourself at least an hour at the old battle site. It's a most impressive and moving place. After the memorial there is an optional two-hour detour to a wrecked Japanese aircraft with its paintwork still clearly visible. It's a steep climb and you'll need a guide.

Back on the main track you'll pass the abandoned village of Deniki on your way to Kokoda.

Shortcuts

If you're looking for the Kokoda experience without taking on the full challenge, you could take a PMV from Port Moresby to the village of Madilogo, which avoids two hard days' walk from Owers' Corner to Naoro. It takes about two hours to reach the track from Madilogo; from there it's one to 1½ hours to Naoro.

For a little taste of the track you can walk down to the Goldie River from Owers' Corner in just an hour or so. If you have the energy, struggle up what was once the Golden Stairs to Imita Ridge.

Another option would be to fly in to Kagi, Efogi or Manari, walk a section and fly out. Flying to Kagi and walking to Manari (one day) would be interesting. These trips are serviced by expensive charter flights only.

A cheaper option is to get to Kokoda (by flight to Popondetta then PMV to Kokoda) and walk to the Isurava Memorial and back. If you're fit, you can walk there and back in a day (10 hours or so). Or overnight in Isurava village or at the Isurava Memorial trekkers hut.

Regions at a Glance

Port Moresby

Culture
Cuisine
Shopping

Traditional Culture

The *haus tambaran*–style Parliament Haus provides a window into PNG culture, while the nearby National Museum showcases the arts and crafts of this diverse country. Many traditional customs of Moresby's original inhabitants can still be observed in the stilt villages of Hanuabada and Koki.

Unparalleled Dining

The nation's capital obliges travellers with the best opportunities for fine dining and multicultural restaurants. There are also plenty of local food outlets to tempt the taste buds.

Markets & Handicrafts

It's worth planning a trip around the fantastic Ela Beach market, held once a month. At other times, there are smaller markets selling weavings and carvings from all across the country.

p44

Central, Oro & Milne Bay Provinces

Villages
Water Sports
Trekking

Sustainable Stays

Move from village to village, staying in thatch-roof guesthouses, and spending your days birdwatching, snorkelling, hiking and relaxing on beaches. Tufi and the islands of Milne Bay are the gateways.

Aquatic Adventure

There's superb diving at Tufi and Tawali Resorts, DIY snorkelling in the Trobriands and paddling trips up the Dawadawa River. The Milne Bay Canoe & Kundu Festival is spectacular.

Bushwalks

Home to the Kokoda Track, Central Province offers unforgettable adventure. There are great day hikes near Tufi and challenging walks all over Milne Bay – from one-day jaunts to multiday treks.

p62

Morobe & Madang Provinces

Diving & Snorkelling
Surfing
Festivals

Underwater Worlds

Madang boasts excellent diving and snorkelling with a legacy of submerged WWII wrecks, spectacular coral walls and drift dives, and a number of coral-fringed islands for shore-based adventures.

Reef Breaks

North of Madang city, Ulingan Bay boasts seasonal surf during the northern monsoon. Enjoy uncrowded reef breaks and PNG's own slice of sandy nirvana.

Singsing Fests

Singsing (celebratory dance or festival) groups from around the country converge on Lae in their ceremonial wigs, cowrie shell breastplates and *arse-gras* skirts for the region's premier event, the Morobe Show.

p82

The Highlands

Festivals
Trekking
Culture

Highland Fests

First held in the early '60s, the Highland shows have evolved into one of the world's greatest displays of indigenous culture. Expect hundreds of *singsing* participants elaborately dressed in feathers, shells and leaves.

Mountain Treks

With so many mountains on offer, why not tackle the tallest of them all – Mt Wilhelm. No less ambitious goals include exploring the remote Crater Mountain Wildlife Management Area and Lake Kutubu.

Traditional Culture

Beating drums and blood-curdling war songs, the Highlands holds some of the most resilient cultures in PNG, including the feathery Huli wigmen and the ghostly masked Asaro mudmen.

p102

The Sepik

Surfing
Culture
Arts

Monsoon Surf

From mid-October to late April, monsoon-induced swells reach PNG's remote northern coast, generating fine surf breaks. Vanimo is the region's best pick, attracting a growing trickle of experienced riders.

Ancient Rituals

The Sepik River is a 1126km-long cultural smorgasbord, and old customs die hard here. Young men are still cut so that the resulting scars imitate a crocodile's skin; local women are still denied entry into the mysterious spirit houses.

Traditional Arts

Traditional art and spiritual beliefs collide in the Sepik. Skull racks, story boards, cassowary thighbone daggers and unusual masks have made the Sepik villages powerhouses of artistic expression.

p124

Island Provinces

Diving
Surfing
Adventure

Wrecks & Reefs

You can go wreck diving and explore the coral wonders of Kimbe Bay, book into a celebrated dive resort at Walindi and discover New Ireland's profusion of reefs and marine life.

Wonder Waves

With a good range of breaks, Kavieng has fantastic surf and a management plan that ensures the waves never get too crowded. You can also head out near Lavongai where you can surf, fish for dinner and enjoy simple island life.

Island Adventures

Adventure abounds on the islands: trek up volcanoes near Rabaul, ride a bike along the scenic Boluminski Hwy to peaceful villages and take a memorable hike through the mountain wilderness of Bougainville.

p147

Solomon Islands

Diving
History
Getaways

Undersea Marvels

The Solomons are as beautiful below the waterline as on land. The country is famous for its world-class sunken wrecks, incredible reefs and abundance of marine life.

WWII Artefacts

A fleet of WWII ship and plane wrecks rest on the sea floor between Guadalcanal and Tulagi. Tanks, amtracks, memorials and anti-aircraft guns are scattered in the jungle throughout the archipelago.

Enchanting Escapes

We've all dreamed of the ultimate getaway: a vision of dense jungle, a turquoise sea, a few scattered bungalows, healthy local food and the soundtrack of nature. Find yours here.

p176

On the Road

Port Moresby

POP 364,000 / AREA 240 SQ KM

Best Places to Eat

➡ Rapala (p52)

➡ Seoul House (p52)

➡ Fusion Bistro (p55)

➡ Duffy's (p54)

➡ Cellar (p52)

Best Places to Stay

➡ Airways Hotel & Apartments (p51)

➡ Raintree Lodge (p50)

➡ Mapang Missionary Home (p49)

➡ Loloata Island Resort (p60)

➡ Ela Beach Hotel (p51)

Squeezed between the dusty hills and the deep blue sea, gritty Port Moresby is unlikely to be most travellers' idea of an enchanting capital. A spread-out collection of neighbourhoods, the city illustrates the stark divide between PNG's haves and have-nots. Modern office buildings in Town and Waigani and a glitzy marina full of yachts contrast with squatter shantytowns, without electricity or running water, that cling to the hillsides and scruffy marketplaces where barefoot higglers from nearby villages sell their modest wares.

Expensive, dangerous (or so many expats will tell you) and not easily walkable...it's easy to see why many visitors are tempted to spend as little time here as possible. But as Moresby's charms reveal themselves – a superb museum, a beautiful green space in the corner of the city, friendly locals, a gourmet meal after weeks in the provinces – the city may well grow on you.

When to Go
Port Moresby

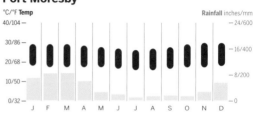

Year-round Hot year-round; average highs between 28°C and 32°C.

Dec–May Wet season with hotter, rainier days.

Jun–Nov Dry season, with slightly lower temperatures.

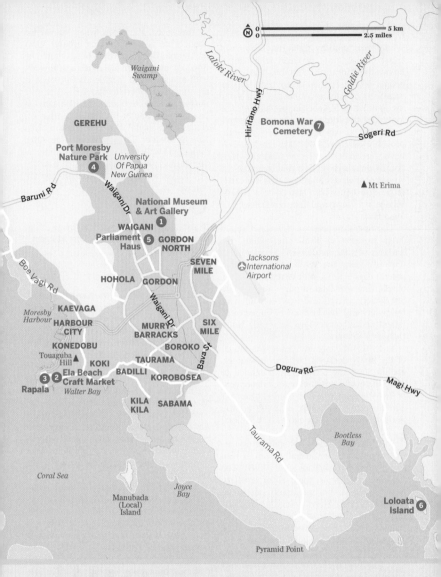

Port Moresby Highlights

① Discovering cultural treasures tucked inside the terrific **National Museum & Art Gallery** (p46).

② Loading up on one-of-a-kind indigenous art at the colourful monthly **Ela Beach Craft Market** (p57).

③ Dining out at Korean, Chinese, Italian, Japanese,

Indian and fine-dining restaurants, like **Rapala** (p52), in PNG's culinary hot spot.

④ Marvelling over trees shrill with fruit bats and an explosion of orchids at **Port Moresby Nature Park** (p47).

⑤ Checking out the towering mosaic facade of **Parliament**

Haus (p46), in Sepik *haus tambaran* (spirit house) style.

⑥ Boating to **Loloata Island** (p60) for snorkelling, diving and waterfront relaxing.

⑦ Driving out to solemn **Bomana War Cemetery** (p59) to contemplate the tragic losses wrought by WWII.

History

While Port Moresby today has dozens of tribal groups, only two can truly call it home: the Motu and Koitabu. The native people of the Port Moresby area are descendants of Polynesian people, unlike the predominantly Melanesian population. The Motu are traditionally a sea-going people and didn't arrive until relatively recently, probably less than 2000 years ago. Motu villages were built on stilts over Moresby Harbour. Hanuabada ('Great Village') was the largest of their communities and still exists today. Stilt houses can also be seen at Koki Village near Town and Tubuseraia down the Magi Hwy.

The first European to visit was Captain John Moresby in 1873, after whom the harbour was named. Moresby explored extensively along the south coast and spent several days trading with villagers at Hanuabada. One year later, the London Missionary Society arrived and was soon followed by traders and 'blackbirders', who recruited indentured labourers and were little better than slave-dealers.

In 1888 Port Moresby became the capital of the newly declared British New Guinea, and in 1906 the territory was handed to Australia, itself only five years independent of British rule. Sir Hubert Murray took over administration of Papua, as it was known, until his death in 1940, aged 78, at Samarai Island while still on duty.

Port Moresby was overshadowed by Lae, the supply base for the gold rushes in Wau and Bulolo, and Rabaul until WWII. The Japanese quickly occupied all of northern New Guinea and were rapidly advancing south when Port Moresby became the staging post for Allied troops fighting along the Kokoda Track. Port Moresby remained in Australian hands throughout the war.

After the war, Papua and New Guinea were administered as one territory with Port Moresby becoming the capital largely by default – more attractive alternatives such as Lae and Rabaul had been flattened by Allied bombing.

Dangers & Annoyances

Parts of Port Moresby can be dangerous, but it's not the hell on earth that many who've never been here make it out to be. The vast majority of visitors to Port Moresby leave unscathed and, if you use your common sense, you should be fine.

Always ask the locals when you arrive about what is safe. Walking around Town and Boroko during daylight hours should be fine, but most other places it's best to walk with a local. Avoid secluded urban areas at any time; *raskols* (bandits) are not strictly nocturnal. Stay out of the settlements unless you are with one of the residents (that includes Hanuabada). Don't walk around Kila Kila, Sabama or Six Mile at any time. After dark, don't walk anywhere. The most important thing is not to make yourself a target or put yourself in situations where you are vulnerable.

◉ Sights

If you make friends with expat yachties, they may invite you out to explore Moresby's wrecks and islands.

★**National Museum
& Art Gallery**   MUSEUM
(NMAG; Map p56; www.museumpng.gov.pg; Independence Dr, Waigani; admission by donation; ⊙8.30am-3.30pm Mon-Fri, 1-3pm Sun) This superb museum, beautifully remodelled for the country's 40th anniversary of independence, is the best introduction you can get to Papua New Guinea's rich indigenous culture. Subtly lit exhibits are divided by theme: musical instruments, body adornments, ceremonial *kundu* and *garamut* drums, seafaring equipment (including a magnificent Milne Bay outrigger canoe decorated in large cowrie shells and ornate canoe splashboards), elaborate masks and vast totem poles from the Sepik are all present and correct. Take your time.

See if you can spot an *agiba* (skull rack), yam cult masks, kina shell money, a *kawarigit* (carved ceremonial stool from the Sepik), bark cloth masks and colourful shields from New Britain and headgear featuring bird-of-paradise feathers.

Other displays cover the geography, fauna, culture, ethnography and history of PNG.

Parliament Haus   HISTORIC BUILDING
(Map p56; ✑327 7377; Independence Dr, Waigani; ⊙9am-noon & 1-3pm Mon-Fri) FREE The main Parliament Haus building is in the style of a Maprik or Sepik *haus tambaran* (spirit house), while the attached, circular cafeteria follows Highland design principles and a mosaic features unmistakably PNG motifs.

The cavernous lobby is entered through doors whose handles are stylised *kundu* drums (an hourglass-shaped drum with lizard skin). Inside, a towering wood carving represents the four regions of PNG. The receptionists are usually happy to walk and talk you through the building's design and history.

Tucked away, several glass displays showcase the nation's wondrous insect life, including the native Queen Alexandra's Birdwing (the world's largest butterfly, with a 30cm wingspan).

It's possible to visit the chamber and witness parliament when it's sitting.

A taxi from Boroko costs about K40 or K50 from Town. Alternatively, take a PMV along Waigani Dr, get out at the white, empty Pineapple Building, and walk about 2km northeast.

★ **Port Moresby Nature Park**   GARDENS
(National Botanical Gardens; ☑ 326 0248; www. facebook.com/PortMoresbyNaturePark; Waigani Dr, Waigani; adult/child/student K14/7/7; ☺ 8am-4pm) At the northern end of Waigani Dr, by the University of Papua New Guinea, this is an island of calm. More than 2km of walkways thread under and through the jungle canopy, with well-maintained gardens displaying both local and exotic plant species, including native and hybrid orchids. The trees are alive with the clamour of fruit bats, and wildlife displays include tree kangaroos, hornbills, cassowaries and a large aviary that houses parrots and birds of paradise. Take public motor vehicle (PMV) 9.

National Library & Archives   LIBRARY
(Map p56; ☑ 325 6200; Independence Dr, Waigani; ☺ 9am-4pm Mon-Fri, to 1pm Sat, 1-4pm Sun) An independence gift from Australia, this library houses a huge PNG collection.

Hanuabada   AREA
(Map p48) Past the docks to the north lies Hanuabada, the original Motu village. Although it is still built over the sea on stilts, the original wood and thatched houses were destroyed by fire during WWII. They were rebuilt in all-Australian building materials – corrugated iron and fibro-cement – but it's an interesting place and the people have retained many traditional Motu customs.

Find a local guide to take you around, or get a taxi to drive you past.

Koki   AREA
(Map p48) The picturesque stilt village of Koki, at the eastern end of Ela Beach, is worth visiting if you can find a local to take you. The best way to do that is by visiting the

neighbouring **Koki Market**, one of the oldest markets in the city. Fresh produce and fish straight off the boat are sold here and it's a colourful place to watch grassroots-style PNG commerce. PMVs stop outside the market.

Ela Beach   BEACH
(Map p53) On the southern side of Town is the long, sandy stretch of Ela Beach. The beachfront promenade is a popular walk during the day and there are usually some locals frolicking in the water.

St Mary's Catholic Cathedral   CHURCH
(Map p53; Musgrave St, Town) This cathedral has an impressive entrance portal in the style of a Sepik *haus tambaran*.

Paga Point   VIEWPOINT
(Map p53) The harbour headland, Paga Point, is adjacent to Town. It's worth walking to the top of Paga Hill for the fine views over the town, the harbour and the encircling reefs – but don't go alone.

🏃 **Activities**

The diving on offer around Port Moresby is excellent. Bootless Bay has world-class diving over reefs and WWII wreckage. Loloata Island (p60) is a popular holiday spot for divers. For more details on diving in the area, see p32.

Dive Centre   DIVING
(Map p48; ☑ 7202 1200; www.divecentre.com. pg) The biggest dive operator in Moresby is the Dive Centre, currently based at Gateway. It offers full PADI courses (K1700), equipment, air, and a wide range of diving and snorkelling tours. A two-dive outing including gear costs K325. Very professional.

☞ **Tours**

New Guinea Natural Tours   BIRDWATCHING
(☑ 7688 0978; www.newguineanaturaltours.com. pg; from US$300 per day) Originally from Mt Hagen in the Highlands, jovial and bushy-bearded Daniel Wakra is an outstanding birding guide who takes clients to Varirata National Park for day excursions.

Ecotourism Melanesia   TOUR
(Map p56; ☑ 323 4518; www.em.com.pg; Lokua Ave, Boroko; half-day tour per person from US$230) This is one of the better locally owned tour operators. It can customise tours to suit your needs, from half-day tours of Moresby to war history tours of Sogeri Rd.

Greater Port Moresby

Niugini Holidays   TOUR
(Map p56; ☎ 323 5245; www.nghols.com) Offers professionally run day trips, including full-day tours of Port Moresby Town (A$65 per person), full-day Town and Varirata National Park tours (A$145) and day-long taste of Kokoda (A$290) tours.

✯✯ Festivals & Events

★ Hiri Moale   CULTURAL
(☉ Sep) Port Moresby's big event is the three-day Hiri Moale Festival, celebrated around September 16 to coincide with Independence Day. Motu people race giant canoes

and celebrate the shift in trade winds that traditionally brought traders home from the Gulf region where they exchanged earth-fired pots for food. There's a Miss Hiri Queen contest. The festival location is Ela Beach.

🛏 Sleeping

Places to stay are scattered all over Port Moresby and, with very few exceptions, are absurdly overpriced. Boroko and Town are the best places to stay if you want to see something of Moresby, as they are both convenient for PMV routes – particularly Boroko, as almost all PMV routes stop at

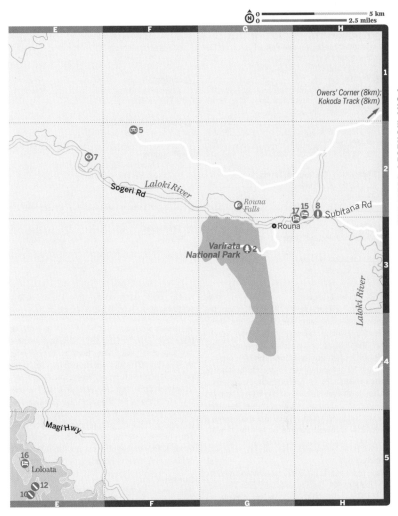

its big bus stop on the Hubert Murray Hwy, one of only two routes into Town. Few room prices include breakfast.

Boroko

★ Mapang Missionary Home
GUESTHOUSE **$**

(Map p54; ☑ 7288 8370; www.mapang.org; Lahara Ave, Boroko; shared/private r per person K200/350; P ❉ @) In central Boroko, this snug guesthouse is clean as a whistle, secure, and run by an affable, knowledgeable American missionary couple. The best budget option in Mores-

by comes with a communal lounge, kitchen and library, and complimentary broadband internet wired to each room. Caters mostly to missionaries; weekends are your best bet. Great ratio of guests per shared bathroom.

Jessie Wyatt House
GUESTHOUSE **$**

(Map p54; ☑ 325 6808; Taurama Rd, Boroko; dm/s/d K100/150/200; ❉) Run by the Country Women's Association, this churchy place is popular with Papua New Guineans. It is clean, quiet and homely with a communal kitchen, free tea and coffee, and a fridge in each room. The rooms are few, spartan in furnishings and in high demand.

Greater Port Moresby

★ **Raintree Lodge** BOUTIQUE HOTEL **$$**
(Map p54; ☑ 7630 7495, 7101 6979; www.the
raintreelodge.com; Ilimo Ave, Boroko; ste K500;
P❊☎) Hiding behind a bamboo stock-
ade like some coquettish ingenue, this
tranquil, intimate boutique hotel consists
of just 12 spacious yet somewhat sombre
suites that sit in an orchid-rich garden. The
Balinese masseuse also works her magic on
nonguests (advance bookings) and Raintree
makes for a peaceful retreat from Moresby's
relentless hubbub. Not to be confused with
concrete monstrosity Raintree Hotel.

Shady Rest HOTEL **$$**
(Map p54; ☑ 323 0000; www.shadyrest.com.
pg; Taurama Rd, Boroko; s/d/ste K299/349/549;
❊☎) The rooms at this secure, intimate hotel
are clean, bright and well equipped (large
flat-screen TV, fridge), but wi-fi costs extra.
Nothing is within easy walking distance, but
on-site you can eat at an excellent Indian restaurant or tapas bar, order takeaway pizza, get
a haircut, withdraw money and sing karaoke.

Paddy's Hotel MOTEL **$$**
(Map p54; ☑ 323 3202; www.paddyshotelpng.
com; Angau Dr, Boroko; r from K520; P❊☎)
Secure, and right in the middle of Boroko's
action, Paddy's is a motel-style set-up spread
across three floors. Rooms probably won't
make your social media posts, but are spa-
cious and modern, and a lively expat crowd
invades the large bar (with pool tables) after

work, particularly on Fridays. There's also a
restaurant on-site. Wi-fi costs extra.

Wellness Lodge HOTEL **$$**
(Map p54; ☑ 7373 4113, 323 8606; www.wellness
lodgepng.com; Vaivai Ave, Boroko; r K249-649;
P❂❊☎) With its no booze or smoking
policy, an on-site spa offering massages, re-
flexology and soqi bed sessions, and a restaurant serving health-promoting dishes and
freshly pressed fruit juices, this hotel pitches
to a specific clientele (you know who you are).
The cheapest, swing-a-cat standard rooms are
tired; K100 extra will get you a much comfier
deluxe. Free (but chaotic) airport pick-up.

Comfort Inn HOTEL **$$**
(Map p54; ☑ 325 5091, 323 0624; www.com
fortinn.com.pg; Mairi Pl, Boroko; s/d incl breakfast
from K290/390, apt K490-650; ❊☎) In a quiet
location two minutes' walk from central
Boroko, the Comfort Inn has friendly service
and comfortable rooms with TVs; ask for a
garden-view room if you're a light sleeper. The
cheapest rooms share facilities.

Be early to the continental breakfast buf-
fet (K30), as it tends to run out. Other meals
(K30 to K40) can be arranged on request.

Town

Weigh Inn Hotel HOTEL **$$**
(Map p48; ☑ 321 7777; Poreporena Fwy, Konedo-
bu; r K350-380; P❊) This ageing place offers
poorly lit standards with cinderblock walls

and boxy but airier 'premier' rooms, all with TV and fridge. There's a restaurant and cosy pub that serves daily specials and is popular with expats and locals alike.

Crowne Plaza
HOTEL **$$$**

(Map p53; ☑ 309 3000; www.crowneplaza. com; cnr Douglas & Hunter Sts, Town; r K590-727, ste K1973; ☞ ❄ @ 🛜 ❄) In the heart of Town, this concrete behemoth has commanding views from its nine floors of neatly fitted-out rooms. The standard rooms are modestly sized, but you could throw a party in the executive suites and apartments, which come with free use of the club lounge. There's a bar, informal cafeteria and one of the best restaurants in town.

Grand Papua
LUXURY HOTEL **$$$**

(Map p53; ☑ 304 0000; www.grandpapuahotel. com.pg; Mary St, near Musgrave St, Town; r K717-843, ste K1006-1996; ❄ @ 🛜 ❄) The high-rise Grand Papua brings yet more luxury to the Town scene, with handsomely appointed but somewhat dark rooms, free wi-fi (hallelujah!), a decent but pricey restaurant with an international menu and excellent breakfast buffet, a British gentlemen's club–style bar and loads of amenities (including spa services). Substantial weekend discounts. Inconsistent service in the restaurant and elsewhere is Grand Papua's Achilles heel.

★ Ela Beach Hotel
LUXURY HOTEL **$$$**

(Map p53; ☑ 321 2100; www.coralseahotels. com.pg; Ela Beach Rd, Ela Beach; r K676-751; P ☞ ❄ 🛜 ❄) This flash hotel has attractively set rooms in a prime beachfront location. The older rooms are nothing special, and the service is decidedly patchy if you wish to order room service or any extras. However, the hotel's redeeming features include the excellent Beachside Brasserie (p53) restaurant and Ozzie's Bar (p55), one of Moresby's best live-music venues.

🛏 Waigani

Holiday Inn & Suites
HOTEL **$$$**

(Map p56; ☑ 303 2000; www.holidayinn.com; Waigani Dr, near Wards Rd, Hohola; r K590-818; P ❄ @ 🛜 ❄) A high-end, pricey option, the Holiday Inn has excellent facilities – a good restaurant, a nightclub (request a room far away from it to avoid being 'lulled' to sleep by pounding bass), an inviting palm-fringed pool – plus modern rooms. The service seems strangely wary of customers.

Across the street, the new Holiday Inn Express is slightly cheaper and has nonsmoking rooms.

Lamana
HOTEL **$$$**

(Map p56; ☑ 323 2333; www.lamanahotel.com. pg; off Waigani Dr, Hohola; r K759-1045; P ❄ 🛜 ❄) The 1970s rooms at Lamana have had a contemporary makeover but the mattresses could also do with revamping, and are fitted sheets too much to ask? The staff is friendly and efficient, the breakfast buffet is excellent, and there's a gym to work off restaurant-acquired calories. But woe betide you if you wish to sleep on weekends; there's a nightclub on-site.

🛏 Near the Airport

Ponderosa Family Hotel
HOTEL **$$**

(Map p56; ☑ 323 4888; Nuana Rd, Gordons; r K250-435; ❄) In a quiet area, this friendly place has simple, tidy rooms (though the cheapest rooms have very old bathrooms and lack air-con). Popular with locals.

Gateway
HOTEL **$$**

(Map p48; ☑ 325 3855; www.coralseahotels. com.pg; Morea-Tobo Rd, Seven Mile; r K320-505, apt K585; P ❄ 🛜 ❄) Located one minute's drive from the airport, this member of the Coral Sea chain is a Moresby institution, with comfortable, if rather worn, standard rooms (go for a newer room) that will do in a pinch for an overnight stay. There are a couple of bars and restaurants; the Palazzio pizzeria downstairs serves passable pizza.

★ Airways Hotel & Apartments
LUXURY HOTEL **$$$**

(Map p48; ☑ 324 5200; www.airways.com.pg; Jackson's Pde, Seven Mile; r K750-950, ste K1050-1250; ❄ 🛜 ❄) The perfect place for the visitor who wants nothing to do with Port Moresby, Airways has spectacular views over the airport and the poolside lounge-and-bar area is lovely. Luxury rooms, two excellent restaurants, two coffee shops and a wonderful spa are reason enough to stop by. The downside? Inconsistency in service and discreet snobbishness directed at casually dressed guests.

Even if you're not a guest, it's worth your while to dine at Baccus, Airways' high-end international restaurant, tuck into an excellent buffet at Vue or scoff some pasta at KC's Deli by the pool.

Eating

After a few weeks in the boondocks eating rice, *kaukau* (sweet potato) and *tinpis* (tinned fish), travellers will find the Moresby dining options a blessing. However, there's little to fill the void between *kai* (fast-food) bars and pricey restaurants. The largest and best-stocked supermarkets are at Harbour City and Vision City.

Boroko

Mr B Coffee Shoppe　　　　　CAFE $
(Map p54; ☑ 325 5411; 1st fl, Brian Bell Plaza, Boroko; mains K5-10; ☺ 9am-4pm Mon-Fri, to noon Sat; ❋) This tiny local favourite set inside the Brian Bell Plaza makes a fine refuge from Boroko's chaotic streets. Mr B serves sandwiches, savoury pies (K5), pastries, lunchtime specials such as chicken and chips, and good Goroka coffee.

Joe's Kitchen　　　　　KAI BAR $
(Map p54; Angau Dr, Boroko; meals K8-12; ☺ 10am-6pm Mon-Sat) While the sheep's tongue stew at this friendly *kai* bar is likely to appeal to gourmets inclined to live dangerously, the roast chicken and chips (K12 for a quarter chicken) is nicely done and the meat pies (K5) make bargain bites.

★ Cellar　　　　　INDIAN $$
(Map p54; ☑ 323 0000; Taurama Rd, Boroko; mains K35-50; ☺ 7am-10pm; ❋ ☑) At the Shady Rest hotel, this refined spot serves authentic Indian dishes. Popular picks include tandoori chicken and vegetable samosas, and the barramundi masala is absolutely stellar; skip the disappointing naan, though.

City Point　　　　　CHINESE $$
(Map p54; ☑ 311 3666; Okari St, Boroko; mains K21-48; ☺ 10am-2pm & 5-9pm; ❋ ☑) Tucked away off the main street, this low-key Chinese restaurant does an excellent value lunchtime menu (K21 to K25) of chicken and rice and other simple dishes. The à la carte menu veers more towards the spicy end of the spectrum, with numerous Sichuan dishes, such as fish poached in chilli broth, twice-cooked pork belly and fried crab with chilli sauce.

★ Seoul House　　　　　KOREAN $$$
(Map p54; Hubert Murray Hwy, Boroko; mains K35-80; ☺ 10am-2pm & 5-9pm Mon-Fri, 10am-2pm Sat, 5-9pm Sun; ℙ ❋ ☑) Skip the so-so Thai food at this refined, minimalist Korean restaurant that overplays its hand, and go straight for the superlative Korean dishes. Bibimbaps and seafood dishes dominate the extensive menu; the spicy squid stands out and fresh oysters on the half-shell with a dash of spicy sauce deliver a knockout punch to your grateful taste buds.

Town

Shakers Coffee　　　　　CAFE $
(Map p53; Cuthbertson House, Armit St; sandwiches K15; ☺ 7.30am-5.30pm Mon-Sat, to 2pm Sun; ❋) Set with picnic-style wooden benches and tables, this unusual cafe serves equally unusual sandwiches (tuna mornay with pesto, smoky sausage...) alongside good Highland coffee, sausage rolls (K6) and cheesecake (K8). It's a popular lunchtime haunt for locals and expats escaping the office.

Tasty Bite　　　　　INDIAN $
(Map p53; ☑ 321 2222; Hunter St, ANG House; thali K15; ☺ noon-3pm & 5.30-9pm Mon-Sat; ☑) This tiny place has a score of loyal expat fans, including a healthy contingent of resident Indians. Expect decent portions of northern Indian dishes; Monday night is all-you-can-gobble buffet night – great value at K59.

Asia Aromas　　　　　ASIAN $$
(Map p53; ☑ 321 4780; ground fl, Steamships Plaza, Champion Pde, Town; mains K35-55; ☺ 11.30am-2pm & 5.30-10pm Mon-Sat; ❋ ☑) Tucked away inside Steamships Plaza and with embroidered dragons and elephants representing its twin cuisines, this low-key restaurant cooks up good, if not hugely memorable, Chinese and Thai dishes. (Hint: the Chinese ones are considerably more authentic; we particularly approve of their braised prawns with butter and garlic and salt and pepper squid.)

★ Rapala　　　　　INTERNATIONAL $$$
(Map p53; ☑ 309 3240; cnr Douglas & Hunter Sts, Town; mains K62-85; ☺ 6.30-9.30pm Mon-Sat) One of Moresby's best restaurants is an elegant, well-dressed, yet somewhat old-fashioned affair inside the Crowne Plaza. The dishes are cutting-edge, though. We particularly like their tasting plates – one-spoon bites of beef kibbeh, lobster tempura, seared scallops and other gourmet loveliness. The veal tenderloin is beautifully tender and the desserts are imaginative multi-part creations. Dress nicely.

Town & Ela Beach

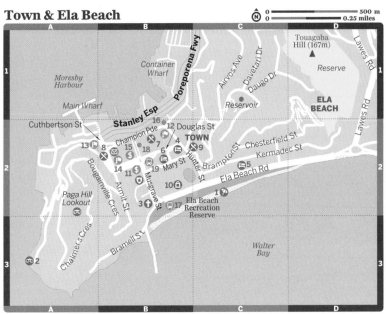

Town & Ela Beach

◎ Sights
1 Ela Beach C2
2 Paga Point A3
3 St Mary's Catholic Cathedral B2

🛏 Sleeping
4 Crowne Plaza B2
5 Ela Beach Hotel C2
6 Grand Papua B2

🍴 Eating
7 Asia Aromas B2
  Beachside Brasserie .... (see 5)
  Rapala .... (see 4)
8 Shakers Coffee B2
9 Tasty Bite C2

🍷 Drinking & Nightlife
  Ozzie's Bar .... (see 5)
  Pondo Tavern .... (see 4)

🛍 Shopping
10 Ela Beach Craft Market B2
  Steamships Arcade .... (see 7)

ℹ Information
  ANZ .... (see 12)
11 Bank South Pacific (BSP) B2
12 French Embassy B2
13 Japanese Embassy A2
14 US Embassy B2
15 Westpac B2

ℹ Transport
16 Air Niugini B2
17 Ela Beach PMV Stop B2
18 PNG Air B2
  Qantas .... (see 8)
19 Town PMV Stop B2

Beachside Brasserie INTERNATIONAL **$$$**
(Map p53; ☑ 321 2100; Ela Beach Rd, Ela Beach; meals K35-80; ⏱ 6.30am-10.30pm; ❄ 🛜 🖉) Aswirl with psychedelic paintings by a local artist, this light, bright brasserie in Ela Beach Hotel serves excellent gourmet pizza as well as chilli prawns, salmon plates, grilled steaks and other international fare.

✕ Waigani

All the Waigani dining options, bar Duffy's, are located inside **Vision City** (Map p56; Sir John Guise Dr, Waigani), Moresby's semi-glitzy shopping mall. Owned by a Malaysian logging company, the mall has been boycotted by eco-minded residents.

Boroko

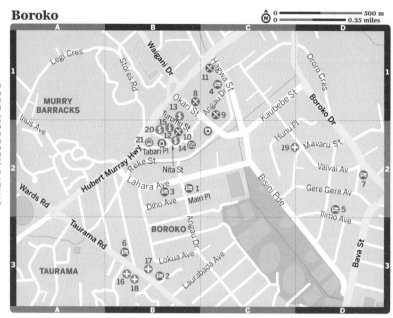

Boroko

Sleeping
1 Comfort Inn B2
2 Jessie Wyatt House B3
3 Mapang Missionary Home B2
4 Paddy's Hotel C1
5 Raintree Lodge D2
6 Shady Rest B3
7 Wellness Lodge D2

Eating
Cellar ....(see 6)
8 City Point B1
9 Joe's Kitchen C1
10 Mr B Coffee Shoppe B2
11 Seoul House C1

Drinking & Nightlife
Paddy's Bar ....(see 4)

Shopping
12 Handicrafts Market B2

Information
13 ANZ B1
14 Bank South Pacific B2
15 Kokoda Track Authority B2
16 Pacific International Hospital B3
17 Paradise Private Hospital B3
18 Port Moresby General Hospital B3
19 Port Moresby Medical Centre
   Clinic C2
20 Westpac B2

Transport
21 Manu Autoport B2

★ **Duffy's** CAFE $
(Map p56; 63 Gabaka St, Waigani; mains K13-22; ⊙8am-4pm Mon-Sat; ❄ 🛜 ✎) Raising Moresby's cafe culture to international levels by its very existence, Duffy's wouldn't look out of place in any Western capital. The decor? Three Cs: cosmopolitan, cool, contemporary. The clientele? Laptop-toting locals and expats keen to tuck into sweet and savoury crepes, salads, quiche, imaginative pies, exotic wraps, eclairs, freshly pressed juices and coffee every which way you want it. Awesome.

Dynasty CHINESE $$
(Map p56; ✆302 8538; Vision City, Sir John Guise Dr, Waigani; mains K22-80; ⊙11am-2pm & 6-10pm; ❄ ✎) Popular with the local Chinese community, this well-regarded restaurant may serve the odd unorthodox dish (Marm-

ite chicken, y'all?) but claypot noodles and black-pepper pork hit the spot. Good lunchtime specials. The yum cha is a major draw on Sunday mornings.

Hog's Breath INTERNATIONAL $$$

(Map p56; Sir John Guise Dr, Vision City, Waigani; mains K44-128; ⊙11.30am-2.45pm & 5.30-10pm; ✹📶) This well-known Aussie diner chain sates the meaty fantasies of the carnivorously inclined with the rib-and-steak combos, lamb cutlets, burgers and more. More eclectic fare includes Tex-Mex combos, seafood gumbo and chilli coconut prawns.

✖ Harbour City

★ Fusion Bistro CHINESE, MALAYSIAN $$

(Map p48; ☑7220 1313, 7192 6666; Poreporena Fwy, SVS Harbour City; ⊙noon-3pm & 5.30-10pm Mon-Sat; ✹📶) Ambitiously promising you offerings from several Asian cuisines, Fusion does Chinese dishes best, though its pandan chicken and sambal fish are well worth a taste. Lunchtime dishes such as claypot chicken are more bargain-worthy, but dress nicely and come to dinner to try the signature salt-and-pepper crab. The chef does wonderful things with tofu, too.

Daikoku JAPANESE $$$

(Map p48; ☑321 0255; 2nd fl, SVS Foodland Bldg, Harbour City; mains K29-70; ⊙11.30am-2pm & 6-10pm Mon-Sat, 6-10pm Sun; 🅿✹📶) This long-running spot with a village-y vibe serves up Moresby's best Japanese fare, with fresh sushi, sashimi, katsu-don, onigiri and other Japanese favourites. Multi-course early-bird specials (K58) are a good deal and the teppanyaki is a highlight, prepared in front of you by chefs with great skill and showmanship. For couples and groups rather than solo diners.

🍷 Drinking & Nightlife

Port Moresby has a few live-music venues and some discos and nightclubs. Some of the latter have a reputation for attracting ladies of negotiable affection.

Paddy's Bar BAR

(Map p54; Angau Dr, Boroko; ⊙5pm-late) After-work happy hour means two-for-one beers at this popular expat hangout with pool tables. Gets particularly raucous on Friday nights.

Figaro COFFEE

(Map p56; 1st fl, Vision City, Waigani Dr; coffee from K8; ⊙9am-6pm; 🛜) An excellent selection of Highland coffees and delectable cakes in refined yuppy surroundings on the 1st floor of Vision City Mall. And did we mention that they've got free wi-fi, too? There's an airport branch in the domestic terminal.

Pondo Tavern BAR

(Map p53; ☑309 3000; cnr Douglas & Hunter Sts, Town; ⊙11am-4.30am) Low-key spot underneath the Crowne Plaza with live music on Thursday nights, and decent pub grub (mains K22 to K35) served on the enclosed patio.

Cosmopolitan CLUB

(Map p56; ☑302 8611; www.cosmopolitanpng. com; Vision City, Waigani Dr; ⊙10am-midnight Tue & Wed, to 4am Thu-Sat) Ritzy, glitzy superclub – the only one in PNG! – that attracts a well-heeled young local crowd and expats ready to party. Think tons of neon, a massive bar with decent but wallet-unfriendly cocktails and either DJ sets or live music, depending on the night.

Royal Papua Yacht Club CLUB

(Map p48; ☑321 1700; www.rpyc.com.pg; Poreporena Fwy) This large, airy place is the last bastion of post-colonial white elitism, with expats and a few visiting yachties mixing over cold beer and good bistro fare (mains K35 to K65) on the deck overlooking the harbour. You can only get in if a member signs you in, so sweet-talk some expat yachties beforehand.

Gold Club CLUB

(Map p56; ☑323 2333; Lamana Hotel, off Waigani Dr, Hohola; ⊙10am-4am) This club at the Lamana hotel has live music courtesy of in-house bands a couple of nights a week, but otherwise it's given over to DJs and local rappers. The two open-air dance floors surrounded by layers of bars create a festive ambience. Monthly appearances by international DJs.

Ozzie's Bar CLUB

(Map p53; ☑321 2100; Ela Beach Hotel, Ela Beach; ⊙9am-2am) With live music Wednesday, Friday and Saturday nights, Ozzie's is a laid-back and unprepossessing place where you can mix it with older locals who love to dance.

Waigani

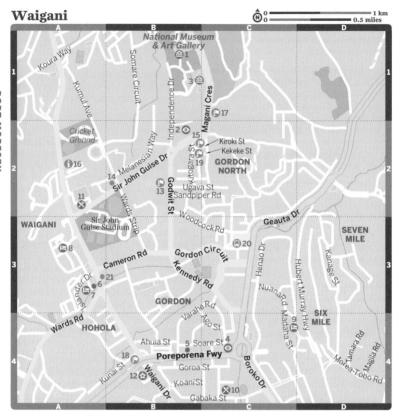

Waigani

☆ Entertainment

The *Post Courier* publishes the 'What's On' entertainment guide on Wednesdays.

Waigani Central Cinema CINEMA
(Map p56; www.facebook.com/paradisecinema png; Waigani Dr) Inside the Waigani Central Mall, this multi-screen cinema screens Hollywood blockbusters.

🔒 Shopping

Handicrafts Market MARKET
(Map p54; Tabari Pl, Boroko; ⊙8am-5pm) Boroko's dusty central square is a good place to buy *bilums,* a selection of Sepik carvings, stone axes, kina-shell breastplates, shell jewellery and the like. Moresby's sellers are used to the ways of tourists and will happily engage in some friendly negotiation, but protracted haggling is considered rude.

Ela Beach Craft Market MARKET
(Map p53; Ela Beach Rd, Ela Beach International School; ⊙7am-noon last Sat of month) This is the best market in PNG, with items from all over the country – with more carvings, baskets, stone tools, adornments, shells and weavings than you can wave a *koteka* (penis gourd) at. (There are penis gourds from the Upper Sepik too.) Barbecued food and traditional dancers (at about 10am) contribute to the carnival atmosphere.

Port Moresby Grammar School Craft Market MARKET
(Map p48; ☑323 6577; Bava St; ⊙8am-noon 2nd Sat of month) A monthly event with carvings, tribal adornments, *bilums* and other paraphernalia from different parts of PNG. Good crowds and a party atmosphere.

ℹ️ Information

EMERGENCY
Ambulance (☑111)
Fire (☑110)
Police (Map p53; ☑000)

INTERNET ACCESS
Pretty much only the priciest hotels offer wi-fi or internet access. Moresby's internet cafes are practically nonexistent, so either invest in a local Digicel SIM card with data, or haunt the 7 C's cafe inside Airways Hotel or Figaro (free wi-fi for customers).

MEDICAL SERVICES
Pacific International Hospital (Map p54; ☑7111 4000, 7998 8000; www.pihpng.com;

Stores Rd, Boroko) Expensive private hospital with 24/7 emergency care. Best in the country.
Paradise Private Hospital (Map p54; ☑325 6022; Taurama Rd, Boroko; ⊙24hr) Private hospital with 24-hour emergency service.
Port Moresby General Hospital (Map p54; ☑324 8200; Taurama Rd, Boroko) Overstretched public healthcare services. You may be waiting for quite some time.
Port Moresby Medical Centre Clinic (Map p54; ☑325 6633; cnr Vaivai Ave & Mavaru St, Boroko; ⊙24hr) Best place in an emergency. Can arrange medivac and has a decompression chamber on-site.

MONEY
ANZ and Westpac are more efficient than Bank South Pacific (BSP), where you'll likely grow old waiting to change your money. If you're changing cash, ask for the international desk.

Town
ANZ (Map p53; cnr Champion Pde & Musgrave St, Town) Reliable ATMs.
Bank South Pacific (BSP) (Map p53; ☑321 2444; cnr Musgrave & Douglas Sts) Charges K15 per ATM withdrawal.
Westpac (Map p53; ☑322 0888; cnr Musgrave & Douglas Sts) Agent for Amex. ATMs work for Visa, MasterCard, Cirrus, Visa/PLUS and Maestro. K20 charge to change cash.

Boroko
Bank South Pacific (BSP; Map p54; ☑323 2288; cnr Nita St & Angau Dr, Boroko) K15 charge to withdraw cash from ATM.
Westpac (Nita St, Boroko) Reliable ATMs.

POST
Boroko Post Office (Map p54; ☑300 3794; Tabari Pl, Boroko; ⊙8am-4pm Mon-Fri, to 11.30am Sat) Busy post office.
Post Office (Map p53; ☑300 3797; cnr Cuthbertson St & Champion Pde, Town; ⊙8am-4pm Mon-Fri, to 11.30am Sat) Main postal services.

TOURIST INFORMATION
Kokoda Track Authority (KTA; Map p54; ☑323 6165; www.kokodatrackauthority.org; 2nd fl, Brian Bell Bldg, Boroko; ⊙9am-4pm Mon-Fri) Statutory body that administers activities related to the Kokoda Track – it collects and distributes trekking fees, liaises with landowners etc. Good place to contact if you're looking for a guide or want to join a trek.

ℹ️ Getting There & Away

AIR
Jacksons International Airport (☑324 4704) PNG's busiest air hub is located to the northeast of the city. It has international connections

to Cairns and Brisbane (Australia), Singapore, Tokyo (Japan) and Manila (Philippines), most served by Air Niugini, and domestic services to every part of the country.

Air Niugini (Map p53; ☑ 321 2888; www. airniugini.com.pg; ground fl, MMI House, Champion Pde, Town)

PNG Air (Map p53; ☑ 321 3400; www. pngair.com.pg; 1st fl, Pacific Place, Musgrave St, Town)

Qantas (Map p53; ☑ 308 3222; www. qantas.com.au; Cuthbertson St, Town)

Travel Air (Map p56; ☑ 7090 3887; www. travelairpng.com; Steamships Compound, Waigani Dr)

BOAT

There are no regular passenger boats sailing out of Port Moresby. Many freighters do have passenger facilities but none of the shipping companies officially allow passengers. If you want to go to the Gulf, ask around the smaller boats at the jetties north of the main wharf. Heading east towards Milne Bay, you could go to Kupiano and look for a small boat or canoe.

CAR

You currently can't really drive anywhere else from Port Moresby (except Sogeri Rd), though the government is (slowly) building a coastal road to eventually connect to Alotau. There are

several companies renting cars and 4WDs in Port Moresby.

PMV

Rural PMVs leave from Gordons Market and head west as far as Kerema (K45, five hours) and east along the Magi Hwy. PMV 16 also leaves here for Bomana War Cemetery and destinations along the Sogeri Rd.

ℹ Getting Around

TO & FROM THE AIRPORT

The hotel minibus is an easy and free way to get between the airport and where you're staying. All but the smallest establishments have one; contact them ahead, or call for free from the NCD Tourist Office in the international arrivals area. In the domestic terminal, buy a phonecard from the shop beside the cafe.

Taxis wait outside both terminals; negotiate the fare before you leave. A taxi to Waigani or Boroko costs around K40, and to Town about K50 to K60.

CAR & 4WD

The airport is full of companies renting cars and 4WDs, and the major names also have offices in several top-end hotels. Prices start at around K265/1855 per day/week for a manual Toyota Corolla and K365/2004 for an all-wheel drive

DOMESTIC FLIGHTS FROM PORT MORESBY

DESTINATION	COST (K)	TIME (HR)	FREQUENCY	AIRLINE
Alotau	341-591	¾-1¼	2-4 daily	Air Niugini, PNG Air, Travel Air
Daru	551-701	1-1¼	1-2 daily except Thu & Sun	Air Niugini, PNG Air
Goroka	361-641	1-1¼	4-5 daily	Air Niugini, PNG Air
Kavieng	540	1½	9.50am Sun	Air Niugini
Kieta	692	3	Mon, Wed & Fri	Air Niugini
Kiunga	621-901	2-3	1-2 daily	Air Niugini, PNG Air
Lae	302-521	¾-1	11-12 daily	Air Niugini, PNG Air, Travel Air
Losuia/Kiriwina (Trobriands)	551-821	1¼- 2¼	Tue, Thu, Fri & Sun	Air Niugini, PNG Air
Madang	427-664	1	2-3 daily	Air Niugini, PNG Air
Mendi	739	1½	4 weekly	Air Niugini
Mount Hagen	361-641	1-1½	7-8 daily	Air Niugini, PNG Air, Travel Air
Popondetta	301-397	½	2-4 daily	Air Niugini, PNG Air
Rabaul	492	1¼-2	2-3 daily	Air Niugini
Tabubil	721-1049	2-3	daily except Sun	Air Niugini, PNG Air
Tari	621-1021	1½-1¾	1-2 daily	Air Niugini, PNG Air
Tufi	392-732	1¾	Mon, Wed & Fri	PNG Air
Vanimo	926	3¼	1-2 daily	Air Niugini
Wewak	469-829	2-3	2-3 daily	Air Niugini, PNG Air

Toyota Rav4 (plus optional insurance at K25 per day for a collision damage waiver excess of K2000). Port Moresby can be a confusing place to navigate, so be sure to have a map and take out full insurance. Police checkpoints are common after dark but shouldn't be a problem if you have your licence.

Avis (Map p48; ☑324 9400; www.avis.com. pg) Offices at the airport (domestic and international terminals).

Hertz (Map p48; ☑325 4999; www.hertz. com) Desks at the airport and Gateway Hotel.

Thrifty (Map p56; ☑325 5550) Offices at the airport, Airways Hotel & Apartments and Lamana Hotel.

PMV

Port Moresby has an efficient PMV (public motor vehicle) service. They're quite safe provided you stick to certain routes and be careful about where you disembark. PMVs run frequently from about 6am to 6pm but stop suddenly at nightfall; be careful not to be caught out. The flat fare is K1 to K2 for trips around Moresby. The main interchange point is **Manu Autoport** (Map p54) in Boroko; look for the pedestrian overpass and crowds of people. In Town, the main stops are on Douglas St and on Ela Beach, and at Gordons near Gordons Market. PMVs get crowded at peak hours and especially on Friday evening.

PMVs run set routes and have route numbers (and sometimes the destination itself) painted on the front. They go both ways. Some useful routes include the following:

Route 4 From Hanuabada, through Town, Koki and Boroko to Gordons Market.

Route 7 From Gerehu, past Waigani, Gordons and Erima to Seven Mile.

Route 9 From Gerehu and Waigani to Four Mile/Boroko, East Boroko and then to Three Mile (this is the bus to get from Boroko to the Botanical Gardens).

Route 10 From Hanuabada to Town, Badilly, Sabama, Manu, Three Mile, Four Mile/Boroko (Jessie Wyatt House; past the hospital and the CWA Hostel), and on to the airport at Seven Mile. Avoid getting on or off in the Kila Kila and Sabama areas, which are relatively unsafe.

Route 11 From Town to Two Mile Hill, Boroko, Waigani (not all stop at the government offices) and Morata.

Route 12 From Gerehu to Waigani, Hohola, Three Mile and Manu.

Route 15 From Tokarara to the government buildings in Waigani, Gordons, Erema, Seven Mile, Six Mile, Five Mile and Four Mile/Boroko to Hohola.

Route 16 From Gordons Market out to Bomana Prison, past the War Cemetery.

Route 17 From Gordons to Four Mile/Boroko, Three Mile, Sabama and Bari.

TAXI

Port Moresby has no shortage of taxis, and you'll usually be able to find one outside a hotel or the airport, and in Boroko. Practically none will agree to use meters, so negotiate the price before setting off. Sample fares: Town to Boroko or Waigani, K40; Town to the airport, K50 to K60.

While reputable companies allegedly include **Ark Taxis** (☑323 0998, 7122 5522) and **Scarlet Taxis** (☑7220 7000, 323 3286), they very rarely answer the phone. So if you find yourself stranded at a restaurant or at your lodgings, ask security to go and round up a taxi for you or if you come across a reliable taxi driver, treasure his number as if it's gold dust. Hailing a taxi on the street is pot luck; many of Moresby's taxi drivers are fresh arrivals from the Highlands, a number of whom only speak Pidgin and don't know the city well, so it's up to you to give them directions.

Joe (☑7113 5391) Reliable, helpful taxi driver.

Thomas (☑7686 4743, 7121 0193) Recommended taxi driver.

AROUND PORT MORESBY

Sogeri Road

There are some interesting areas near Port Moresby along or just off the Sogeri Rd, which veers to the right (east) off the Hubert Murray Hwy a couple of kilometres past the airport. It's quiet during the week, so it's best to travel on the Sogeri Rd with a local, though there haven't been any robberies since the road's been paved.

It's 46km to Sogeri but there is enough to see to make it a full-day trip.

◉ Sights

Bomana War Cemetery CEMETERY
(Map p48; ☑328 1536; ⊙8am-4pm) A turn-off near Fourteen Mile takes you to the large and carefully tended Bomana War Cemetery, where 4000 unknown PNG and Australian WWII soldiers are seeing out eternity, overlooked by a vast rain tree. American soldiers who died in PNG were generally shipped home for burial. The inscriptions on identical white gravestones read: 'A soldier of the 1939–1945 war. Known unto God.' It's a serene yet sobering place. PMV 16 from Gordons Market runs past the gate.

National Orchid Gardens GARDENS
(Map p48; ☑325 5049; adult/child K15/10; ⊙8am-4pm Sat & Sun) Around Fourteen Mile,

WORTH A TRIP

LOLOATA ISLAND

About 20km east of Port Moresby, in Bootless Bay, the appealing **Loloata Island Resort** (Map p48; ☑ 325 8590, 7276 8687; www.loloata.com; s with/without air-con US$292/264, d US$462/424; ❉) is a popular weekender getaway. It's also a destination in its own right for divers who plumb the depths of its 29 dive sites. Accommodation consists of large, comfortable beachfront bungalows with panoramic views northeast across Bootless Bay and the Owen Stanley Range. Pick-up is offered for daytrippers.

As well as first-rate diving, the resort also offers snorkelling, fishing and kayaking. A day trip, including return boat from Tahira Marina, lunch and a diving/snorkelling trip to the reefs around nearby Lion Island, costs K180; pick-up from hotels in Moresby an additional K60. Diving costs US$60 for one or US$150 for three dives (including equipment); night dives and PADI courses are also available. Loloata also offers a range of tours (such as Varirata National Park, Sogeri and Owers' Corner).

To get there, drive out on the Rigo Rd (which meets the airport road in Six Mile) to the Tahira Marina on Bootless Bay. The resort's boats depart the marina at 9am and 2.30pm daily. Alternatively, call ahead and the resort bus will collect you from the airport or your hotel. At time of writing, the resort was being completely remodelled.

next door to the humdrum Adventure Park PNG (look out for the Ferris wheel) are the excellent National Orchid Gardens. Apart from getting up close and personal with numerous flowering orchids, your entry price allows you to visit the adjoining aviary to see such feathered delights as cassowaries, cockatoos, splendid Victoria crown pigeons and brightly plumed birds of paradise.

Laloki River Gorge HILL
(Map p48; Sogeri Rd) A few kilometres past the Bomana War Cemetery cemetery, the road winds up the impressive Laloki River gorge and you're soon more than 600m above sea level. There are several viewing points looking into the gorge and up to the Rouna Falls and power station.

Hombrum Bluff Lookout VIEWPOINT
(Map p48; Hombrum Bluff Rd) Some kilometres down the rough Kokoda Track road (barely navigable in a 2WD and in dry season only) is a turn-off left (west) back towards Port Moresby. This is the Hombrum Bluff road that runs along the top of the Laloki River canyon wall. It leads to Hombrum Bluff Lookout that rises 1300m and was used as a retreat for the military brass during WWII. Below is Seventeen Mile, which was an important base camp for more than 400 soldiers.

★**Varirata National Park** NATIONAL PARK
(Map p48; admission K5) Right after the small store at Laloki River Gorge is the turn-off to Varirata National Park which, at 1000 hectares and more than 800m high,

is the highlight of the Sogeri Rd. It's 8km from the turn-off and you'll find several clearly marked walking trails among the pine trees, ranging from 45 minutes to three hours, and some excellent lookouts back to Port Moresby and the coast. Birdwatchers may spot kingfishers and Raggiana birds of paradise.

It's possible to camp here, but unless you're in a large group, it's potentially unsafe. The best place is on the grass outside the derelict huts. There are pit toilets. Speak to the ranger-in-charge (if you can find him!).

McDonald's Corner MONUMENT
(Map p48; Kokoda Track Rd) On the rough Kokoda Track road you can drive past McDonald's Corner where there's a small memorial that marks the start of the Kokoda Track. It was here that Australian WWII soldiers disembarked their trucks and began the long muddy march. Later the rough road was pushed further through to Owers' Corner, from where it's possible to do day hikes along the Kokoda Track (bring a guide).

🛏 Sleeping & Eating

Kokoda Trail Hotel LODGE $$
(Map p48; ☑ 323 6724; www.kokodatrailhotel. com; s/d from K205/250, apt K450; 🅿❉) The plushest option on the Sogeri Rd is this Aussie-owned lodge that's often booked out by trekkers. Amid lush landscaping, the rooms here are bright and nicely equipped (fan, TV and fridge), and the restaurant (mains K30 to K60) has tasty dishes, includ-

ing pan-fried barramundi, and superb views over the river. The lodge doesn't arrange Kokoda guides.

Sogeri Lodge GUESTHOUSE **$$**
(Map p48; ☑7093 8254, 325 5440; sogent@global.net.pg; s/d with shared bathroom K175/250; ❄) Popular with Kokoda trekkers, Sogeri has clean, simple, fan-cooled rooms and a pleasant restaurant (mains K20 to K50) with a terrace offering fine views. There's an absorbing mini-museum of WWII relics in the lobby and Kokoda guides can be arranged next door.

❶ Information

Sogeri Enterprises (Map p48; ☑7265 0138, 325 1887; www.kokodatreks.com) Next door to Sogeri Lodge, this local company can arrange a trekking guide for the Kokoda Track. Prices start from around K3000 per person.

❶ Getting There & Away

PMVs leave from Gordons Market semi-regularly. The road is surfaced to Sogeri and all the way down to the Varirata National Park, but the section from Sogeri to Owers' Corner – the start of the Kokoda Track – is suitable for 4WDs only.

Central, Oro & Milne Bay Provinces

POP 732,600 / AREA 67,940 SQ KM

Best Places to Stay

➡ Ulumani Treetops Lodge (p74)

➡ Nuli Sapi (p76)

➡ Butia Lodge (p81)

➡ Tufi Resort (p68)

➡ Tawali Resort (p74)

Best Village Stays

➡ Garewa (p68)

➡ Kofure (p68)

➡ Okaiboma Beach Huts (p81)

➡ Kaibola Beach Guesthouse (p81)

➡ Orotaba (p68)

Why Go?

In these eastern provinces, the legendary Kokoda Track zig-zags relentlessly through the jungle-clad mountains, throwing down the gauntlet to those who wish to walk in the footsteps of WWII's fallen. Further east, amid the fjords of the rugged coastline, some of the world's most biologically diverse reefs have divers gasping through their mouthpieces. Coastal villagers welcome visitors with old-fashioned hospitality and can show them the sacred skull caves of their ancestors.

North across the Solomon Sea, the Trobriands are a world apart: yams rule supreme, 'free love' is occasionally practised, magicians bring rain and cricket is played aggressively.

Head south and the land dissolves into thousands of islands, islets and atolls, where the adventurous can spend weeks island-hopping. This watery world celebrates its seafaring heritage during the Milne Bay Canoe & Kundu Festival, during which island warriors race their splendidly decorated ocean-going canoes.

When to Go
Kokoda

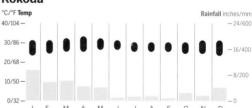

Jun–Aug Catch the raucous Milamala Festival on the Trobriand Islands.

May–Sep Dry, cooler weather in Central Province, ideal Kokoda trekking weather.

Oct–Dec Calm, dry weather in Milne Bay – best for diving and snorkelling.

History

The coastal people and islanders of this region have traded for centuries in extensive barter networks. The *hiri* trade between Motuans in Central Province and villages further around the gulf was conducted in huge two-masted *lakatois* (sailing boats).

In 1606 Spanish mariner Luis Vaéz de Torres, after whom the Louisiade Archipelago was named, abducted 14 children and took them to Manila in the Philippines to be baptised. He was followed by an array of explorers, including the famous Frenchman Antoine d'Entrecasteaux, but it wasn't until 1847 that Europeans sought to settle the region. In that year, Marist missionaries arrived on Muyua (Woodlark) Island, but the locals, it seems, were unenthusiastic about Christianity and the Marists were gone within eight years. Apparently undeterred, the London Missionary Society (LMS), Catholics, Anglicans, Methodists and finally Seventh-Day Adventists opened for business between the 1870s and 1908. Most notable among them was Reverend Charles W Abel, a dissident member of the LMS, who in 1891 founded the Kwato Extension Association on Kwato Island, providing skills training to the indigenous people of Milne Bay.

Apart from men of God, the region attracted 'blackbirding' opportunists who forcibly removed local men to work in northern Australian sugar plantations well into the 20th century.

On the north coast early European contacts with the Orokaiva people were relatively peaceful, but when gold was discovered at Yodda and Kokoda in 1895, violence soon followed. A government station was established after an altercation between locals and miners, but the first government officer was killed shortly after he arrived. Eventually things quietened down and the mines were worked out. Then came WWII.

Milne Bay became a huge Allied naval base and the gardens and plantations inland from Buna and Gona had barely recovered from the war when Mt Lamington's 1951 eruption wiped out Higaturu, the district headquarters, killing almost 3000 people. The new headquarters town of Popondetta was established at a safer distance from the volcano.

Geography

The region stretches down the 'dragon's tail' at the eastern end of mainland Papua New Guinea and out into the Coral and Solomon Seas, taking in the hundreds of islands and atolls of Milne Bay Province.

The mainland is divided by the Owen Stanley Range, which rises rapidly from the northern and southern coasts to peaks of 3500m to 4000m. Major roads are few: the Magi and Hiritano Hwys extend from Port Moresby, while in Oro Province the only road of any length runs from Popondetta to Kokoda.

Mt Lamington, near Popondetta, remains a mildly active volcano and further east there are volcanoes near Tufi. The section of coast around Cape Nelson has unique tropical 'fjords' *(rias);* their origin is volcanic rather than glacial.

The islands of Milne Bay Province are divided into six main groups: the Samarai group; D'Entrecasteaux group; the Trobriand Islands; Muyua (Woodlark) Island; the Conflict and Engineer groups; and the 300km-long Louisiade Archipelago. They range from tiny dots to mountainous islands such as Fergusson, Normanby and Goodenough; the last, while only 26km wide, soars to 2566m at the summit of Mt Oiautukekea, making it one of the most steeply sided islands on earth.

CENTRAL PROVINCE

Stretching for more than 500km either side of Port Moresby, Central Province lives in the shadow of the national capital. Overlooked by tourists and long ignored by politicians, infrastructure is, even by local standards, *bagarap* (buggered up).

Kokoda

POP 550

The Owen Stanley Range rises almost sheer as a cliff face behind the Oro Province village of tiny Kokoda, where the northern end of the infamous Kokoda Track (p35) terminates. The grassed area in the centre of town houses a small **museum** that has photos and descriptions of the campaign. Ask around to have it opened. Postmistress Grace Eroro (p66) is a great source of information. Opposite the post office is a branch of the Kokoda Track Authority where trekking permits can be bought if you haven't already done so in Port Moresby. Trekkers finishing the trail should also report here to be officially stamped off the trail.

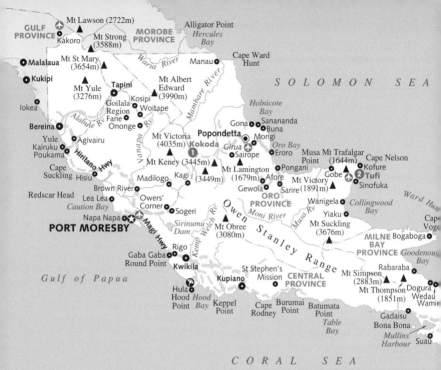

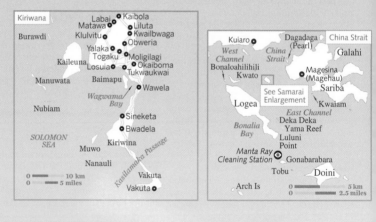

Central, Oro & Milne Bay Provinces Highlights

1 Retracing WWII battles over the rugged Owen Stanley Range along the infamous Kokoda Track to **Kokoda** (p63).

2 Staying in a seaside village among the amazing volcanic *rias* (fjords) of **Tufi** (p67).

3 Seeing yam houses, meeting the rain magician and catching a wildly colourful cricket match on the **Trobriand Islands** (p78).

4 Visiting skull caves, snorkelling and wandering around historic settlements in the **Samarai Islands** (p74).

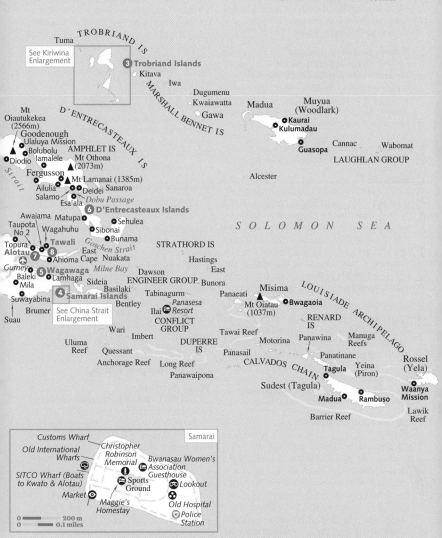

5 Snorkelling around a ghostly wrecked ship, canoeing, and just hanging out at the Edenesque Ulumani Treetops Lodge in **Wagawaga** (p73).

6 Hiking to waterfalls, snorkelling coral reefs and spying birds of paradise on the remote **D'Entrecasteaux Islands** (p76).

7 Watching spirited dance groups followed by a magnificent canoe race at the Milne Bay Canoe & Kundu Festival in **Alotau** (p69).

8 Taking in the abundance of marine life on a dive at **Tawali** (p75).

🛌 Sleeping & Eating

Most resthouses allow you to pitch your tent on their camping grounds for a fee. Limited food and, mercifully, beer is usually available from Kokoda's trade stores.

Kokoda Memorial Hospital GUESTHOUSE $
(☑ 7368 3197, in Australia 1300 514 811; camp39. wix.com/kokodamemorialhospital; dm & camping per person K100) The first guesthouse after exiting the trail (to your right) is part of the Kokoda Memorial Hospital, which has some dormitories with toilets, showers, gas stoves and kitchen utensils. Money goes towards much-needed medical supplies and donations are welcome. Meals can be arranged.

Camp 39 GUESTHOUSE $
(☑ 7382 3309, in Australia 1300 514 811; camp39.wix. com/camp-39-b; dm & camping per person K200) Named after the legendary 39th Battalion, Camp 39 is a friendly, pleasantly sited spot with a grassy lawn (for camping) and a large open thatch-roof building where you can sleep on a mat. Meals are included in the price and there's a shop on-site for snacks. Hot showers and flushing toilets seal the deal.

Grace Eroro's Guesthouse GUESTHOUSE $
(☑ 7113 6598; r per person K100) About 2.5km along the road to Popondetta is Grace's place, run by the big-hearted portmistress Grace Eroro. Grace welcomes travellers in her bunkhouse (a bed for the night and a mosquito net, though flush toilets and showers are still in the planning), or you can camp on the lawn and bathe in the river. Meals extra.

★ Oro Haven Kokoda Retreat GUESTHOUSE $$
(☑ 325 4423, in Australia 0415 499 495; www. orohaven.com; dm/r K100/400) By far the best place to stay in Kokoda, right next to the airstrip and with its own generator. Six traditional huts can sleep guests dorm-style, with individual mosquito nets, but if there's availability, you can book a hut all to yourself. There's wood-fired pizza for dinner and cold beers at the Wantok bar. Weekend packages from Moresby arranged (K1400).

❶ Getting There & Away

Trekkers tackling the Kokoda Track either book group charter flights directly to Kokoda, fly into Popondetta or else finish their trek in Kokoda after hiking from Sogeri Rd. Public motor vehicles (PMVs; K20, 3½ hours) leave Kokoda for Popondetta around the ungodly hour of 3am.

ORO PROVINCE

Oro Province is sandwiched between the Solomon Sea and the Owen Stanley Range. It's physically beautiful but few travellers make it here apart from dedicated Kokoda Track hikers.

The province is famous for the world's largest butterfly, the Queen Alexandra's birdwing. You might think that you've seen some big butterflies in PNG, but these are monsters, with wingspans of nearly 30cm. The first specimen collected by a European was brought down by a shotgun! That butterfly, a little damaged, is still in the British Museum. The Queen Alexandra's birdwing is now a threatened species.

Popondetta

POP 10,200

Popondetta is a ragged yet low-key sprawl of a town, without much appeal for tourists, although some come to see the area's WWII history – Buna and Gona are within an easy day trip. The Oro Guesthouse and Birdwing Butterfly Lodge can provide information and help arrange guides. Japanese tourists come here in search of the remains of their WWII fallen. Bushwalkers can trek up the looming 1679m **Mt Lamington** with a local guide, provided the trails are intact.

🛌 Sleeping & Eating

★ Oro Guesthouse GUESTHOUSE $$
(☑ 7644 8513, 7108 2463; ogh.popondettapng@ gmail.com; r incl breakfast & dinner K176-280; ✳) Easily the best option in Popondetta (not that it's much of a horse race), Oro is set back from a quiet street amid lush vegetation. The somewhat worn rooms are clean, comfortable and come with small bathrooms, excellent local information and two square meals (we hope you like yam). It's a 10-minute walk from town; ask PMVs to drop you off here.

Comfort Inn HOTEL $$
(☑ 629 7222; r K312-442; ✳) The most central option has a rather dingy lobby with a correctional-institution vibe and staff that may not honour your booking. Simple rooms with tile floors, fridge and TV open onto a garden-like exterior. It has the only restaurant in town (mains K30 to K65) but don't get too excited.

YAMS, SEX & CRICKET

Bronislaw Malinowski's celebrated books *The Argonauts of the Western Pacific*, *Coral Gardens and Their Magic* and *The Sexual Life of Savages in Northwestern Melanesia* were published after WWI, and revealed much about the intricate trading rituals, yam cults and sexual practices of the Trobriand Islands. Malinowski found a matrilineal society, in which the chief's sons belong to his wife's clan and he is succeeded by one of his oldest sister's sons. The society is strictly hierarchical, with distinctions between hereditary classes and demarcations in the kind of work each person can perform.

Yams

Yams are far more than a staple food in the Trobriands – they're a sign of prestige and expertise, and a tie between villages and clans. The quality and size of your yams is important. To be known as a *tokwaibagula* (good gardener) is a mark of great prestige.

The yam cult climaxes at the harvest time (usually July or August). The yams are first dug up in the gardens, then displayed, studied and admired. At the appropriate time, the men carry the yams back to the village, with the women guarding the procession.

In the villages, the yams are again displayed before being packed into the highly decorated yam houses. Each man has a yam house for each of his wives and it is his wife's clan's obligation to fill his yam house. The chief's yam house is the biggest, most elaborate and first to be filled.

Sex

Malinowski's tomes on the Trobriand Islanders' customs led to Kiriwina Island receiving the misleading title of 'Island of Love'. It's not surprising that such a label was applied by inhibited Europeans when they first met Trobriand women, with free-and-easy manners and short grass skirts, but it led to the inaccurate idea that the Trobriands were some sort of sexual paradise. The sexual customs are not without their own complicated social strictures.

Teenagers are encouraged to 'make friends' (have as many sexual partners as they choose) until marriage, when they settle down with the partner who is chosen as suitable and compatible. A couple is only considered married if they are seen to be dining together. Some men have more than one wife. Males leave home when they reach puberty and move into the village *bukumatula* (bachelor house). Here, they are free to bring their partners back at any time, although they usually opt for somewhere more private. Even married couples, subject to mutual agreement, are allowed to have a fling when the celebrations for the yam harvest are in full swing.

Aside from all this activity, it's said that few children are born to women without permanent partners. Most people do not believe there is a connection between intercourse and pregnancy – most believe that in order for a woman to become pregnant, she must first be infused with the spirit of a departed ancestor.

All this apparent freedom has negligible impact on visitors. Freedom of choice is the bedrock of Trobriand Islands life, so why would any islander choose unattractive, pale *dimdims* who can't speak like civilised humans, don't understand the most fundamental laws and will probably be gone tomorrow?

Cricket

Trobriand Islands cricket developed after missionaries introduced the sport as a way of taking the islanders' minds off less-healthy activities. It's since developed its own style, which is quite unlike anything the Marylebone Cricket Club ever had in mind. There is no limit to the number of players, meaning you can wait days for a bat. Trobriand cricket is played rather aggressively, with much dancing, singing and whistle blowing, making it rather difficult to concentrate on line and length. When we asked what the song meant, it was translated to us as 'I don't know why we are dancing, the fool is already out!' Games tend to coincide with the yam harvest time.

now preferable to betel nut. The paramount chief presides over the island's oral traditions and magic. He oversees the important yam festival and *kula* rituals, and can often be found sitting on a chair under his house.

Togaku
VILLAGE

A half-hour's walk from Butia Lodge, this village is notable for its particularly splendid yam house – the tallest on the island, painted in the traditional white, red and black and lavishly decorated with strings of large cowrie shells. There's also a large magic stone with a face carved into it, the presence of which brings prosperity to the village.

Luyo
VILLAGE

Trobriands Islanders believe in the power of certain individuals to bring rain. This power is passed on from father to son, and during periods of drought villagers bring gifts to the Rainmaker, who then performs a secret ceremony. It's possible to meet the Rainmaker here; a small gift (K20) is expected.

Kaibola Beach
BEACH

(admission K20) At Kaibola village, at the northern tip of Kiriwina, you can swim and snorkel at the picture-postcard white-sand beach (bring your own snorkelling gear). Locals charge visitors K20 to visit their beach, encouraged by monthly cruise ship visits. PMVs run from Losuia to Kaibola (K5, one hour, several daily).

Sacred Cave
CAVE

(admission K10) A 15-minute walk from Butia Lodge, there's a sacred cave of crystal-clear water that's popular with locals. You can swim in the cool water provided you get permission from the owner.

BANANA LEAF MONEY

The Trobes is the only place in PNG where local women still trade among themselves using *doba* (banana leaf money). They make it by taking leaves from a specific type of banana tree, placing them over a wooden board with a pattern carved into it (each woman has her own unique pattern) and then running a scraper over the leaf. The leaves are then dried and tied into bundles of 10, with each bundle worth K1. *Doba* bundles are also given away during feasts. Ask for a demonstration (around K20) to see how *doba* is made.

Plane Wreck
MONUMENT

Various WWII relics, including the fairly intact remains of an American plane, can be seen near Butia Lodge.

Wawela
BEACH

On the road south of Losuia, Wawela is on a beautiful, curving sand beach edging a cool, deep, protected lagoon. On a falling tide, beware of the channel out to sea from the bay: the current can be very strong. You'll need to charter a 4WD from Butia Lodge.

Kaileuna Island
ISLAND

Of the islands off Kiriwina, Kaileuna Island is the easiest and cheapest to access as boats carrying *buai* (betel nut) travel from Losuia most days. The villages of Kaisiga, in the south, and Tawema to the north have beautiful white-sand beaches.

Festivals

Milamala Festival
CULTURAL

Milamala celebrates a bountiful crop of yams, harvested between June and August. Festivities culminate in a week of canoe racing, cricket matches, ribald dancing and free love. Before you get excited, note that visitors with boiling loins usually have to make their own entertainment because, while yams are considered objects of great beauty, *dimdims* (white people) are not.

Mention to any mainlander that you are off to see the Milamala Festival and you'll be greeted with smirks and puns along the lines of exactly whose yams are ripe for harvesting. Ever since Malinowski published his provocatively titled *The Sexual Life of Savages in Northwestern Melanesia* (1929), the West has been fascinated with the thought of sex-starved, bare-breasted maidens in a tropical paradise, but the reality is different.

The crop yield (along with the chief's whim and, increasingly, monetary incentives from the government) dictate whether or not there will even be a Milamala, and dates are notoriously difficult to pin down.

Sleeping & Eating

Accommodation options have electricity by generator usually from about 6pm to 10pm. Restaurants are nonexistent; most visitors eat at their guesthouse. Butia Lodge and Losuia Lodge can arrange village stays for around K100 per night.

Cindarella's
GUESTHOUSE $

(☑ 7313 6538, 7135 5414; r per person with full board K160) Opposite the cricket field at 'the station', smiling widow Cindy and daughter Janet welcome visitors into their home. The small house has two bedrooms, sleeps three or four, and is the heart of her extended family's compound. The home-cooked meals are a treat!

★ **Butia Lodge** LODGE $$
(☑ 7126 5653; kwepa.clark@gmail.com; s/d incl 2 meals K250/350) Near the airstrip, this is the most comfortable accommodation in Kiriwina. The restaurant – an attractive, open-sided building supported by 18 posts, each carved with a Trobriand legend – serves terrific local food that mixes tubers, fish and masses of mouthwatering mud crabs. The lodge van can be hired for day excursions (K500 including Gum the terrific guide and driver).

Losuia Lodge LODGE $$
(☑ 7360 8603; losuialodge@gmail.com; r K200-375; ❄) A 10-minute drive from Losuia, this lodge has 18 simple but pleasant rooms opening onto a shared veranda. The waterside restaurant (meals K25 to K35) serves good meals. The lodge also has an old minibus for hire (per day K400). The staff can arrange dinghy hire to visit other islands (K250 per day, plus fuel).

🛍 Shopping

Trobriand Island carvings are famous throughout the whole of PNG. A master carver is a position of high prestige in the Trobriands and it's a role bestowed upon people at birth. Other than wood carvings (found in most villages) and lime pots, you can get shell money and *doba* (banana leaf money incised with patterns). Artisans meet arriving planes hoping to sell their wares. They'll also come and find you wherever you're staying!

Obweria Village CARVINGS
Obweria village specialises in intricately carved ebony walking sticks, many decorated with pearl-shell inlays. Ebony is an extremely hard and brittle timber, and difficult to work, so carving it requires exceptional skill and months of work from the artisan. Prices start from around K1000.

Bwetalu Village FURNITURE
Bwetalu village produces particularly fine stools and tables made of kwila, a local hardwood. You may get away with carrying a small stool home.

Yalaka village HANDICRAFTS
Yalaka village sells striking lime pots (gourds decorated with a distinctive black pattern and

VILLAGE STAYS

Staying in a village is a uniquely memorable experience. You can arrange a village stay yourself by speaking with the chief of the village that you'd like to stay in.

Overlooking the gorgeous strip of white sand that is Kaibola Beach, the **Kaibola Beach Guesthouse** (☑ 7306 5753; r per person K100) consists of three simple rooms. Emmanuel and his wife provide home-cooked meals and Emmanuel can take you spear-fishing. Ask your lodgings to contact Tobulowa at Okaiboma to spend the night in one of his basic **beach huts** (per person with full board K80).

fitted with a boar's tusk stopper). Prices vary, depending on size and quality (from K10).

ℹ Information

Butia and Kiriwina lodges are your best sources of information; ask about any cricket matches, weddings, mortuary feasts and other events. Butia employs Gum, a terrific local guide, while at Losuia, Rebecca Young is very helpful. Both can arrange *singsing* (celebratory dance or festival) groups and a 'mini-Milamala' with their village contacts (though it won't be cheap).

ℹ Getting There & Away

AIR

Air Niugini (www.airniugini.com.pg) Direct flights to Port Moresby (K674, 1¼ hours) on Tuesday and Friday.

PNG Air (www.pngair.com.pg) Flights to Port Moresby (K551, 2½ hours) via Alotau (K312, 45 minutes) on Tuesday, Thursday and Sunday.

BOAT

Located at 'the station', the island's wharf is your best bet for finding passage on a local boat to Alotau or the D'Entrecasteaux Islands.

ℹ Getting Around

The island's few PMVs meet all arriving flights. Butia Lodge and Losuia Lodge can organise vehicle hire with driver. All private vehicles operate as de facto PMVs; you may get a ride with one of them to the village of your choice and then walk back.

Kiriwina's main roads are unpaved but in reasonably good condition. Cycling is a great way to see the island – Kiriwina Lodge may have bicycles for hire. Otherwise, do what the locals do and walk.

Morobe & Madang Provinces

POP 1.2 MILLION / AREA 62,470 SQ KM

Best Places to Stay

➜ Madang Lodge (p93)

➜ Lae Travellers Inn (p85)

➜ Jais Aben Resort (p98)

➜ Tupira Surf Club (p99)

Best of Activities

➜ Morobe Show (p85)

➜ Niugini Diving Adventures (p92)

➜ Tupira Surf Club (p99)

➜ Kalam Culture Festival (p101)

Why Go?

Geographically speaking, Morobe and Madang are similar – both rise from azure seas off Papua New Guinea's northern coast into a series of thickly forested hills towards imposing mountain ranges. Both also offer plenty of scope to grab a snorkel and banana boat your way to palm-lined bays and coral islands.

Lae grew up hard through a notorious 1920s gold rush. In the 1940s Lae was invaded by the Japanese and bombed by the Allies. Grappling with growing pains and wrapped in razor wire, modern Lae is now a booming economic and industrial hub – a crucible of PNG's rapid social change.

Madang, situated on a small peninsula jutting into a tranquil harbour, is far more relaxed and prettier than bustling Lae. Despite facing occasional *raskol* (bandit) issues in modern times, Madang has retained much of its carefree disposition to match its postcard vistas, easily accessed coral reefs and fascinating wreck dives.

When to Go
Madang

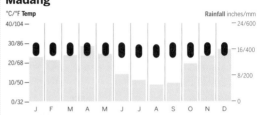

Jun–Sep The dry season offers the best visibility for divers in Madang.

Jun–Aug During the Lae–Finschhafen area's wet season there can be lots of rain.

Late Oct The Morobe show draws *singsing* groups from around the country.

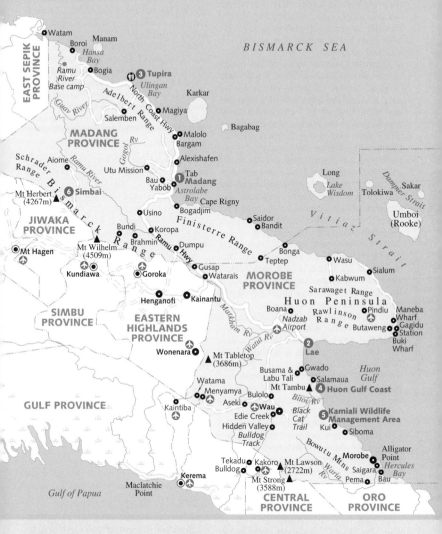

Morobe & Madang Provinces Highlights

1 Diving the wrecks and carnage of WWII or snorkelling over the psychedelic reefs around **Madang** (p92).

2 Paying your respects to the fallen at the War Cemetery, and watching Anga warriors dance at the Morobe Show in **Lae** (p84).

3 Catching a wave on the clean **Ulingan Bay** break opposite the Surf Club in Tupira (p99).

4 Bouncing in a banana boat as it speeds along the **Huon Gulf Coast** (p89) to your very own Robinson Crusoe hideaway.

5 Watching leatherback turtles scramble ashore at **Kamiali Wildlife Management Area** (p89) under a full moon.

6 Witnessing the beetle-bejewelled *singsings* of the isolated **Simbai** (p101) villages high in Bismarck Range.

History

Some of the earliest remains of human civilisation in PNG have been found in Morobe Province. Ancient axe heads suggest people have been living in this part of PNG for about 40,000 years.

The first European to spend any length of time on the PNG mainland was Russian biologist Nicolai Miklouho-Maclay. He arrived at Astrolabe Bay, south of the present site of Madang, in 1871 and stayed for 15 months before leaving to recover from malaria. More rapid change occurred when the German New Guinea Company established a settlement at Finschhafen in 1885. It was a disaster, with malaria, boredom and alcohol taking a heavy toll. The company moved north, first to Bogadjim on Astrolabe Bay, and then Madang, before finally conceding defeat to the mosquitoes and decamping for the relative comforts of New Britain.

The legendary prospector 'Sharkeye' Park is credited with discovering gold near Wau in 1921. By the mid-1920s the gold hunters were flooding in, arriving at Salamaua and struggling for eight days up the steep and slippery Black Cat Trail to Wau, a mere 50km away. Malaria, the track itself and unhappy tribesmen claimed many lives.

In 1926 a richer field was discovered at Edie Creek, high in the hills above Wau. To squeeze the most out of these gold-rich streams, the miners turned to aircraft and within a few years more air freight was being lifted in PNG than the rest of the world combined.

Lae was a tiny mission station before the gold rush but soon became a thriving community, and during WWII Lae, Salamaua and Madang became major Japanese bases. In early 1943 the Japanese, reeling from defeats at Milne Bay and the Kokoda Track, attempted to take Port Moresby by attacking towards Wau, after marching over the mountains from Salamaua. The Battle of Wau was fought hand-to-hand after the ammunition ran out.

MOROBE PROVINCE

Morobe Province is the industrial heart of PNG and gateway to both the Highlands and Islands. The province curves around the beautiful Huon Gulf where a string of village guesthouses provides a great opportunity to get off the beaten track. Outdoor enthusiasts relish the challenge of the historic Black Cat Trail, but tensions remain around the villages along the trail and, at the time of writing, it remains inadvisable to tackle this trek.

Intense WWII fighting has bequeathed a legacy of battlefield relics from submerged shipwrecks to downed aircraft. Culturally the region boasts 171 distinctive languages and is home to the Anga people, renowned throughout PNG as fierce warriors.

Lae

Lae is PNG's second-largest city and, despite having a sizeable industrial base, is more attractive than Port Moresby. Like other PNG cities, the streets are filled with people and it can be hard to imagine what the crowds are doing. No one seems to be in a rush; everyone's happy to chat with friends and amble around town.

Most shops can be found in either of the two commercial mini-centres – Top Town and Eriku. There are also a few shops down the hill in China Town; named after the Chinese community who once lived here.

◉ Sights

Botanical Gardens   GARDENS
(📞 472 4188; Milford Haven Rd; admission K10; ⊙8am-5pm) The Botanical Gardens offer a pleasant stroll through a patch of rainforest and grassland in the centre of Lae. Butterflies flutter and reptiles scuttle as you amble beneath the huge, vine-cloaked trees hosting flocks of colourful birds. The gardens also feature an exotic orchid collection. Officially it's closed on weekdays, but the guards at either the main northern gate (near the RAAF DC-3) or the southern gate (near Lae War Cemetery) usually let you in. Avoid coming here alone.

Lae War Cemetery   MEMORIAL
(Memorial Ave; ⊙7am-4pm) The Lae War Cemetery, just south of the Botanical Gardens, is meticulously maintained by the Australian government. There are 2808 graves here, 2363 of which are Australian, the rest being Indian, New Zealand or British. An Anzac (Australian and New Zealand Army Corps) Day dawn service is held on 25 April commemorating those who lost their lives during WWII. If the war seems rather distant and unreal, pay a visit and read some of the headstones; the tributes can be quite moving.

IN THE FOOTSTEPS OF HISTORY

Two of the most historic and famous tracks in PNG remain on the to-do list for adventurous trekkers, but at the time of writing they were closed following an incident on the Black Cat Trail. Check the latest news with the PNG Tourism Promotion Authority (www.papuanewguinea.travel) and trekking companies.

Black Cat Trail

The Black Cat Trail was used by miners in the 1920s and its difficulty lies in the precipitous 'no-matter-what' route straight from Salamaua to its objective – the Black Cat mine, northeast of Wau. The miners took eight days to cover the 50km, and parts of the track were later used by Australian soldiers during WWII.

More recently the Black Cat Trail was famed as one the PNG's greatest adventure challenges and was gaining in popularity among those who wanted to test their endurance in an unforgiving environment. All that changed in September 2013 when a trekking party was attacked by a gang of *raskols* (bandits). Three porters died, others were seriously injured and some of their Western clients received injuries. Such attacks take a long time to heal, particularly in tribal parts of PNG where payback runs in parallel with official law and order. Since the attack the trail has been closed and not actively promoted by the PNG Tourism Promotion Authority.

Should the situation change by the time you read this, the following are two companies with plenty of Black Cat experience: **Executive Excellence** (www.executiveexcellence.com.au) and **Papua New Guinea Trekking Adventures** (☑ 325 1284; www.pngtrekkingadventures.com).

Bulldog Track

The WWII Bulldog Track, intended to link Wau with the south coast, winds its way from Edie Creek to Bulldog, from where you had to travel by river. When completed in 1943 the track was actually a road capable of bearing large trucks. It has deteriorated since and has been cut by landslides and jungle. Depending on how much of it you want to walk, the Bulldog Track takes from three to nine days and passes through a stunning array of landscapes and villages. It is a bona fide adventure requiring considerable fitness and should not be undertaken lightly.

The Hidden Valley mine has denied track access, making it logistically difficult to undertake without the assistance of a tour company.

MOROBE & MADANG PROVINCES WAU & BULOLO

a Japanese convoy near Lae, crashed while searching for the Wau airstrip. The remains of the aircraft are in fairly good condition and lie on a hillside, a four-hour return trek from Biawen Junction, 13km from Wau. However, note that the trail was not open at the time of research. Do not attempt this trail without a local guide or permission from landowners. Several fees may be payable.

🛌 Sleeping & Eating

Pine Lodge LODGE $$
(☑ 474 5220; r K330) In Bulolo, Pine Lodge has passable rooms and food. Each room sleeps two and comes with private facilities.

Valley View Guesthouse GUESTHOUSE $$
(☑ 474 6312, 7258 3616; r per person without bathroom incl meals K275) A 10-minute walk from

Wau on the road to Bulolo, this informal, breezy guesthouse has large rooms, comfy beds and enough of the owner's personal effects scattered about to give it a very homey atmosphere.

ℹ Getting There & Away

AIR
North Coast Aviation (www.nca.com.pg) based in Lae has a service every Tuesday to Wau (K290), and further down the Garaina Valley (Garaina, Garasa, Omora and Kira). It also provides charter services to Wau or Bulolo.

PMV
PMVs to Lae (K22, four to five hours) leave Wau between 6am and 7am most days from near Donna's Stoa. They travel via Bulolo (K20, three hours).

MADANG PROVINCE

Madang Province is PNG in miniature. It has islander, coastal and mountain cultures plus modern resorts and timeless villages. The fertile coastal strip looks out onto smoking volcanic islands and is backed by some of the most rugged mountains in PNG – the Adelbert and Schrader Ranges to the north, and the Finisterre Range to the south.

Madang

Madang was once dubbed the 'Prettiest town in the Pacific' – not least due to its position on a peninsula, surrounded by azure waters sprinkled with picturesque islands – and while it did suffer wartime ruination it retains much of its natural charm.

Madang's warm, wet climate and fertile soil produce luxuriant growth. Many of the huge casuarina trees that tower over the Madang streets support raucous colonies of flying foxes. Madang was virtually destroyed during the Japanese occupation and subsequent fighting during WWII, so much of what you see today was built after the war.

Sights

Madang Museum MUSEUM
(☑422 3302; Modilon Rd; admission K5; ☺8am-noon & 1-4.30pm Mon-Fri) In the same building as the Madang Visitors & Cultural Bureau, this small but fascinating museum is worth visiting. Learn about the 1660 eruption of Long Island. Look for the ceremonial headdress from Bosmum village on the Lower Ramu River. These are worn during the 'cleansing of the blood', the time in which blood is drawn from a boy's tongue and penis during initiation to manhood.

Coastwatchers' Memorial Beacon MEMORIAL
(Kalibobo Point lighthouse) The 30m-high Coastwatchers Memorial Beacon, visible 25km out to sea, is a reminder of those who stayed behind enemy lines during WWII to report on Japanese troop and ship movements. It's a rather ugly concrete memorial, but the 3km beachfront road south of the memorial is the most pleasant walk in Madang, with views across Astrolabe Bay.

Flying Fox Roosts WILDLIFE
(Kasagten Rd) You can't miss Madang's bats. They're everywhere; wheeling overhead all day, constantly disturbed by the town noises below. Locals told us that these *kwandi* (spectacled flying foxes) moved into town in the mid-1970s.

Activities

Excellent visibility, stunning tropical coral and fish life, and countless WWII wrecks make the diving and snorkelling around Madang world-famous. Local favourites include **Barracuda Point, Magic Passage, Planet Rock** and **Eel Gardens**. There's also good DIY snorkelling just off **Family Beach** and off the rocks at Madang Lodge and Smugglers Inn Resort, but watch the swell and the tides because the rocks, coral and sea urchins can be hazardous. For more on diving in the area, see p31.

The best swimming beaches are along Coronation Dr, particularly Family Beach and **Machine Gun Beach**, but these are more rock than sand. If you want to throw down a towel on actual sand, head to nearby Krangket Island (p97).

Niugini Diving Adventures DIVING
(☑422 2655; mtsoperations@mtspng.com; Coastwatchers Ave, Madang Resort Hotel) Niugini Diving Adventures is currently the only operation in town and has plenty of local experience. Prices listed here are based on a minimum of two divers; solo divers pay a surcharge (K80). Rates include: PADI open-water certification (K1400), one-/two-dive packages (K175/330) and snorkelling excursions (K90 including gear). Night diving and speciality courses are available. Dive gear costs K70 per day to hire.

In addition to diving, you can hire sea kayaks and sailing catamarans.

Tours

Madang Visitors & Cultural Bureau (p96) offers plenty of suggestions and practical advice for day tours and excursions.

Melanesian Tourist Services TOUR
(MTS; ☑424 1300; www.mtspng.com; Coastwatchers Ave; half-day village tour or harbour cruise K100) Madang Resort Hotel's Melanesian Tourist Services runs **village tours** to the south coast stopping at lookout points, war memorials and Bilbil village to buy pottery. Its **harbour cruise** uses banana boats to visit wreckage of Japanese landing craft before calling at Krangket Island for snorkelling. The *Kalibobo Spirit*, a 29m, luxurious liveaboard boat is available for diving, fishing and Sepik exploratory cruises.

Half-day tours have a minimum of two people; full-day tours are also available.

✯✯ Festivals & Events

Madang Festival   CULTURAL

(www; ☉ 1st weekend Jun) This festival on the Queen's Birthday weekend in June celebrates the diverse cultures of Madang Province from the mountains to the sea. Activities include vibrant floats, canoe races and *singsings* (celebratory dances or festivals) on Laiwaden Oval.

Divine Word University
Cultural Show   FESTIVAL

(admission K15; ☉ Aug) Usually held on the third or fourth Saturday in August (check with the Madang Visitors & Cultural Bureau), the Divine Word University Cultural Show is smaller than its highland cousins but still a riot of colour, feathers and traditional attire. At the end the highland *waipa* dance is celebrated with gusto and performers won't rest until everyone is dancing.

The official start is at 9am, but it's usually under way by 11am.

🛏 Sleeping

If you're looking for further budget options, the guesthouses on Krangket Island (p97) are worth considering and easily reached.

★ Madang Lodge   HOTEL $

(☎ 422 3395; www.madanglodge.com.pg; Modilon Rd; budget s/d without bathroom K140/210, s K490-560, d K560-630; ❋ 🗢 🗷) With something for everyone and with great snorkelling nearby, this is one of the best places to stay in PNG. The budget rooms are the best value in town. Although small and fan-cooled they are absolutely spotless and you get free wi-fi plus a great swimming pool. At the top-end, the semidetached bungalows have a kitchenette, cable TV and air-con.

Scattered about the manicured grounds you'll find a gym, an inviting seaside pool, carver's workshop, coffee shop (with internet-connected computers) and a wonderfully situated waterfront restaurant that serves delicious meals. A hotel shuttle can run you into town (K5), or jump on a PMV that stops outside.

CWA Guesthouse   GUESTHOUSE $

(☎ 422 2216; madang.cwa@global.net.pg; Coastwatchers Ave; dm/s/tw/f K80/135/165/255) Occupying a prime slice of real estate on the waterfront near the town centre, this church-run guesthouse may be rather basic and well worn, but is clean and breezy and the staff genuinely friendly. You can borrow a book (K1) and there is a Saturday morning (10am to noon) coffee shop on-site. Meals aren't served but there's a communal kitchen.

Coronation Drive Guest Haus   GUESTHOUSE $

(Fabies Guesthouse; ☎ 7035 2903; fjenjet@gmail.com; Coronation Dr; d K280, s/d without bathroom K180/200; ❋) This welcoming guesthouse is still locally known by its former name of Fabies. It has spic-and-span bedrooms that share a communal TV lounge in a renovated family home. It's opposite Machine Gun Beach and the only place in this price range with air-con.

Lutheran Guesthouse   HOSTEL $

(☎ 422 2589; lghm@global.net.pg; Coralita St; dm/d incl breakfast K130/185) Clean, simple and friendly sums up this guesthouse. Dorms have either two beds or three beds, and each room, although basic, has its own bathroom. It is likely that you will get a room to yourself. If fully occupied, solo travellers are expected to share. A self-contained unit sleeps five. Breakfast is included and additional meals are around K25.

Coastwatchers Hotel   HOTEL $$

(☎ 422 2684; www.coralseahotels.com.pg; Coastwatchers Ave; r incl breakfast K310-388; ❋ 🗢 🗷) As the name implies, this hotel enjoys ocean views – but not from every room. It's a modern, comfortable complex adjacent to the Coastwatchers' Memorial Beacon and the golf course. The rooms are large (standard rooms sleep three) while others are split over two storeys – ideal for families or groups.

There's excellent dining in **Coasties Restaurant & Bar** upstairs on the open-air veranda. On a muggy night it catches a pleasant breeze, and the lazy fans and cane furniture add to the tropical ambience.

Madang Resort Hotel &
Kalibobo Village Resort   RESORT $$$

(☎ 422 2655; www.mtspng.com; Coastwatchers Ave; s incl breakfast K320-760, d K370-810, ste K1500; ❋ @ 🗢 🗷) Madang Resort and Kalibobo Village are owned by the same people, sit side by side, share facilities and are run jointly. Both share the enormous waterfront grounds, three pools, brilliant orchid gardens, poolside bars and restaurants and an integrated tour desk and dive shop. This is the most tourist-oriented accommodation in the province.

Madang

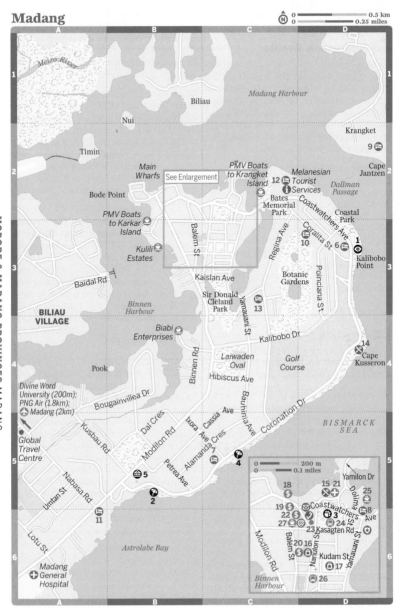

Madang Star International Hotel HOTEL $$$

(☑ 422 2656; www.madangstar.com.pg; Regina Ave; r/apt incl breakfast K450/550; ✳ ⧉) The landowners of Star Mountain (where the Ok Tedi mine is located) have used some of their profits to invest in hospitality. Aimed squarely at the business end of the markets the rooms are spacious and immaculate. However, there was no internet service when we visited, and there isn't much in the way of shady gardens.

Madang

MOROBE & MADANG PROVINCES MADANG

✖ Eating

The overall standard for restaurant dining in Madang is probably PNG's best outside of Port Moresby. All of the major hotels have attached restaurants and bars that are the most sophisticated places to dine in town. We thoroughly recommend the restaurants at the Madang Lodge, Coastwatchers Hotel and Madang Resort.

Eden Restaurant　　　　　CHINESE $$
(☑ 422 3198; Coronation Dr; meals K18-56; ⊙ 10.30am-2pm & 5.30-10pm Mon-Sat, 5.30-10pm Sun) Admittedly this restaurant doesn't make much of an impression; it's right on the foreshore but designed to have no views and be stiflingly hot. People don't come for the view, however, but for the enormous selection of Chinese cuisine with a few Thai and Southeast Asian dishes thrown in. The beer is cold and you can buy wine by the glass.

For views, pop next door to the Madang Country Club.

Ocean Restaurant　　　　　ASIAN $$
(☑ 422 1384; Coastwatchers Ave; mains K24-48; ⊙ 11am-2pm & 6-10pm Mon-Sat) Get here early to secure a table on the small harbourside veranda at lunch – for our money, the most atmospheric dining in town. The menu is dominated by Chinese cuisine, but there are a few inspiring Filipino dishes and a smat-

tering of Western pub-style meals. The lunch specials (K16 to K38) are from the Chinese or Western selection.

Next door is the Madang Club; officially you need to be member, or at least be signed in by one, but a bit of bravado will usually see you pass security for the Friday quiz night.

🛍 Shopping

Bilbil clay pots are a local speciality. Highlanders come down with some *bilums* (string bags) and hats, and you'll see *bukaware* (baskets) and items from the Sepik. Have a look through the market and in the carvers' huts attached to Madang Lodge and Madang Resort Hotel for souvenirs.

Market　　　　　MARKET
(⊙ closed Sun) The market has fruit and vegetables as well as some clothing, *bilums* and local shell jewellery.

Beckzle Plaza　　　　　DEPARTMENT STORE
(Madang Department Store; Nanulon St) It's possible to buy snorkelling gear from the sports shop in Beckzle Plaza.

ⓘ Information

EMERGENCY
Ambulance (☑ 111)
Police (☑ 422 3233; 149 Yamauani St)

INTERNET ACCESS

Veniba Internet Cafe (Kasagten Rd; per hr K19; ⊗8am-4pm Mon-Fri, 9am-1pm Sat) This cafe is upstairs in a nondescript building opposite the large and conspicuous Kasagten Haus building. Fast satellite connections, CD writing capabilities but no Skype.

MEDICAL SERVICES

Pharmacies are well represented.

Family Clinic (☑ 422 1234; Coastwatchers Ave; ⊗9am-noon & 2-4pm Mon-Fri) This small clinic beside the Madang Club has Dr John Mackerell, an Australian doctor, on the staff.

MONEY

All major hotels cash travellers cheques, often at a rate that's competitive with the banks, and major credit cards are widely accepted. Westpac, ANZ and Bank South Pacific have ATMs that accept international credit cards.

ANZ (☑ 422 2866; Coastwatchers Ave) Opposite BSP and has ATMs. Charges 1% commission on travellers cheques.

Bank South Pacific (☑ 422 2477; Coastwatchers Ave) Charges around K50 to change travellers cheques. It has an ATM lobby in the Beckslea Plaza on Nanulon St.

Westpac (☑ 422 2213; Nuna St)

POST

Post Office (☑ 422 2006; cnr Coastwatchers Ave & Nuna St)

TELEPHONE

Telikom (Nuna St) Next to the post office. It has public phones outside.

TOURIST INFORMATION

Madang Visitors & Cultural Bureau (☑ 422 3302; www.tourismmadang.com; Modilon Rd, Madang) This is one of the best resourced information centres in the country. The friendly staff have up-to-date information on accommodation and attractions throughout the province, including hard-to-reach destinations such as Simbai and Karkar Island.

Melanesian Tourist Services (MTS; ☑ 424 1300; www.mtspng.com; Coastwatchers Ave, Madang Resort Hotel) Runs local tours and books airline tickets.

TRAVEL AGENCIES

Global Travel Centre (☑ 4241859; globaltravel @dwu.sc.pg; Divine Word University) This reliable travel agent unfortunately charges 25K for quotes and ticketing services – so it is better to go the airlines directly. It is inside the grounds of the Divine Word University, to the left of the main entrance.

ⓘ Getting There & Around

TO/FROM THE AIRPORT

The airport is 7km from Madang. Most of the hotels and guesthouses have complimentary airport transfers and will meet your flight when you arrive; otherwise 8B PMVs run along Independence Dr and into town (K2).

AIR

Planes don't fly between 5pm and 8pm (when the flying foxes leave their roosts) for fear of bat strike. **MAF** (☑ 422 2229) and **Island Airways** (☑ 422 2601) are both based at the airport and service small communities in remote areas. Their schedules vary with passenger requirements, but if you are heading to the Finisterre or Bismarck Ranges or the Ramu Valley (Aiome, Simbai or Teptep), these are the guys to see. It is possible to arrange charter flights with either company.

Air Niugini (☑ 422 2699; www.airniugini.com. pg; Nuna St) Has twice-daily direct flights to/ from Port Moresby (K450, one hour), daily direct flights to/from Wewak (K360, 40 minutes), and Wednesday and Saturday flights to/from Manus (K530, 30 minutes). Other destinations connect through Port Moresby.

PNG Air (☑ 790 45893; www.pngair.com.pg; airport; ⊗7am-4pm) PNG Air flies directly to/ from Wewak (K340) and Lae (K340) on a daily basis. Many other connections are available through Lae.

Travel Air (☑ 422 1838; www.travelairpng. com; Nanulon St, Beckzle Plaza) Flies to/from Madang (K230) daily; and to Port Moresby (K455) on Monday, Thursday and Saturday; to Wewak (K230) on Tuesday and Saturday; and Mt Hagen (K335) on Wednesday only.

BOAT

Small boats run to the islands in Madang harbour from an inlet behind the CWA Guesthouse and next to the Madang Resort, hourly or so from 7am to 5.30pm (K1 to K5).

Star Ships (Rabaul Shipping; Balam St) Star Ships has a vessel, the *Carlvados Queen*, that sails west to Wewak (K200) and east to Wasu (K160), in Morobe Province. Timings vary so check the current timetable posted outside the ticket office, on an intersection beside Ela Plaza.

PMV

On the north coast the road is sealed to Bogia. PMVs travel to Siar village (K4, 35 minutes), Riwo/Jais Aben (K4, 45 minutes), Malolo (K7, one hour) and Bogia (PMV 17L or 17M; K25, five hours) from the **PMV stop** (Kasagten Rd) opposite the Ho Kid store. Bogia-bound PMVs usually leave between 1pm and 2pm.

Heading south along Madang's main thoroughfare, the road becomes the Ramu Hwy and rises over the tortuous Finisterre Range into the vast Ramu Valley on its way to Lae; and via the Highlands (Okuk) Hwy, deep into the central mountains. This is very spectacular driving and the only 'interstate' in the country.

Buses gather around the market at 8am and the door guys yell out their destinations 'LaeLaeLaeLae' and 'HagenHagenHagen' with a great sense of theatre. The fare to Lae is K40 (five hours) and to Goroka K50 (five hours). The overnight buses to Mt Hagen (K80) rendezvous with Lae buses at Watarais, where they form a convoy – presumably for safety.

Local buses include the 6A, which runs to Barasiko market at the Lae junction; 6B, which continues 3km up the North Coast Hwy; and 6C, which goes to Yabob village. All cost K1 to K3.

TAXI

It's possible to count the taxis in Madang on one hand and you could go for weeks without actually seeing one. If you do need a taxi or a hire car, call **Ark Taxis** (☏ 721 42315, 422 1636) or **Turatravelinx** (☏ 7234 3755).

Around Madang

Krangket Island

Krangket Island, across Dallman Passage from Madang, is a large island with several villages and a beautiful lagoon ideal for swimming and snorkelling. There's a popular picnic spot, which was a former rest area for wounded Australian soldiers in the days following the Japanese surrender in WWII. The **snorkelling** (bring your own snorkelling gear) near Krangket Island Lodge is well worth the K5 locals charge day-trippers.

Boats from Madang (K1, 15 minutes) drop their passengers about 45 minutes' walk from the Krangket Island Lodge, though you should be able to negotiate passage to the lodge end of the island.

🛏 Sleeping

Laidex Guesthouse GUESTHOUSE $
(☏ 7925 4340; r K25) The island's best and friendliest accommodation is Laidex Guesthouse, a very simple village guesthouse operated by Makos Los. There's a total of three rooms – all fairly basic – and a kitchen for preparing your own food.

Krangket Island Lodge GUESTHOUSE $
(☏ 7294 0264; bungalow K80) At the opposite end of the island from Laidex Guesthouse,

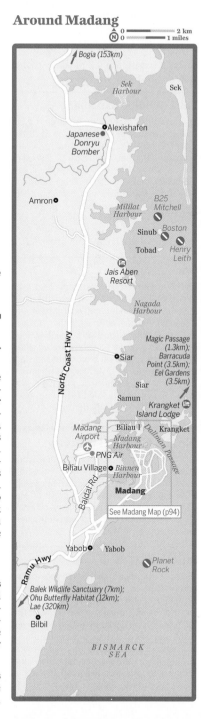

Around Madang

MOROBE & MADANG PROVINCES AROUND MADANG

the Krangket Island Lodge is operated by the Dum (pronounced 'doom') clan. The caretaker/toll collector will demand K5 just to walk on the land to inspect the accommodation. It consists of a few run-down cottages tucked away from the village.

Balek Wildlife Sanctuary

This **wildlife management area** (☑715 34883; admission K10; ☺7am-5pm) is 10km south of Madang. It's featured in scenes from the 1996 film production of *Robinson Crusoe* with Pierce Brosnan. There's a sulphur creek that flows from a huge limestone formation. Spirits are said to inhabit the site and the water has curative properties. The water is incredibly clear and you can feed eels and turtles with bananas and fresh meat. Catch a 15A/B PMV from town (K2).

Ohu

The **Ohu Butterfly Habitat** (☑726 85248; admission K10; ☺7am-3pm), 15km southwest of Madang, is a community conservation and research project where butterflies, including PNG's famous birdwing varieties, feed on the nectar of the flowering *aristolochia*. The butterflies are best seen in the morning from 7am to 10am. If you haven't organised your own vehicle, catch a 13B PMV (K2) from Madang to the 'Medo' drop-off, from where it's a 70-minute (5km) walk.

North Coast Highway

The north coast offers a necklace of pristine beaches, excellent diving and snorkelling, and some luxurious resorts and rustic villages to explore. The road runs north of Madang as far as Bogia, from where you catch banana boats to Angoram and ultimately make your way to Wewak.

Jais Aben Area

Divers rave about the north-coast sites (p31), such as the US freighter *Henry Leith* in 20m of water near Jais Aben Resort, and the nearby minesweeper *Boston*. The 'waterhole' is an enclosed lagoon connected to the open sea by a large underwater tunnel and offers dramatic snorkelling. Pig, Wongat and Tab Islands are also recommended snorkelling spots. Jais Aben Resort offers harbour tours, snorkelling, fishing and land-based tours. At the time of research, the resort's dive shop was closed; however, a new operator was being sought. In the meantime, Madang's Niugini Diving Adventures (p92) can arrange diving (and snorkelling) trips to all these sites.

🛏 Sleeping & Eating

★**Jais Aben Resort**   RESORT **$$$**
(☑423 3111; www.jaisabenresort.com; r K395-450, special weekend rate K249; ✳@🛜🏊) This lovely resort resides on its own pretty peninsula, with private swimming beaches and sweeping lawns. The beachside bungalows are airy and comfortable, with enclosed verandas and seafront outlooks. The 'deluxe' bungalows have air-con. A beachfront bar fronts an excellent swimming beach and serves burgers, steaks (K26 to K40) and drinks. The fine-dining **Cocos restaurant** boasts a seasonal menu incorporating local and international dishes.

The resort is 20km from Madang, 3km off the highway. Town and airport transfers are free for guests. PMV 17A runs along the main road from Madang (K1) but stops 1km shy of the resort.

Alexishafen

Alexishafen Catholic Mission is set off the North Coast Hwy to the right, 23km north of Madang. The name 'Alexishafen' is derived from the combination of the German word for harbour, *hafen,* and the first name of a Russian princess, Alexis. The graveyard here stands as a reminder of the early missionary period. Beyond the mission you can see the old overgrown missionary-built airstrip.

Like so much of the area, Alexishafen was badly damaged during the war. The WWII Japanese airstrip (a little off the road to the left, between the mission airstrip and Alexishafen) is now overgrown by the encroaching jungle. Only bomb craters and the odd aircraft wreck hint at the saturation bombing that destroyed the base. The most impressive of these aircraft wrecks is a **Japanese Donryu bomber** (☑7949 7136; Alexishafen; admission K5) that was waiting to taxi with crew when it was strafed by Allied aircraft. Though the wreck has been vandalised for its aluminium, the machine-gun bullet holes are very evident and it is a poignant site. The caretaker/landowner is George Nalul, who charges a reasonable K5 for access.

History

In 1930 Mick Leahy and Mick Dwyer came to the Highlands searching for gold and walked into the previously 'undiscovered' Eastern Highlands. Three years later, Leahy returned with his brother Dan and they stumbled upon the huge, fertile and heavily populated Wahgi Valley.

The film *First Contact* (1983) includes original footage of this patrol by Mick Leahy and is a priceless record of the first interaction between Highlanders and Europeans.

Missionaries followed the Leahy brothers, and government stations were built near present-day Mt Hagen and in the Simbu Valley, near present-day Kundiawa, although gold was never discovered in any great quantities.

Even during WWII, the mountains largely protected the Highlanders from the foreign forces. Not until the 1950s were outside influences really felt, and many areas remained largely unaffected until the 1960s and even into the '70s. The construction of the Highlands (Okuk) Hwy had a huge impact on the lives of Highlanders, as did the introduction of cash crops, particularly coffee. The Highlanders had long been traders and skillful gardeners and adapted to the cash economy with remarkable speed.

Dangers & Annoyances

Parts of the PNG Highlands are genuinely high in altitude. You should give yourself a few days' acclimatisation at lower altitudes before taking on any serious mountain climbing or excessive physical activities if you are to avoid acute mountain sickness.

Bus travel through the Highlands is not necessarily dangerous, but there is an element of risk. Very occasionally there are hold-ups, buses are ambushed and the passengers are robbed. Ritual warfare has always been an integral part of Highlands life and to this day payback feuds and land disputes can erupt into major conflicts. During times of political tension and tribal war, seek advice from the police and locals in each town before heading to the next town in a PMV (public motor vehicle). West of Mendi can be particularly volatile, so either avoid overland travel or seek local advice.

Parts of the Highlands are designated 'dry regions' and alcohol cannot be purchased outside licensed premises, such as hotels, clubs and resorts. However, there's a booming black market in beer and all of PNG has a problem with wickedly strong, home-brewed alcohol and associated violence.

EASTERN HIGHLANDS PROVINCE

Undulating grass-covered hills and neat villages of low-walled round huts are the defining characteristics of the Eastern Highlands. Listen carefully for the secrets whispered by the tufts of grass fixed to the peaks of the roofs of these houses.

The most heavily populated of all the provinces, the region has had longer contact with the West than the other Highland provinces, and was the first to feel the impact of the missionaries, prospectors, mercenaries and misfits who have visited these parts.

Goroka

Goroka has grown from a small outpost in the mid-1950s to a major commercial centre, and is now the main town in the Eastern Highlands Province.

Mountains encircle the town, which in turn almost encircles the airport. At 1600m, Goroka enjoys a pleasant year-round climate of warm days and cool nights. More relaxed than Mt Hagen, safer than Lae and endowed with essential services, Goroka is one of PNG's more attractive towns.

Goroka's main cash crop is coffee and you'll see it growing under the canopies of larger trees in the hills throughout the district.

◉ Sights & Activities

JK McCarthy Museum   MUSEUM
(cnr Makinono & Morchhauser Sts; admission by donation; ⊙ 8am-noon & 1-4pm Mon-Fri, by arrangement Sat & Sun) JK McCarthy was one of PNG's legendary patrol officers and wrote one of the classic books on New Guinea patrolling – *Patrol into Yesterday*. Among the exhibits are pottery, weapons, clothes and musical instruments, and even some grisly jewellery – Anga mourning necklaces of human fingers. 'Peer through the mists of time' courtesy of a fascinating collection of photos in the Leahy wing, many taken by Mick Leahy in 1933. There are also WWII relics, including a P-39 Aircobra mounted out behind the museum.

Raun Raun Theatre   HISTORIC BUILDING
(☑ 532 1116; Wisdom St) The theatre is a superb building, which blends traditional

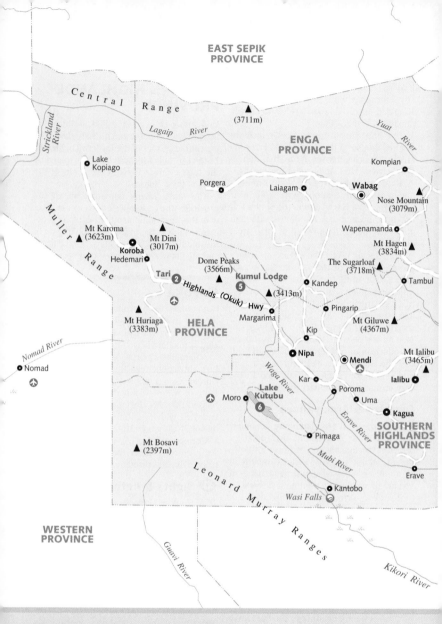

The Highlands Highlights

❶ Photographing the extravagantly adorned performers at one of the Highland's celebrated shows, such as **Goroka** (p107) or **Mt Hagen** (p114).

❷ Immersing your senses into the colour and culture of the Huli wigmen villages around **Tari** (p121).

❸ Scrambling up **Mt Wilhelm** (p111) in the

predawn gloom to catch the sunrise light up both the north and south coasts.

❹ Sharing a traditional *mumu* feast of meat and vegetables slowly cooked in

an earth oven in a highlands
village near **Kundiawa**
(p111).

⑤ Exploring the jungles
around **Kumul Lodge** (p116)
at first light in search of the

flamboyant and legendary
birds of paradise.

⑥ Chilling out at the seldom-
visited **Lake Kutubu** (p120)
and visiting the local villages.

materials and modern architecture. It's located on parkland about 500m due north of the post office. Performances by the Raun Raun Theatre Company are irregular, but you might get lucky.

Mt Kis Lookout   VIEWPOINT

A motorable track just off Wisdom St climbs to an excellent lookout, Mt Kis, so-called because it's the lovers' leap of Goroka. There are two large water tanks halfway there, and a ladder you can climb to catch spectacular views of the distant valleys through the pine trees. Unfortunately the area is also a favourite hideout of *raskols* (bandits), so

you must check with locals before heading up there, and never go alone.

★Asaro Mudmen   CULTURAL VILLAGE

Asaro village, northwest of Goroka, is famous for its mudmen – warriors who traditionally covered themselves in grey mud and wore huge mud masks before heading off on raids. It's a very striking image, best witnessed in a village setting rather than one of the big shows. The Asaro men re-create the scene for tourists; the number of mudmen in direct proportion to the number of kina-paying tourists. Local tour companies (p107) can arrange mudmen tours.

Goroka

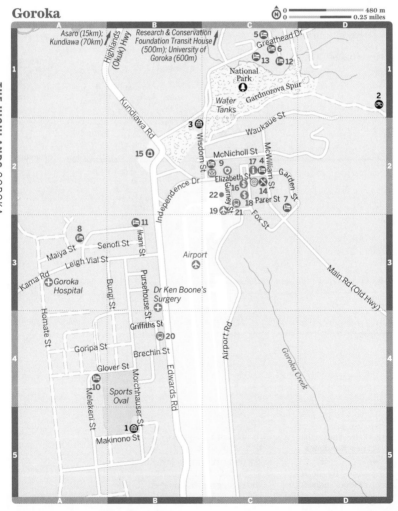

⟟ Tours

Many of the local tour operators are small operators, without an office but with a mobile phone and freelance guides. Most of them are trustworthy while others have achieved local notoriety for failing to pass on tourist fees to the villages they visit. Day trips include visits to the Asaro Mudmen, *mumu* feasts, Simbu villages, and local caves and waterfalls. Most can also arrange treks to the peaks of Mt Wilhelm, Mt Hagen and Mt Giluwe.

Goroka Trek & Tours   CULTURAL TOUR
(☏ 532 1281; www.pngexplorers.com; shop 12B, Bird of Paradise Hotel, Elizabeth St) A prominent local tour operator with a souvenir shop and office at the Bird of Paradise Hotel. Has Japanese- and English-speaking guides.

Niugini Adventure Trekkers   ADVENTURE TOUR
(☏ 7347 2948; www.travelthewild.com) A one-man operation run by Raphael 'Siwi' Kogun who has many years' experience working for larger companies. In addition to cultural tours he specialises in treks, short and long, such as Goroka to Madang and Goroka to Simbu and Mt Wilhelm.

PNG High Country Tours   ADVENTURE TOUR
(☏ 7111 5877; www.pnghighcountrytours.webs. com) Samuel Lulu runs tours and treks around the jungles and caves of the Eastern Highlands and out towards Simbu. He offers

village accommodation in the Namasaro Unggai district west of Goroka.

PNG Highlands Adventures   ADVENTURE TOUR
(☏ 7046 8746; pnghighlandsadventures@gmail. com; PO Box 611, Goroka) A well-connected in-bound operator that specialises in the High-lands, and is particularly good at organising village performances in Simbu (p111). Can also organise country-wide tours and treks.

✹ Festivals & Events

★ Goroka Show   CULTURAL SHOW
(www.papuanewguinea.travel/events; adult 1-/2-/3-day pass K100/150/250; 📷) The Goroka Show is held over the Independence Day weekend (mid-September) at the National Sports In-stitute's Sports Oval. It attracts more *singing* (celebratory dance/festival) groups than the Mt Hagen show and there are also bands and other cultural activities. Make accom-modation arrangements early as many plac-es (especially top-end hotels) are booked out months in advance. Prices, like a Highland headdress, go sky-high.

The show is the glamour event on the so-cial calendar for many performers and it is extraordinary how many feathers one per-son can squeeze on a headdress. Performers receive a payment from the proceeds and you are neither expected nor encouraged to tip individuals. There are also some ele-ments of an agricultural show.

THE HIGHLANDS GOROKA

Goroka

🛏 Sleeping

Research & Conservation Foundation Transit House

GUESTHOUSE $

(RCF; ☑532 3211; www.rcfpng.org; Kyle St; dm K80) The dorm-style accommodation has three or four beds per room, free laundry, an excellent shared kitchen and a TV in the common room. Profits go to support the community development within the Crater Mountain Wildlife Management Area and staff can help you plan a trip there. Catch town bus 3 and get off near the university.

Lutheran Guesthouse

GUESTHOUSE $

(☑532 1171; luthguesthausgka@global.net.pg; Mc-Nicholl St; dm incl breakfast K120) Right in the centre of town behind the post office. The two-storey house is clean and austere and the tidy shared rooms come with two, three or four beds, so a couple may get their own room. Dinner costs K30.

National Sports Institute

HOSTEL $

(☑532 2391; natspoin@daltron.com.pg; Glover St; s/d K88/154) If you don't mind being this far from the town centre, this is a good option. Bathroom and kitchen facilities are shared, while the 106 simple rooms are segregated into buildings for men and women. The spacious grounds are peaceful except when the Goroka Show or a rugby match is on. Meals are available from the cafeteria (K20 to K35).

Nimba Lodge

GUESTHOUSE $

(☑532 1882; ncklmerimba6@gmail.com; Numune Pl; s/d without bathroom K100/150) Nimba has simple and tiny bed-in-a-box rooms with shared bathrooms and no atmosphere or TVs. If a large group books rooms then a cook can be hired; otherwise the kitchen is free to use by guests.

DARTS

Darts is serious business in the Highlands and great fortunes are won and lost on a single throw. Men play darts at roadside 'clubs' where a dozen dartboards are fixed to posts sticking out of the ground. The rules are more or less the same as for regular darts, but you stand a lot further away – Highlands darts is something between regular darts and javelin throwing. Sometimes you can see men in traditional costume playing at village darts clubs.

GK Lodge

HOTEL $$

(☑532 3819; gkklos@global.net.pg; Garden St; s K198, d K220-330) This central place is clean and well kept with large and homey rooms and a decent restaurant. The cheaper standard rooms, including the small singles, are in the old wing. Better 'premium' rooms are in the new wing. The rate for solo travellers is a bit steep, but it's fair value for couples.

Red River Lodge

HOTEL $$

(☑525 1842; redriverlodge@live.com; Greathead Dr; r K220-330) Featuring an ever-so-slight American theme, this attractive red-planked building is set in an attractive leafy garden. Rooms are pleasant, clean and bright, except those few that have inside-facing windows that are rather dark; avoid these if possible. There is a restaurant on-site.

Diwai Hut Lodge

HOTEL $$

(☑532 3840; fax 532 3850; Greathead Dr; r K295-350) The Diwai has a leafy, valley-side outlook within earshot of the Zokozoi River (you can't actually see it), about 10 minutes' walk from the town centre. Rooms are secure, modern and comfortable, if a little plain, and have tea- and coffee-making facilities and a small fridge. There is a quality restaurant on-site (mains K40 to K64).

Emmanuel Lodge & Apartments

HOTEL $$

(☑7040 8185, 532 1393; emmanuellodge@global.net.pg; Greathead Dr; r K280-380) This new lodge boasts a restaurant and very modern and comfortable rooms in a secure, if a little austere, enclosure. Note that the leafy Pacific Gardens Hotel is close by for a social drink or meal. The same owners have a block of ageing apartments on Ikan St, also called Emmanuel Lodge. Be sure you are booking the correct building.

Kanda Resthouse

HOTEL $$

(☑532 2944; kanda@global.net.pg; Numune Pl; r/ste K350/450) The whole place is bright and breezy; freshly painted on the outside with notably large, airy rooms (each with a double and single bed). The suites have kitchens complete with fridge, gas cooker and microwave, although there's also a small restaurant on-site (breakfast K30 to K40, dinner mains K40 to K55). Airport transfers are complimentary and the owners also run a hire-car company.

Pacific Gardens Hotel

HOTEL $$$

(☑532 3418; www.pacifichotel.com.pg; Mokara St; r K280-515, ste K650; @ 🛜) In the grounds of a leafy expats residential estate, this hotel's premier rooms (K515) are the best in town and cheaper than those on offer at the Bird. Airport transfers are included in the tariff and a shuttle to town will cost K20. The garden-fronting restaurant (meals K35 to K65) and congenial bar are also highly regarded.

Bird of Paradise Hotel HOTEL $$$
(☑532 1144; thebird_reservations@coralsea hotels.com.pg; Elizabeth St; r K471-1002, apt K977; @☎☒) 'The Bird' is overdue for a renovation. The tired rooms are large, comfortable and decorated with an assortment of mismatched furniture. Besides the inclusion of an ironing board, there is little difference between the standard and premier rooms. Either way, the rooms facing the garden are better than those facing the street. The restaurant, bars and pool are its top selling points.

✗ Eating

Besides *kai* (fast-food) bars, eating options outside the hotels are few. The market sells an array of fresh fruit and vegetables, peanuts and probably a cuscus or two.

Mandarin Restaurant CHINESE $$
(☑532 2888; Elizabeth St; meals K20-43; ☉10am-2.30pm & 5-9.30pm) Opposite the Bird, and a popular lunch spot for hotel guests, the Mandarin serves tasty, veggie-packed dishes that would do the home country proud. Meals are served in a variety of sizes and are prepared to be shared. A small plate with a side of rice or noodles is enough for one.

★Deck Bistro INTERNATIONAL, BUFFET $$$
(Bird of Paradise Hotel, Elizabeth St; mains K30-64; ☉breakfast, lunch & dinner; ☎) The Bird's Deck Bistro overlooking the pool is *the* place to rendezvous and central to the social life of Goroka's well heeled. There's a nightly themed buffet (K60), of which the Sunday carvery is the pick, and a popular lunch salad buffet (K35). The 'Grill' has à la carte steaks in varying sizes and cuts.

🛍 Shopping

There are several supermarkets and shops clustered between the post office and the Bird of Paradise Hotel. Souvenir sellers camp outside the Bird, stringing up their *bilums* (string bags), hats, spears, bows, masks, *bukaware* (basketry) and jewellery on the wrought-iron fence of the provisional government building. Mild haggling is acceptable here.

Market MARKET
(☉closed Sun) The open-air market is interesting to walk through and you'll see piles of potatoes and exotic leafy greens as well as more familiar tomatoes, capsicums (bell peppers) and avocados. *Bilums* and Highland hats are sold, as are spools of intensely colourful twine and string used in *bilum* manufacture. Watch out for pickpockets.

ℹ Information

EMERGENCY
Ambulance (☑111)
Police (☑532 1443; Elizabeth St)

INTERNET ACCESS
Internet Cafe (1st fl, DJ Haus Bldg, Elizabeth St; per 15min K5; ☉8am-4.30pm Mon-Fri, to 1.30pm Sat) Upstairs, opposite the Bird of Paradise Hotel.

MEDICAL SERVICES
There are several pharmacies in town.
Dr Ken Boone's Surgery (☑532 3544, 7243 9318; Edwards Rd; ☉24hr) A safer bet than the Goroka Hospital.
Goroka Hospital (☑531 2100; Leigh Vial St) Also houses the PNG Institute of Medical Research.

MONEY
The bigger hotels accept major credit cards, as do ATMs. Travellers cheques can be cashed at the bigger hotels as well as banks.
ANZ (☑732 2000; Elizabeth St)
BSP There is a BSP ATM outside the Bird of Paradise Hotel.
Westpac (☑732 1140; Fox St) Also maintains a more private ATM in the lobby of the Bird of Paradise Hotel.

POST
DHL (☑732 3555; Elizabeth St)
Post Office (☑732 2470; Elizabeth St; ☉8am-4.30pm Mon-Fri)

TRAVEL AGENCY
Travel Connections (☑532 3422; travel connect01@gmail.com; shop 17, Bird of Paradise Hotel, Elizabeth St) Ticketing agent for international and domestic flights.

TOURIST INFORMATIOM
East Highlands Province Tourism Bureau (Elizabeth St, Goroka) This office presumably springs into action during the Goroka Show, but it is usually closed and it looks doubtful it would have much in the way of information.

WORTH A TRIP

CRATER MOUNTAIN WILDLIFE MANAGEMENT AREA

In the tri-border area, where the Eastern Highlands, Simbu and Gulf provincial borders meet, is the Crater Mountain Wildlife Management Area (www.rcfpng.org). This is one of the best places in PNG to experience the spectacular countryside, wildlife and village culture.

The area encompasses 2700 sq km, ranging from lowland tropical rainforests on the Purari River to alpine grasses on the slopes of Crater Mountain. You can hike between the various villages, but it's serious trekking. There are three villages (Haia, Herowana and Maimafu) with basic **guesthouses** (per person K30) that provide beds (bring your own sleeping bags) and kerosene stoves (bring your own food). The Research & Conservation Foundation Transit House (p108) in Goroka can radio each village and help organise guides and flight arrangements with one of the three charter airlines servicing the area.

❶ Getting There & Around

AIR

Air Niugini (☑ 532 1444; www.airniugini.com.pg) All of Air Niugini's flights are routed via the twice-daily Port Moresby flights (K520).

PNG Air (☑ 532 2532; www.apng.com) Flies to Lae (K280), Mt Hagen (K380) and Port Moresby (K480) daily.

CAR & PMV

Goroka is well served by PMVs and the Highlands (Okuk) Hwy. It's an easy trip to Mt Hagen (K30, four hours) via Kundiawa (K15, two hours) in the west, or down to the coastal cities of Lae (K40, five hours) and Madang (K50, five hours) in the east.

PMVs gather near the market area early in the morning, and more leave as the day wears on. A dedicated PMV bus station is being planned and may be in use by the time you read this. The road out to Mt Hagen is fairly flat through Asaro, but it then hairpins its way up to Daulo Pass (2450m). The pass is cold and damp, but the views are spectacular.

Although the town is small enough to walk around, PMVs run up and down the stretch of main road, Edwards Rd, aka Highlands (Okuk) Hwy, and to the university (K1).

TAXI

Goroka Taxi Service (☑ 7249 7709; ⊙ 24hr)

SIMBU PROVINCE

Simbu (pronounced *chim*-bu, and sometimes spelt that way) derived its name from when the first patrol officers gave steel axes and knives to the tribespeople, who replied *simbu* – very pleased. Despite its rugged terrain, it's the second most heavily populated region in PNG. The people have turned their steep country into a patchwork of gardens spreading up every available hillside. However, you won't see any form of terracing. Population pressures are pushing them to even higher ground, threatening remaining forests and bird of paradise habitats. Most people in the province speak a similar language – Simbu dialects make up PNG's second-largest language group.

Kundiawa

Kundiawa was the site of the Highlands' first government station, but has been left behind by Goroka and Mt Hagen. Although it's the provincial capital, and the crossroads for the Highlands (Okuk) Hwy and the road to Kegsugl, Kundiawa is pretty small. There's a bank, post office, small supermarket, bakery and several hotels. Surrounding Kundiawa are numerous villages with extraordinary cultural traditions. It's worth your while investigating the village homestay and hikes in the region if you want to do more than scratch the surface of this diverse province.

🛏 Sleeping

Greenland Motel   HOTEL **$$**
(☑ 525 1760; greenland49kundiawa@gmail.com; r standard/deluxe K250/350) Greenland is the best option in town, with a pleasant outlook over town from its hilltop locale. Rooms, all with en suites, are bright and clean and catch the breeze. The on-site restaurant is nothing fancy but produces wholesome and generous dishes (breakfast K25; dinner mains K30 to K50).

Mt Wilhelm Hotel   HOTEL **$$**
(☑ 535 1062; ctambagle@live.com; r standard/deluxe K220/300) An institution in Kundiawa as a conference hotel, the rooms are clean but disappointing and run-down; the standard

rooms are not good value at all. The 'Tribal' coffee shop has colourful murals, espresso coffee (K6) and a small selection of cakes, while the 'Million Dollar' restaurant has a selection of generously proportioned meals (K50 to K70) including Mt Wilhelm trout (K60).

ⓘ Getting There & Away

AIR
The airport is quite spectacular, on a sloping ridge surrounded by mountains. The airport was under maintenance when we visited. Would-be passengers were instead heading to Goroka or Mt Hagen.

PMV
There are PMVs to Goroka (K15, two hours) and Mt Hagen (K20, 2½ hours). The trip to Kegsugl (for Mt Wilhelm) takes 4½ hours and costs K30 to K50, depending on the driver and passenger numbers. PMVs for Kegsugl (Land Cruiser Troop Carriers, usually) leave from the Piunde (Interoil) petrol station; others stop on the highway near the police station.

Around Kundiawa

Several villages west of Kundiawa offer the type of cultural experience for which Simbu Province is famous, including traditional dances, singing and *mumu* feasts. Some performances may seem overly contrived, but it must be appreciated that the tourist dollar is the only funding that is helping keep many of these traditions alive in modern times.

At **Kona** village, nearby to the larger Minima village, you get the opportunity to experience village life first-hand as well as hike to a **flying-fox cave**, ancient **burial grounds** and a traditional **singsing site**. Bruce Mondo and Vero Mondo, of the **Kona Village Cultural Group** (☑ 7004 7839, 7241 7499), run all these activities and also offer village guesthouse accommodation for independent travellers. Also nearby, the village of **Bamugl** is renowned for its painted **skeleton dancers** that re-enact the rescue of a young boy from the scary-looking mountain spirit, Omo Massler. Performances such as these can be seen at the large Goroka and Mt Hagen shows; however, they are much more powerful when performed in the home village for a small group of spectators.

Diugal Cave is a limestone overhang that was once the place where leprosy sufferers were banished to help limit the spread of the disease. The **Kunabo Women's Skeleton Group**, in the village of Diugal right below the Diugal Cave, is committed to retaining

local *kastom* (culture) through song and dance. Members will explain the cave's prominence and perform for a negotiated fee. Other caves around Kundiawa invite exploration, but as many were used as burial places you shouldn't visit them without consulting locals as they may be *tambu* (forbidden).

Village visits and performances are best organised through local tour companies such as those in Goroka (p107).

Mt Wilhelm

For many, climbing to the 4509m summit of Mt Wilhelm is the highlight of a Highlands trip. On a clear day, you can see both the north and south coasts of PNG. It is the tallest peak in PNG and often billed as the tallest in Oceania (even though several mountains in Indonesian Papua surpass it as, technically, all of Indonesia belongs to Asia).

Even if you don't intend to tackle the summit, the region around the base offers fantastic walking and dramatic landscapes.

🛏 Sleeping

★ East Kegsugl
Guesthouse   GUESTHOUSE $
(☑ 276 7513, 7281 0831; r without bathroom per person K80) Across the road from the Kegsugl airstrip, this guesthouse is a great option. The hosts, Josephine and Arnold (Rambo to his friends), make guests feel welcome with small touches such as strawberries and honey from their garden. There are seven rooms with two beds in each and enough blankets to keep an Eskimo warm in a blizzard.

The shared bathroom is outside but has plenty of solar-heated hot water with an electric back-up. Two to three meals with home-grown veggies, local honey and trout cost an extra K20 per person per day.

Pindaunde Lakes Huts   HUT $
(per person K80) Halfway up Mt Wilhelm from Kegsugl are two very basic huts (A-Frame and ANU) that are used for overnighting and the essential altitude acclimitisation. There are mattresses and pillows provided, though you will need your own sleeping bag and food provisions. There is no electricity, but you can cook over the bottled-gas stove provided.

Hut accommodation will be organised by your hotel and guide. Your guide will be given the key for one of the huts when you pay your hut fee down in Kegsugl. Guides and porters stay free.

CLIMBING MT WILHELM

While not technically difficult, this popular **climb** (trekking fee per person K20) is hard work. Preparation is important and the dangers should not be underestimated. Climbers in this region have died and you'll pass the skeletal remains of a previous trekker and a memorial plaque to another about an hour from the summit. Don't try to climb the mountain on your own no matter how fit you are – a guide is essential.

Would-be guides are plentiful and you'll be approached by men offering their services the moment you reach Kundiawa. It is better (and cheaper) to wait until you arrive in Kegsugl before hiring someone. This way you're guaranteed to get a local who knows the landowners and has climbed the mountain many times before. Most guesthouses can arrange guides (K150 per day; one guide per trekker; minimum three days) and porters. Porters (or carriers, as they are locally called) will only haul your bag as far as the base camp huts (K30 per trip). Whomever you hire will expect to share your food, so bring enough to feed everyone.

If the weather is fine, the climb takes two days, but frequently the weather causes delays. The dry season (April to October) is the best time to climb. If you've just come up from the coast, allow yourself time to acclimatise to help avoid altitude sickness – the main reason why many don't make it to the summit. It is advisable to take an extra day exploring around and above the lakes (3500m) before tackling the summit.

The final ascent starts in the black of early morning so that climbers get to see the dawn and both coasts before the clouds roll in. It can get very cold on the mountain (and may even snow), and can easily become fogbound. Sunburn and hypothermia are hazards.

You need to take sufficient food, equipment, warm clothing, water containers (there's no water past the lakes), a torch (flashlight), gloves, candles, toilet paper and a warm sleeping bag. The base camp huts are stocked with kerosene stoves, cooking utensils and musty mattresses. Besides the DIY approach we've just described, it is also possible to book an organised, all-inclusive trek with a tour company:

➡ Goroka Trek & Tours (p107)

➡ Niugini Adventure Trekkers (p107)

➡ Paiya Tours (p114)

➡ PNG Holidays (www.pngholidays.com.au)

➡ PNG Trekking Adventures (p38)

The Climb

Beginning at the end of the road just past the Camp Jehovah Jireh guesthouse at **Kegsugl**, a track leads up through a mountain rainforest and then along an alpine grass-land glacial valley to the twin lakes of **Pindaunde** and two huts collectively known as **Base Camp**. It is customary to spend at least one night here before tackling the summit the next morning. Some say it's better to spend another day acclimatising and exploring the area before the final push. If you catch an early morning PMV from Kundiawa, it is possible to reach Kegsugl by noon and walk (four to five hours) to Base Camp in the afternoon.

From the Pindaunde Lakes Base Camp, it's a long, hard walk to the summit – anything from five to nine hours. Parts of the trail are treacherously steep so take care with your footing at all times. It can get cold, wet, windy and foggy at the top, so bring warm clothes, a hat and some gloves. Clouds roll in after dawn so summit-climbers start out as early as 1am.

The summit itself isn't particularly impressive and isn't visible until you are only 30 minutes from it and, if you are to make it (many don't), go slow! Even if you don't make it all the way to the top, the views of the craggy **Bismarck Range** and the silvery Pindaunde lakes below – from even halfway up – are worth the sweat, and possibly a few tears.

The descent back to the huts takes about four hours, but some people go all the way back to Kegsugl, a further 3½ hours downhill.

Betty's Place   GUESTHOUSE **$$**

(☑7100 5432; bhiggins905@gmail.com; Kekla village; per person with/without meals K280/150) Betty's Place is on a ridge surrounded by bird-filled forest, about 1km from Kegsugl at the start of the trail. While the lodge and bedrooms are looking a little ramshackle, the fireplace, hot showers, delicious meals and home-style furnishings give it a cosy and friendly ambience. A generator provides electricity and there's a trout farm, piggery and vegetable gardens.

Camp Jehovah

Jireh   GUESTHOUSE **$$**

(☑7261 1484; Kekla village; per person incl meals with/without bathroom K250/150) Camp JJ is close to Betty's Place, and boasts the best rooms in this neck of the woods. Rooms are not endowed with much atmosphere, but are bright and clean. The lodge has 14 bunkrooms, so you are likely to score one for yourself, plus six rooms with en suites. The jungle grounds have nature walks, orchid gardens and valley views.

Breakfast and dinner are included in the tariff but you will need to bring your own lunch supplies.

❶ Getting There & Away

Kegsugl is 57km northeast from Kundiawa along a razorback road that has to be seen to be believed. PMVs to Kegsugl (K30 to K50, 4½ hours) leave Kundiawa from the Piunde (Interoil) petrol station. They return to Kundiawa about 6am the following day. Some will do drop-offs and pick-ups from Kekla village with advance notice.

Most guesthouses can send a private car to collect you from Kundiawa, Mt Hagen or Goroka, although it will be expensive.

Kegsugl to Madang

The erstwhile three-day trek from the Highlands to Madang has now become a road plied by PMVs and the journey can be completed in a day. From Kegsugl to Bundi (K70, three hours) the road is still pretty rough; the turn-off to Madang is between Kegsugl and Gembogl. From Bundi to Usino costs K20 (1½ hours), though you may have to change vehicles at Brahmin (K10, 30 minutes). From Usino to Madang (K15 1½ hours) there are many PMVs and the road is sealed.

WESTERN HIGHLANDS & JIWAKA PROVINCES

The people in this area are fiercely proud, with strong tribal loyalties and complicated clan affiliations. In part, it was because of such divisions that three districts split from the Western Highlands and formed Jiwaka Province in 2012.

Mt Hagen is by far the region's largest town and it wasn't that many years ago when farmers could be seen proudly strutting through Hagen's market in traditional clothing. The men favoured wide belts of beaten bark with a drape of strings in front and a rear covered by a bunch of leaves attached to a belt (known collectively as a *tanket* or *arse gras*). Women wore string skirts and hung cuscus fur 'scarfs' around their necks. Such attire is now reserved for *singsings* (celebratory dances or festivals) and political rallies, but the proud swagger lives on. *Singsings* are still an integral part of life and a great opportunity to witness the Highlanders' singular sense of style – make every effort to see one.

Mt Hagen

Despite its environs and economic prominence, Mt Hagen is not nearly as attractive as Goroka. PNG's third biggest city, 'Hagen', as it's often called, was a patrol station before WWII, and has boomed in the last 40 years as Enga and the Southern Highlands have opened up. Now it's an unruly city with major squatter settlements, potholed roads and many itinerant people. As in Lae and Port Moresby, Hagen's streets are packed with people.

The city's ambience can vary from the usual PNG relaxed vibe to periods of heavy tension during elections or inter-clan disputes.

◎ Sights & Activities

Hagen Market   MARKET

(◷8am-4pm Mon-Sat) This is one of PNG's biggest and most varied markets and a great place to buy *bilums* and Highland hats. There's also a vast range of fresh produce on sale and you may also see sorry-looking cuscuses, pigs and birds trussed up on poles or in enclosures. It's busy each day and thieves work the crowd. They're mostly kids working in tandem – one might distract you while another snatches a bag or wallet.

The atmosphere in the market can be edgy, and the best way to make friends is to buy stuff.

Tours

Paiya Tours — TOUR
(☑542 3529, 7685 8183; www.paiyatours.com) Locally run from the Magic Mountain Nature Lodge (and Travellers Hut). Can arrange birdwatching and trekking to the peaks of Mt Hagen, Mt Wilhelm and Mt Giluwe.

PNG Eco-Adventure Tours — CULTURAL TOUR
(☑7165 1482; www.pngtourism.com) A Port Moresby–based operation that specialises in tours to remote villages, including those around Lake Kutubu.

Trans Niugini Tours — TOUR
(☑542 1438; www.pngtours.com; Kongin St) One of the main inbound tour companies (p241) in PNG, it arranges tours and activities across the country. It's well organised, professional and rather expensive. Its packages include meals and activities, and guests are ferried to its seven lodges by private aircraft and stay in luxury, including Mt Hagen's very own Rondon Ridge (p116).

Festivals & Events

Mt Hagen Show — CULTURAL SHOW
(adult 1-/2-day pass K150/300; ⊙3rd weekend Aug) It's not as big as the Goroka Show, but the Mt Hagen Show is definitely a must-see. It's held at the showgrounds, 13km northeast of town. Tickets can be brought from Trans Niugini Tours and major hotels prior to the show. The performers are happy to pose for photographs (they don't charge) but at times it can feel like a photographic free-for-all.

Cheap 'general admission' passes are designed for locals and won't allow you access to the *singsing* groups until 11am, and then only from the surrounding banks. The two-day pass allows you to arrive early (around 8am) and see the groups dressing and donning their feathered headdresses. Vigorous impromptu performances at this time can often be more powerful, even ribald, compared with the formal stuff dished up in the arena. Contrary to what you might be fearful of, there's no general bird-of-paradise slaughter just before show time – the feather headdresses and costumes are extremely valuable and rarefied heirlooms.

There are some quality artefacts on sale outside the showgrounds and *mild* bartering here won't offend local sensibilities. Locals prefer the live bands and contemporary music on stage in a natural bowl just outside the showgrounds – follow your ears and watch your camera in the crowds.

Sleeping

During the weekend of the Mt Hagen Show, rooms are scarcer than tree kangaroos in Port Moresby. Be sure to book at least three months ahead.

Travellers Hut — GUESTHOUSE $
(☑7685 8183; www.paiyatours.com; Kunda St; r standard/deluxe K100/150) This new project by the couple running Magic Mountain Nature Lodge was still under construction when we visited. Nonetheless, it is already a great budget addition to Mt Hagen's options, with clean and comfortable en suite rooms and an on-site restaurant. The bonus is having such knowledgeable hosts who can arrange cultural, birdwatching and trekking tours.

Mt Hagen Missionary Home — GUESTHOUSE $
(☑7096 5496, 542 1041; mhmhpng.weebly.com; Kumniga Rd; dm/r K120/320; 🛜) Each room sleeps four in two bunk beds and has its own bathroom. It's friendly, secure, squeaky clean and central. There's an excellent kitchen free to use, plus it is only a short walk to the Hagen Club. Transport can be arranged to the Mt Hagen Show for K30 per person.

Lutheran Guesthouse — GUESTHOUSE $
(☑542 2137; Moka Pl; r K150-200) Right in the middle of town, this is a rather noisy option and no longer kept as clean as it once was. Nonetheless, of the town cheapies, this is a safe bet with good security and rooms that will sleep up to four. A laundry service and meals (breakfast K5 to K25, dinner K20 to K45) are also available. Key deposit is K20.

Hotel Poroman — HOTEL $$
(☑542 3558; www.hotelporoman.com.pg; Moka Pl; r standard/deluxe K330-440) The Poroman may have fairly basic rooms, and the deluxe rooms are not exactly sumptuous, but the staff is super-friendly and the gardens are a good place to unwind after the crowds on Mt Hagen's streets. There's a bar and the excellent Jara's Restaurant (meals K26 to K58) and a Saturday BBQ lunch.

Mt Hagen

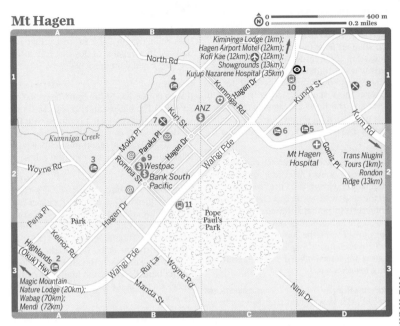

★ **Magic Mountain Nature Lodge** LODGE **$$**
(☑ 542 3529, 7685 8183; www.paiyatours.com; r & bungalow K200) Magic Mountain is more than just a bed for the night. Guests are usually booked on other activities for which this is an ideal base. Surrounded by jungle and gardens, the 10 traditionally built cottages provide all the essential comforts while retaining a genuine ecofriendly vibe. The main lodge also has three en suite rooms plus a veranda for meals and views.

Pym Memindi, the owner, has years of experience and can arrange everything from village visits, including the Paiya Village Moka (a festival on the day before the Mt Hagen Show), to mountain peak treks. The lodge is a 30-minute drive (transfers K150 if not included in package) out of Mt Hagen on the road to Wabag.

Kimininga Lodge HOTEL **$$**
(☑ 542 2399; www.wampnga.com.pg/kimininga; Highlands Hwy; r K300-440; @ 🛜) Run by a local landowner group, Kimininga Lodge has a variety of rooms. The cheapest of the 38 self-contained rooms, in quasi huts, are barely comfortable. You are better off spending more. Airport and town transfers are included in the accommodation price,

Mt Hagen

◎ Sights
1 Hagen Market.................................. D1

◉ Activities, Courses & Tours
Paiya Tours .... (see 6)

🛏 Sleeping
2 Highlander Hotel A3
3 Hotel Poroman A2
4 Lutheran Guesthouse B1
5 Mt Hagen Missionary Home D2
6 Travellers Hut C2

🍴 Eating
7 Best Buy B1
8 Hagen Club D1
Palmuri Restaurant .... (see 2)

ⓘ Transport
9 Air Niugini B2
Budget .... (see 2)
10 PMVs to Airport, Kundiawa &
Goroka C1
11 PMVs to Wabag, Mendi & Tari B2

and there's an attractive restaurant (mains K46 to K70) on-site where an Indian chef creates numerous tasty curries, pizza and espresso coffee.

Hagen Airport Motel HOTEL $$
(✏ 545 1647; hagenairportmotel@gmail.com; Highlands Hwy; r K250-280, unit K440; ▣) This motel, situated near the airport, has 20 rooms that sleep three in double and single beds, plus two self-contained units. It's clean and friendly, although nothing out of the ordinary. The restaurant (meals from K25 to K55) and the hotel are 'alcohol-free zones'. You can grab a lift on the hotel truck, which travels into town daily.

Highlander Hotel HOTEL $$$
(✏ 542 1355; www.coralseahotels.com.pg; Highlands Hwy; s/d from K566/644; @⬚▣) The Highlander, part of the Coral Sea chain, has all the amenities you'd expect from a top-end hotel (except perhaps the razorwire-topped fence), including a pool-side restaurant and bar, an ATM in the lobby, plus a 24-hour foreign-exchange desk. The 60 comfortable rooms are self-contained and are easily the smartest in town.

Rondon Ridge LUXURY HOTEL $$$
(✏ 542 1438; www.pngtours.com; all-inclusive s/d US$853/1266; @⬚) Rondon Ridge is a luxury lodge run by Trans Niugini Tours. It's located at 2164m on Kum Mountain, 13km southeast from Hagen. There are magnificent views of the mountains and the Wahgi Valley to be enjoyed from each of the 12 units. Up here it's comfort all the way, and all guest activities, transfers and meals are included in the tariff.

WORTH A TRIP

KUMUL LODGE
....
Kumul Lodge (✏ 542 1615; www.kumullodge.com; s K170-200, d K210-250), located 40 minutes from Mt Hagen, just inside Enga Province, is geared towards birdwatchers, and you can see birds of paradise in the grounds of the lodge. The bungalows, built from bush materials, are very comfortable, self-contained and have large windows and balconies overlooking the surrounding forest.

The cosy, warm bar and communal restaurant are perfect for sharing stories and snapshots of the local bird population. Most guests arrive on a package, but independent travellers can arrange transfers (K70) and birding guides at the lodge.

✕ Eating

The town centre has lots of *kai* (fast-food) bars selling lamb flaps so greasy that not only are they capable of clogging your arteries, they could dam the Sepik.

Best Buy SUPERMARKET $
(Paraka Pl; pies K4; ⊙ 7am-6pm Mon-Fri, to 4pm Sat & Sun) The biggest and best-stocked store in town, although it can't compete with the market when it comes to veggies and fruit. The on-site bakery is good value with a good selection of pies, sausage rolls and cakes.

★ Kofi Kave CAFE $$
(Banz Kofi; near Airport; mains K25-55, coffee K8-12; ⊙ 8am-4.30pm Mon-Fri, 8am-2pm Sat) If you're wondering where the expat community hangs out, you'll find them sipping coffee and nibbling cheesecake (K12) in this uber-trendy cafe. Turn right (southeast) when you reach the airport and look for the Banz Kofi sign and high stone walls. Knock on the metal gates and someone will let you in.

Hagen Club PUB FOOD $$
(✏ 542 1537; Kum Rd; mains K30-65; ⊙ 11am-2pm & 4-10pm Mon-Sat) Serves cold beer and good pub-style light meals during lunch, and cold beer and European dishes during dinner. The Mt Hagen Ball is held here to coincide with the Mt Hagen Show. Bring your tux, and dancing shoes, and see the manager for a ticket.

★ Palmuri Restaurant INTERNATIONAL $$$
(✏ 542 1355; Highlander Hotel, Highlands Hwy; mains K40-70; ⊙ breakfast, lunch & dinner) The Palmuri is Hagen's most upmarket restaurant. It offers delectable delicacies such as Mt Wilhelm trout, pasta, steaks, triple-stacked pancakes, a seafood-style buffet (K85) every Thursday and a separate pizza menu (K40 to K65).

❶ Information

Aside from *raskols* (bandits), tribal warfare can break out over land disputes, pigs or gardens. Clan warfare never embroils outsiders, confining itself to the protagonists, but it can make people tense and unpredictable. During the day, Mt Hagen is reasonably safe. Nobody hassles or asks for money, but the town is thronged with security guards and dogs around banks and shops. Don't approach the dogs – they are not accustomed to unfamiliar people.

It's not, however, safe at night and the market area is rife with pickpockets at any time.

ASCENDING MT GILUWE

Mt Giluwe is a striking mountain when seen from the Highlands (Okuk) Hwy between Mt Hagen and Mendi. It attracts climbers from around the world who are committed to summitting the highest volcanic peaks on all seven continents – the Volcanic Seven Summits. As part of the Indo-Australian continental plate, PNG has been contiguous with Australia in past ice ages, and is considered part of the Australian continent. And at 4367m, this old shield volcano holds the title. From the trailhead near the highway it takes about six hours to reach the cave generally used as base camp (bring your own tent and supplies). From the cave, it is about three hours up to the peak. Paiya Tours (p114), based in Mt Hagen are recommended organisers of this trek.

Mt Giluwe Lodge (☑ 7926 3383; Mendi; r with/without bathroom K150/250) sits on the highway between Mt Hagen and Mendi (take PMV K10 from either direction). It has clean and comfortable rooms and a restaurant (breakfast/lunch/dinner K25/20/30). The lodge can organise the all-essential local mountain guides (K150). Don't underestimate the cold temperatures, altitude and exposure of this trek. Many trekkers first tackle Mt Hagen in an effort to acclimatise for the altitude.

EMERGENCY
Ambulance (☑ 001)
Police (☑ 542 1222; Kumniga St)

INTERNET ACCESS
Kumul Electronics (Paraka Pl; per 15min K6) Above the red Digicel shop and next to the obvious Brian Bell shop.
Pilgrims Office Supplies (Hagen Dr; per 15min K7) Located beside the Western Highlands Tourism Bureau.

MEDICAL SERVICES
There are several pharmacies in town.
Kujup Nazarene Hospital (☑ 546 2341, 546 2228; Kujup) Located 45 minutes east on the Highlands (Okuk) Hwy, Dr Jim Radcliff comes recommended by the local missionaries.

MONEY
Besides the ATMs at banks, there is also an ATM inside the Highlander Hotel that allows you to withdraw money in comparative safety.
ANZ (☑ 542 1622; Hagen Dr)
Bank South Pacific (☑ 542 1877; Romba St)
Westpac (☑ 542 1056; Romba St)

POST
Post Office (☑ 542 1270; Paraka Pl)

❶ Getting There & Around

AIR
The airport is at Kagamuga, about 10km from Hagen's centre. Minibuses run often from the small market next to the airport to the Hagen Market (K2). For an additional K1 the driver will often drop you at your hotel. Major hotels provide transfers.

Air Niugini (☑ 542 1183, 542 1039; www.airniugini.com.pg; Paraka St) Has flights three times daily to/from Port Moresby (K510).
PNG Air (☑ 545 1407, 542 1547; www.apng.com; Airport) Has flights that connect Mt Hagen to Port Moresby (K370) daily; Lae (K429), Wewak (K445) and Tabubil (K549) on Tuesday, Thursday and Saturday; and Tari (K290), Kiunga (K549) and Goroka (K250) on Monday, Wednesday, Friday and Sunday.
MAF (Mission Aviation Fellowship; ☑ 7373 9900; png@maf.org.au; MAF-papuanew guinea@maf.org; Airport) Offers charter connections to numerous remote destinations. Mt Hagen is MAF's principal base.

CAR
There are no taxis in Mt Hagen but a number of car-rental agencies are located near the airport. Expect to pay around K1000 per day for a 4WD, double cab or Toyota HiLux.
Avis (☑ 545 1350; www.avis.com.pg; Airport)
Budget (☑ 542 1818; reservations@budget.com.pg; Highlander Hotel, Highlands Hwy)
Hertz (Eagle Hire; ☑ 542 3544; Airport)
Wangdui Hire Cars (☑ 545 1112; wang dui7469@gmail.com; Airport)

PMV
Roads heading west from Mt Hagen towards Mendi and Wabag have been prone to ambushes in the past and it is worth seeking advice from your place of accommodation before jumping on a west-bound PMV to Mendi (K20, 3½ hours) or Wabag (K20, four hours). It is possible to reach Tari (K50, 11 hours) in one day if you start early.

In the other direction there are buses to Kundiawa (K20, 2½ hours) and Goroka (K30, four hours).

PMVs going east, to Kundiawa and Goroka, leave from the market. PMVs going west, to Wabag, Mendi and Tari, leave from the highway beside Pope Paul's Park.

ENGA PROVINCE

Enga is the highest and most rugged of all PNG's provinces, and even other Highlanders refer to Engans as 'mountain people'. The provincial capital of Wabag is more of an outlying town to Mt Hagen than a major centre. The two other main centres are Wapenamanda and Laiagam.

Enga is unique in that it has only one major linguistic and ethnic group, and the shared ethnicity of the Enga speakers overshadows the province's minority tribes such as the Ipili speakers (around Porgera) and Nete speakers.

Porgera, the giant and controversial gold and copper mine in the far west, has brought about rapid change for some, but most people still grow cash crops – coffee, pyrethrum and cool-weather European vegetables – in their steep mountain gardens.

Wabag

Wabag has little to attract tourists, except for an excellent cultural centre and the mighty Lai River barrelling through town, but the hills around Wabag are stunning, featuring jagged mountains, gushing rivers and picturesque villages nestled in the mountains.

◉ Sights

Enga Take Anda Cultural Centre   CULTURAL CENTRE
(☑ info 547 1128; ☺ 8am-4pm Mon-Fri, 9am-2pm Sat) FREE At this large and fascinating cultural centre, art gallery, museum and workshop, you'll find a grand building with informative displays, including artefacts and archival photos. Insights include excellent descriptions of tribal politics and inter-clan warfare, and the history-changing introduction of the sweet potato from South America around 350 years ago. At the nearby gallery you can watch young artists making sand paintings.

✦ Festivals

Enga Cultural Show   CULTURAL
(☺ mid-Aug) The main (and cynics might say, only) reason to visit Wabag is the annual Enga Cultural Show, a smaller version of the Mt Hagen and Goroka Shows. Like the Mt Hagen Show, it is held in mid-August, presumably with the hope of drawing some of the Hagen crowds to Wabag. It's a tactic that seems to work.

While this show doesn't draw as many *singsing* groups, those groups that do attend are no less spectacular, and the setting, largely free of tourists (especially on the first day), is more intimate. It's held at the sports ground.

🛏 Sleeping & Eating

Wabag Lodge   GUESTHOUSE $$
(☑ 547 1210; Wabag; r K200-250, r without bathroom K100-150) This secure guesthouse is the best option in Wabag with clean if unexceptional rooms provided with soap and towel, tea and coffee, and a TV. The kitchen is well equipped, while breakfast (K30) and dinner (K49) can be provided. If you are asking for directions in Wabag, note that the lodge was formerly the Wabag Guesthouse.

Dae Won Wabag Hotel   HOTEL $$
(☑ 547 1140; fax 547 1033; Highlands Hwy; r K130-240) Wabag's only formal hotel and owned by a Korean trading company, this place is bare-bones minimalist and low on comforts. It's on the Mt Hagen side of town and there's a communal lounge area and kitchen, as well as a restaurant and very, very high fence.

Green Haus Restaurant   CAFETERIA $
(2nd fl, Ipatas Centre; mains K10-50) In the large, green Ipatas building that dominates the town is this cafeteria run by the same folks at Wabag Lodge. The menu includes 'live' or 'frozen' chicken with chips and there is wine by the glass (K15).

❶ Getting There & Away

AIR
Although the Wabag airstrip is closed, **Air Niugini** (☑ 547 1274) flies to/from Wapenamanda (an hour's drive away on the highway towards Mt Hagen on a K8 PMV) and Port Moresby daily for K615.

PMV
PMVs travel between Mt Hagen and Wabag (K20, four hours) via Wapenamanda (from Mt Hagen K15, three hours). The road to Porgera and the mine is in good condition, but PMVs rarely go there. A few PMVs go to Mendi via Laiagam and Kandep over a very rough road with frequently washed-out bridges.

four bunk beds. Men are welcome and while meals aren't usually provided, arrangements can be made. Otherwise, there are shared cooking facilities. The manager can also give you directions to other women's guesthouses in the area, including ones at Hoiyabia, Paikela and Tigibi.

★ Lakwanda Guesthouse
& Cultural Centre
GUESTHOUSE **$$**

(☏ 7140 5705; Hedemari; s/d without bathroom K100/200) In the village of Hedemari, midway between Tari and Koroba, in the heart of Huli country, is the beautiful Lakwanda Guesthouse. Run by Thomas Tayapi, a wigman of some status, this is the best place to stay to organise cultural tours. Rooms are in comfortable traditionally made huts. Thomas is also an excellent cook and the soup and vegetable dishes are top-notch.

Ring Thomas for an airport pick-up, or catch a PMV (K5) from Tari. Local cultural tours of nearby Huli villages cost from K50 per person.

★ Ambua Lodge
LUXURY HOTEL **$$$**

(☏ 542 1438; www.pngtours.com; all-inclusive s/d US$853/1266; @) The showpiece of the Trans Niugini Tours operation (p114), Ambua Lodge offers commanding views across the Tari Basin and Huli homelands. At 2100m, the lodge enjoys a refreshing mountain climate and attracts many birdwatchers

and orchid enthusiasts. Guests are accommodated in luxury, bush-material huts or in one of the new-wing rooms, beside the restaurant. All rooms have superb 180-degree views.

The lodge is about 45 minutes east of Tari on the Highlands (Okuk) Hwy, near Tari/Ambua Gap, and the surrounding forests have a network of trails ideal for birdwatching. Most guests come as part of a Trans Niugini package on its private planes.

❶ Getting There & Away

AIR

Air Niugini (☏ 540 8023; www.airniugini.com.pg) Air Niugini flies to/from Port Moresby (K890) on Monday, Wednesday, Friday and Sunday.

PNG Air (www.apng.com) Flies direct to Port Moresby (K810) on Tuesday and Thursday and via Mt Hagen (K290) on Wednesday, Friday and Sunday.

PMV

PMVs leave Tari from the market early each morning (excluding Sunday) and pass Ambua Lodge on their way to Mt Hagen (K50, 11 hours) via Mendi (K30, seven hours). PMVs also run from Tari to Koroba for around K10. Between Tari and Mendi the road passes through Nipa and Poroma where there are occasional tribal battles and armed road hold-ups. For safety, check with the Tari police before embarking on this road journey.

THE HIGHLANDS TARI

The Sepik

POP 698,900 / AREA 79,100 SQ KM

Best Places to Stay

➡ In Wewak Boutique Hotel (p130)

➡ Naigboi Guest House (p131)

➡ Vanimo Surf Lodge (p133)

➡ Karawari Lodge (p146)

Best for Sepik Culture

➡ Garamut & Mamba Festival (p128)

➡ Sepik River Festival (p143)

➡ Crocodile Festival (p29)

➡ Middle Sepik *haus tambarans* (p141)

➡ Maprik *haus tambarans* (p132)

Why Go?

The mighty Sepik is one of the great rivers of the world. In serpentine fashion it flows for 1126km through swamplands, tropical rainforests and mountains. However, the Sepik is more than just a river – it's also a repository of complex cultures, a place where some men have crocodile skin while others place masks on yams in celebration, where mysterious rituals live on in *haus tambarans* (spirit houses) and master carvers still create the most potent art in the Pacific.

As you make your way around one of the endless river bends, the scale of the river, the bird life, the eerie lagoons and the traditional stilt villages make it easy to believe that you've travelled clean out of the 21st century and into a timeless, wondrous place.

On the coast, the two main towns attract a small trickle of intrepid surfers who come to tame the seasonal swells.

When to Go
Wewak

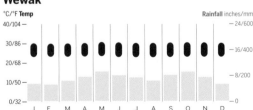

Jul–Sep Festival time: yam harvests in Maprik, Sepik River Festival and Crocodile Festival.

Oct–Apr Monsoon swells bring waves; bring your surfboard to Vanimo.

Dec–Apr The wet season is a good time to see birdlife, and high water levels make it easy to get around.

History

The Sepik's first contact with the outside world was probably with Malay bird-of-paradise hunters – the feathers from these beautiful birds were popular in Asia long before fashionable European millinery incorporated them into late-19th-century women's headwear.

The first European contact came in 1885, with the arrival of the German New Guinea Company. The Germans established a station at Aitape on the coast in 1906, and in 1912 and 1913 sent a huge scientific expedition to explore the river and its vast, low-lying basin. They collected insects, studied local tribes and produced maps of such accuracy that they're still referred to today.

The early 1930s saw gold rushes in the hills behind Wewak and around Maprik, but development and exploration ceased when WWII started.

The Japanese held the Sepik region for most of the war. Australian forces pushed along the coast from Lae and Madang, and the Japanese withdrew to the west. In early 1944 the Americans seized Aitape and the Australians moved west from there. When a huge American force captured Hollandia (now Jayapura in West Papua) in April, the Japanese in Wewak were completely isolated. A year later, in May 1945, Wewak fell and the remaining Japanese withdrew into the hills. Finally, with the war in its last days, General Adachi surrendered near Yangoru. The formal surrender took place a few days later on 13 September 1945 at Wom Point near Wewak. Of 100,000 Japanese troops, only 13,000 had survived.

EAST SEPIK PROVINCE

East Sepik Province is much more developed than Sandaun Province and includes the most-visited and heavily populated sections of the Sepik, as well as several large tributaries. It was here, in 1945, that the Japanese finally surrendered to the Allies and various vehicles of war can still be seen, rotting where they were left.

Wewak & Around

POP 37,800

Wewak was once the site of the largest Japanese airbase in mainland New Guinea, and subject to a barrage of bombs during WWII.

A short distance inland the coastal mountains of the Prince Alexander Mountains separate the Sepik Basin from the narrow band of flat land and headland peninsula on which Wewak is built.

Wewak itself is a rather disjointed place, with most services concentrated in the tiny Town and the rest spread along the coast, en route to the airport. While the majority of visitors pause only long enough to arrange their Sepik expedition and to stock up on provisions, the town does have its charms.

◉ Sights

Mission Point to Cape Boram
WATERFRONT

Near the main wharf lie the rusting remains of **MV Busama** (Map p130). Further down at Kreer, on the road to the airport, there's the wooden hulk of a **Taiwanese fishing junk**. On the beach between Kreer Market and the hospital are some rapidly disappearing rusting Japanese landing **barges**. There's a gorgeous **beach** stretching pretty much all the way to the airport, with gentle waves, clean sand and good swimming.

Japanese Memorial Peace Park
PARK

(Map p130) This peace park marks the mass grave of many troops. The soldiers' bodies were later exhumed and returned to Japan. Here you'll find a memorial and a fish pond. Tok Pisin doesn't have a word for peace; 'peace' sounds like *pis*, which means fish. Thus, most locals refer to the park as *pis park*, which is perhaps appropriate given the fish pond and the general ambivalence that many modern Papua New Guineans have towards WWII.

Cape Wom International Memorial Park
MEMORIAL

(admission K10; ⊗ 7am-6.30pm) Fourteen kilometres west of Wewak, Cape Wom International Memorial Park is the site of a wartime airstrip and a war memorial that marks the spot where Japanese Lieutenant General Adachi signed the surrender documents and handed his sword over to Australian Major General Robertson on 13 September 1945.

To get here, catch a Dagua-bound PMV and get off at the turn-off to the cape at Suara. From the turn-off it's a 3km walk to the memorial park.

There's a ranger at the gates but you shouldn't come here alone.

The Sepik Highlights

1 Trailing your fingers in the legendary **Sepik River** (p135) as your canoe threads through narrow channels to remote villages.

2 Being invited inside a sacred *haus tambaran* (spirit house) at a **Middle Sepik** village (p141).

3 Buying masks, totems and carvings from master craftspeople in a traditional village such as **Palambei** (p142).

4 Spotting splendid birds-of-paradise along the remote **Wagu Lagoon** (p145).

in Wewak, a reliable local operator. Friendly Alois Mateos also owns Ambunti Lodge on the Upper Sepik and specialises in all-inclusive tours based there.

PNG Frontier Adventures (⌨ 7366 4075, 7383 1130, 456 1584; www.pngfrontieradventures. com) Experienced outfit composed of local guide Chris Karis and a British couple. They can organise everything from a single guide to a full-blown tour. Be clear on the inclusions before you set out.

Sepik Spirit (⌨ 542 1438; www.pngtours. com; 4-day package per person all-inclusive s/ tw US$3680/6360) Owned by Trans-Niugini Tours, this luxurious boat contains nine rooms, each with their own toilet and shower, and a communal lounge and bar area. Guests board faster, smaller craft to explore the villages, primarily along the Karawari and Krosmeri rivers, and around the Black Lakes, returning to overnight on the boat.

Melanesian Travel Services (MTS; ⌨ 422 2776; www.mtspng.com; per person from A$3999) The owners of the Madang Resort Hotel operate charters to the Sepik River on the super smart, 98ft *Kalibobo Spirit*. Price includes all meals and wine.

Joseph Kone (⌨ 7121 4829; joseph.kone6@ gmail.com) Knowledgeable guide who specialises in tours of the Upper Sepik and can also arrange tours of the Highlands. Be clear on the inclusions before you head out.

ℹ Getting There & Away

AIR

MAF Wewak (p131) flies weekly to airstrips at Amboin on the Karawari River and Ambunti. It was not flying during research time because grass on the landing strips was deemed 'too long'.

BOAT

It's possible to catch a betel-nut boat from Angoram to Mandi Bay, Boroi or Awar, all very close to Bogia, where you can spend the night before catching an early morning PMV to Madang.

PMV

The river is only accessible by road at two points – Angoram on the Lower Sepik, and Pagwi on the Middle Sepik. PMVs in these parts are mostly trucks, either with a tarpaulin covering bench seats down each side, or a plain open tray. The 'Sepik Highway' has become a lot safer in recent times, with occasional police patrols; hold-ups are very rare.

From Wewak, catch a 3-8 PMV to Pagwi between 9.30pm and 11.30pm (K30, mostly on Monday, Wednesday and Thursday). These vehicles run through the night in order to meet the waiting canoes at around 6am the next morning. They return to Wewak as soon as they are full, usually between 6am and 8am. The road is paved most of the way to Pagwi, but potholed.

Two to four PMVs bound for Angoram leave from Wewak's market daily, except Sunday (K20, three hours). The road from Wewak to Angoram is the shortest access route to the Sepik. It branches off the Maprik road 19km out of Wewak. The 113km road is partially paved but still bumpy. If you're returning to Wewak, you start very early (around 3am) in order to get the locals to the morning market soon after dawn.

PMVs are scarce on Saturday and don't run on Sunday. Market days are the best days to travel when the trucks (and canoes) are more frequent.

THE SEPIK

CARVINGS & CROCODILE CULTS

The Sepik region is the best known part of PNG outside the country, and Sepik artefacts (carvings and pottery) are displayed in many of the world's great museums. Traditional art was linked to spiritual beliefs. Sepik carvings were often an attempt to make a spirit visible, although decorations were also applied to everyday items (ie pots and paddles).

Today carving is rarely traditional – it's more a mixture of long-established motifs, imagination and commercial tastes – but it's still beautiful, and of excellent quality. Some villages still retain their own signature styles – Kambot makes the famous story boards but even these are not traditional. Story boards were originally painted on large pieces of bark, and now they're carved in relief from timber.

Christianity, as elsewhere in PNG, is blended with many traditional beliefs. Although most Sepik people would claim to be Christian (they go to church every Sunday), it's a very localised interpretation. The religious world is also inhabited with the spirits of ancestors and some Sepik people invest great spiritual power in crocodiles. People around Kanganaman and Korogo villages in the Middle Sepik perform an initiation rite where young men are cut with hundreds of incisions on the back, chest and buttocks to imitate a crocodile's skin.

Middle & Lower Sepik

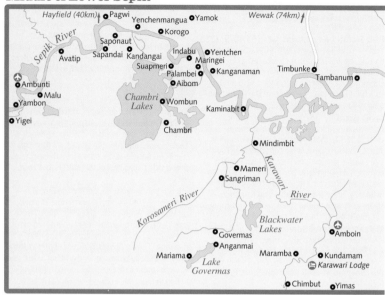

Upper Sepik

Above Ambunti, the villages are small and spread out. The people have had less contact with Western tourists than lower down the river and are more reticent. There's not the same concentration of artistic skills that you find on the Middle Sepik, but nature lovers will find this the most exciting part of the river. From Ambunti the river narrows and the land it flows through becomes hilly with denser vegetation. In many areas, trees grow right down to the water's edge.

There are few villages after Yessan and there is a long uninhabited stretch between Mowi and Tipas. The Upper Sepik is more isolated than the Middle Sepik and, as villages tend to move, there are lots of deserted settlements.

Swagup

Well off the main stream, east of the April River, Swagup is two hours' travel from Ambunti and the home of the 'insect cult' people. Their unique art usually incorporates the figure of a dragonfly, sago beetle, praying mantis or other insects. The ferocious reputation these people earned in former times continues.

Maliwai

This village is on a small lake off the river. The Waskuk people invest spiritual power in cassowaries and these flightless birds are carved into most things, regardless of function. It used to be customary in this village to cut off a finger joint when there was a death in the family. The *haus tambaran* here has collapsed and most artefacts are housed within people's homes. It's 3½ hours' ride from Ambunti.

Ambunti

POP 1690

Ambunti is a scruffy administrative centre but there is an airstrip, police outpost, a very basic clinic and a couple of reliable guides and people who hire motor-canoes. It's well worth peeking inside the local **church**, decorated with carvings from different clans.

The big event here is the two-day Crocodile Festival, sponsored by WWF Papua New Guinea, that attracts *singsing* (celebratory festival or dance) groups from throughout the Sepik Basin. Usually held in August (check www.pngtourism.org.pg for exact dates), the canoe races and cultural performances aim to promote community tourism and crocodile conservation.

The nicest place to stay is the **Ambunti Lodge** (☑ 456 1516, 7259 6349; www.ambunti lodge-sepiktour.com.pg; r K200; ❉), which offers seven double rooms and two shared bathrooms, and has its own generators to run the air-con. There's grilled pork chop or chicken meals (from K30) too. It mainly caters to the clients of Sepik Adventure Tours (p138) but it is possible to stay here if it has rooms available. **Ambunti Catholic Mission** (per person K30), at the bend of the river just before Ambunti Lodge, is a back-up option and can sometimes provide meals.

Middle Sepik

This region starts just below Ambunti and finishes at Tambanum. This area is regarded as the 'cultural treasure house' of PNG. Almost every village had a distinct artistic style but these styles are now merging. The whole Middle Sepik region is interesting but the largest concentration of villages is just below Pagwi and it's possible to visit several on a day trip.

Pagwi

Pagwi is the most important access point to the Middle Sepik. It's not a hugely exciting little place – there are some run-down government buildings and trade stores where you can buy basic supplies, plus houses on both sides of the river.

You can hire motor-canoes here but be mindful that there are some rogues. Day trips to Korogo, Aibom, Palambei, Yentchen and Kanganaman are all interesting and within reach. It's about four hours to Timbunke and another three or four to Angoram.

Sangra Guesthouse (☑ 7364 8450; sangra @ymail.com; r per person K50) is the nicest guesthouse in Pagwi, right by the river and the PMV stop, with a soaring roof like a *haus tambaran* and simple rooms with shared bathroom, electricity and mosquito nets. The owner is a good source of local information and can help organise river tours; meals (K10 to K25) are also available. Alternatively, a two-minute walk upriver brings you to the **Catholic Mission** (per person K30), which has basic beds and mosquito nets.

Korogo

Korogo has an impressive **haus tambaran** with a pair of carved eagles at each end of the roof. Local myth tells of two young women who, while fishing, attracted the lascivious attentions of the Crocodile Spirit. The spirit caused a flood, forcing the girls from their homes and into his waiting jaws. One sister was eaten, the other captured and duly married. The union produced two eggs from which eagles, not crocodiles, hatched. Inside there are colourfully painted pillars and beams, *garamut* drums with river spirit carvings, ceremonial costumes and shell-studded long masks for sale.

There's a pleasant two-hour walk inland to the village of **Yamok**, home to the Sowas tribe and two smaller *haus tambarans*; it's also famous for its hook cult figure carvings. You can also take a canoe to Palenqaui and walk from there (40 minutes).

In Korogo, James Kongon has a small **guesthouse** (per person K100) made of bush materials; meals are included. Korogo is 30 minutes by motorboat from Pagwi.

Yentchen

The soaring **haus tambaran** here was copied from photographs taken at the turn of the century by German explorers of the building standing at that time, but sadly, only the beautifully carved pillars and the roof beams remain on the once-magnificent building.

A small, temporary **haus tambaran** has been built near the ruins of the old one, with hearths inside clay dishes and six *garamut* drums with catfish, crocodile and female figure carvings. Yentchen is noted for its wickerwork dancing costumes – figures of crocodiles, pigs, cassowaries and two-headed men are kept here.

Male initiates have their skin cut into 'crocodile skin' (p139) around Christmas. The ceremony is open to foreigners but be *very* respectful; no photography. You'll have to pay a premium (possibly even K1200, depending on who you talk to) for the privilege.

Yentchen is 1½ hours by motor-canoe from Pagwi and it is possible to stay with Jacob Kambak in his basic **guesthouse** (per person K30).

Palambei

You can't see Palambei village from the river; it's a hot 10-minute walk to this attractive village with two impressive **haus tambarans** at each end of a ceremonial green. The main, two-storey *haus tambaran* features three garamut drums with pig, crocodile and hornbill carvings; upstairs is a treasure trove of shell-inlaid masks, totems, miniature canoe models and wood carvings depicting the

OFF THE BEATEN TRACK

MOUNTAIN ADVENTURE

The craggy Hindenburg and Victor Emmanuel Ranges separate PNG's two mightiest rivers: the Sepik and the Fly. Dotted amid the mountains are the villages of the Min people, among the most isolated in PNG. Connected to the outside world by infrequent supply flights and to each other only by footpaths, they present a unique side of PNG culture, a subject on which anthropologist **Dan Jorgensen** (dwj@uwo.ca) is expert; he may be able to suggest a local guide. There is some spectacular, tough hiking to be done in these mountains; one demanding, week-long hike with a local guide can take you from the tiny Frieda River outpost via Eliptamin to Telefomin, the latter near the source of the Sepik River. Both Frieda River and Telefomin can be reached via charter flight.

legend of a woman being carried by her eagle son; all are for sale. Ask to see the chair that houses the village spirit but don't photograph it. Downstairs are seven hearths, one for each of the village clans.

The second *haus tambaran* has soaring twin roof peaks but a modest interior. The remains of a third *haus tambaran* sit between the other two. It was bombed by the Japanese (or Americans, depending on who you ask) in WWII and all that remains are the large upright posts with carved faces.

Stones, which must have been carried many kilometres, have been set up in the glade. Locals are great *garamut* players and you might see some beating out their powerful and complex rhythms (K40).

Palambei is a 20-minute ride from Kanganaman by motor-canoe and the village has two simple **guesthouses** (per person K30). One is owned by Jacob Kambak and the other by Benny Kusodimi.

Maringei

A pleasant 10-minute walk through a bamboo grove from Palambei, Maringei is an attractive village, with large green spaces between houses. There is a modest **haus tambaran** with masks, a large *garamut* drum and a spirit chair reminiscent of Frosty the Snowman. Just outside are the remains of an older *haus tambaran,* its carved pillars still erect.

Kanganaman

A brief walk from the river, this village is famous for having the oldest **haus tambaran** on the Sepik. Declared a building of national cultural importance, it has been renovated with help from the National Museum. It is a huge, rather open building with enormous carved posts, soaring river birds atop its roof, ceremonial costumes and the spirit chair in the centre of the building.

The second, smaller *haus tambaran* nearby is smoky, covered with long sago leaves and home to a splendid cassowary costume used in ceremonial dances. A female figure with her legs spread welcomes you in; she symbolises rebirth and all men are considered 'reborn' when they exit the spirit house, as they're supposed to leave all negative emotions behind. You'll find carvings and masks for sale in both *haus tambarans.*

SEPIK ART

The Sepik is synonymous with tribal art. It is often described as Papua New Guinea's 'treasure trove', overflowing with masks, shields, figures, canoe prows and story boards. Today carving plays an important part in the river economy.

Like all art forms that are alive and vigorous, Sepik art is constantly undergoing subtle transformations, evolving from traditional forms to reflect current tastes and artistic fashions. Today, just as in the past, a master carver is invested with considerable prestige and is quite capable of producing quality work every bit as unique as his forefathers.

The most artistic villages are concentrated on the Middle Sepik. The villages of Palambei, Kaminabit, Timbunke and Tambanum are all good places to buy tribal art. Remember that a 10kg carving might cost less than K100 but excess baggage or postage charges might be twice the cost of the item.

There is also a dark side to art collecting, and over the years unscrupulous art collectors have plundered the Sepik of some of its most significant and culturally important pieces. Taking advantage of local poverty, the lucrative ethnic art market and toothless laws, traders have been able to strip the area of its cultural treasures, leaving the treasure chest, or more aptly, the skull rack, empty.

Rory Callinan's interesting article on the trafficking of human heads, 'The New Head Hunters', is worth reading at www.time.com.

Launched in 2014, the **Sepik River Festival** (13-15 Aug) takes place in Kanganaman in August, with *singsing* groups from seven different villages. As it was a resounding success, it's due to become an annual feature.

The **guesthouse** (per person K25) in Kanganaman is very basic: without running water but with light in the evening courtesy of the generator. There are plans to build bungalow-style accommodation, complete with shower room and toilet.

Kaminabit

Kaminabit is divided into three villages and it's a fair walk between each. There is a large, well-maintained **Catholic church** in the middle village, with three wings (one for each village) radiating from the central pulpit.

The **haus tambaran** in the central village features a couple of large ceremonial masks, hook cult figures and *garamut* drums. Its centrepiece is a crocodile-tailed guardian with a hornbill on his head and genitalia to make any man proud. It is sought out for good luck before fishing or hunting.

Run by local carver and artist Ronnie, **Bowies Art Centre** by the riverfront in the first (easternmost) village has the best concentration of artefacts on the Sepik, from Tanbanum masks and Minimbit guardian carvings to locally made shell-and-pig-tusk necklaces, penis gourds from the Upper Sepik, yam masks from inland villages and more. Ronnie also does remarkable art with crocodile skulls (from K2000).

Right near Bowies Art Centre in the easternmost village, there's a compact **haus tambaran** that is the cleanest in the area (no cobweb curtains here) and has Albert the wild pig costume in its pride of place, as well as a couple of *garamut* drums.

Experienced guide Cyril Tara runs an appealing **guesthouse** (☑ 7111 0089; per person K50) with baby-blue trim and clean, simple rooms with mosquito nets. Cyril's wife can cook up meals on request. Plan B is the large, rambling and pricier **guesthouse** (per person K80) run by Sebby Kungun, with rather unloved basic rooms.

From Aibom it takes one hour to get here by motor-canoe, and from Palambei it's 1½ hours by motor-canoe.

Mindimbit

This village is near the junction of the Karawari and Korosameri Rivers. The Korosameri leads to the beautiful **Blackwater Lakes** region. Mindimbit is entirely dependent on carving and there is some nice work, particularly the guardian figures with optimistically proportioned genitalia. There is currently no *haus tambaran* because it was washed away when the river altered its course.

THE SEPIK MIDDLE SEPIK

WANDERS IN THE WESTERN PROVINCE

The remote Western Province is a water world characterised by vast swamplands, PNG's largest lake and the watersheds of two major rivers: the Strickland River and the mighty Fly River – the country's second longest. Little-visited by outsiders, it offers remarkable scope for an epic river journey for intrepid travellers with lots of time on their hands.

From Port Moresby, there are Air Niugini (p58) flights to Daru in the Fly River Delta (K626, 1¼ hours, Monday and Friday) where it's possible to find someone with a boat and a guide to take you upriver. Alternatively, you can see if you can catch a ride on one of the **North Fly Rubber Co-op** (wdutton@global.net.pg) boats that ply their leisurely way along the Fly and can get you as far as Kiunga, from where the boat journey along the Fly can be done in reverse. Kiunga is served by direct Air Niugini flights from Port Moresby (K816, two hours) on Saturdays and PNG Air (p58) flights (K621, four hours) on Mondays, Thursdays and Saturdays. You can also fly to Kiunga via Tabubil (K981) on Monday, Wednesday and Friday and from Mt Hagen (K521, two hours) daily.

The best place to stay in town is the **Kiunga Guesthouse** (☑ 649 1188; manager@ ningerum.com.pg), with basic budget rooms that share the common bathroom, and more expensive self-contained rooms; meals are included in the price. If you're a birder, Kiunga Guesthouse can put you in touch with Sam Kepuknai of **Kiunga Nature Tours** (☑ 548 1451; skepuknai@gmail.com); birdwatchers swear that he's the most reliable bird man in PNG for guaranteeing to see the species he promises.

Kiunga is connected to Tabubil in the northernmost part of the Western Province by a 137km 'highway', maintained by the OK Tedi mine. Tabubil, linked to Port Moresby and Mt Hagen via frequent flights, hosts the occasional group of birdwatchers. **Hotel Cloud-lands** (☑ 548 9277; cloudlands@online.net.pg; Newman Rd) is the most salubrious place to stay in town, with clean but overpriced business rooms and an erratic restaurant popular with Ok Tedi mining types.

If you're masochistically inclined, you can ask around for a local guide to take you on a brutally difficult trek over the Hindenburg Range as far as Hotmin Mission in the Sandaun Province, from where you can find a boat to take you down the May River to join the Sepik.

Timbunke

This is a large village with a big Catholic mission, a hospital and a number of other Western-style buildings. There are also some impressive houses and a large jetty.

Timbunke's cobwebby **haus tambaran** is a one-storey structure towards the west end of the village. A Lonely Planet author was the first non-local (and first woman) to ever set foot inside. You'll find some splendid examples of *garamut* drums, some with crocodile heads, some given birth to by female figures.

When tourist boats dock here, locals bring out artefacts and carvings for sale.

Tambanum

This is the largest village on the Middle Sepik and fine, large houses are strung along the bank for quite a distance. The people here are renowned carvers who produce beautiful masks, both painted and inlaid with cowrie shells, as well as guardian figures. Try to avoid Saturday (market day) as more people will be around to show you their wares.

The **haus tambaran** is fairly simple and one-storey, topped with soaring water birds.

Jonathan and his family run a simple **guesthouse** (per person K30) here (with a smiley face on the front), complete with chill-out terrace and guitar (K30 per person).

American anthropologist Margaret Mead lived here for an extended time. From Timbunke, Tambanum is about 30 minutes by motor-canoe.

Lower Sepik

The Lower Sepik starts at Tambanum and runs down to the coast. Angoram is the most important settlement on the Sepik. The Marienberg Mission station, which has been operated by the Catholics for many years, is about two hours downstream from Angoram.

Near the mouth of the river, the Murik Lakes are vast semi-flooded swamplands, narrowly separated from the coast. Villages along this part of the Sepik are smaller, poorer and generally have had less Western contact than many in the Middle Sepik.

The vast volume of water and silt coming down means that the landscape around the mouth of the Sepik changes rapidly. Many villages here are only a few generations old, built on new land.

Angoram

POP 2070

This is the oldest and largest Sepik station. Established by the Germans before WWII, it is now a sleepy, spread-out administrative centre for the Lower and Middle Sepik regions.

Angoram is the most easily accessible of the Sepik villages in terms of public transport from Wewak, and while the Lower Sepik is not as interesting culturally as other parts of the river, the nearby villages are worth a visit.

Wavi Guesthouse (☑ 7161 6330; r K120-150, backpacker r per person K60), run by the daughter of knowledgeable, reliable local guide Francis Tobias, is a short walk from the river. Simple rooms have beds and mosquito nets, and meals (K20 to K35) can be arranged. **Sepik Lodge** (☑ 7908 5609; sepiklodge@gmail. com; r K200), on the outskirts of Angoram, is the swishest option in town (think electricty and your own bathroom). Both places can arrange boat trips and help find PMV boats to Bogia, from where you can hop aboard another boat to Madang (overnighting in Bogia).

Tributaries & Lakes

The Sepik River becomes monotonous as it winds through its vast, flat plain, with *pitpit* (edible wild cane) up to the water's edge. The most spectacular scenery is on the tributaries, and the villages are generally smaller, friendlier and less visited. There are three main accessible tributaries in the Lower Sepik – the **Keram**, the **Yuat** and the smaller **Nagam**.

Kambot & Chimondo

A good day trip from Angoram is to travel south on the Keram River to Kambot, stopping at Chimondo (often spelt Sumundo) on

the way; Wavi Guesthouse can help arrange a boat. While there's little to see in Chimondo besides the skeletal remains of a *haus tambaran*, Kambot is the home of the **Sepik story boards**. The river is narrow and winding, and the banks are crowded with luxuriant growth that attracts many ibises.

It's possible to stay in a simple **guesthouse** (per person K60) at Kambot (ask for David Bamdak). A traveller reported that he was allowed to pitch his tent on the platform in the Kambot *haus tambaran* and spent a magical night camped under its carved struts. It's doubtful that this invitation would be extended to women.

Wagu Lagoon

This lagoon is terrific for birdwatching, though it gets cut off from the river during the dry season when lake levels drop. The Hunstein Range is behind **Wagu** village and the area is covered in lush rainforest. Kaku Yamzu (Mathew) operates the **Toheyo Guesthouse** (per person K60), a simple stilt house with a shared bathroom. Simple but tasty meals are available, and Mathew's tours include trips to see the bird-of-paradise display tree (K20), fishing (K5) and crocodile-spotting at night (K10).

Chambri Lakes

The Chambri Lakes are a vast and beautiful expanse of shallow water. Being only 4m deep, they partially empty in the dry season when things get smelly and the water is unfit for drinking unless treated.

When the water is deep enough there are various routes and shortcuts to Chambri. The deepest route connects the lake with the Sepik just above Kaminabit. To get to Wombun from Aibom when the water is low, you may have to enlist the help of villagers to push the canoe across a shallow part.

AIBOM

Aibom, one of the villages on the lakes, produces distinctive primitive pottery – from cooking hearths and pots to candlesticks – and has a large stone said to be that of a woman who turned to stone resisting a snake that tried to drag her into the water. There's a basic **guesthouse** (per person K30) also (no mosquito nets).

From Suapmeri to Aibom takes 1½ hours by motor-canoe. From Aibom to Kaminabit takes another hour by motor-canoe. There

THE SEPIK TRIBUTARIES & LAKES

are village boats to Kandangai from Pagwi most days.

With the help of French anthropologist Nicolas Garnier and international funding, there is a **haus tambaran** in Wombun, topped with herons, with beautifully carved and painted pillars and with a wealth of masks and carvings for sale inside. The four main totems here are eagles, flying foxes, rats and crocodiles. Although there is no guesthouse, many guides bring tourists here to stay with their *wantoks*.

Amboin

Amboin is usually reached by private flight on Monday, Wednesday or Friday from Mt Hagen or Ambua Lodge (p123). From the village it's a short distance up the river to the luxurious Karawari Lodge. The lodge

river trucks will take you to nearby villages such as **Maramba**, **Marvwak** and **Chimbut**, where traditional Sepik-style tree houses are still used. *Singsings* and re-enactments of the Mangamai skin-cutting ceremonies are all part of the deal. Special birdwatching tours to the Yimas Lakes can be organised.

The **Karawari Lodge** (☑ 542 1438; www.pngtours.com; s/d/tw with full board US$812/1206/1206; @) is a luxury base, operated by Trans Niugini Tours, for exploring the Sepik near Amboin. The main building, built in the style of a *haus tambaran* with impressive carved totem poles and stools, is surrounded by 20 mosquito-proofed bungalows. The lodge has dramatic views across the Karawari River and a vast sea of jungle. Tourists arrive as part of a larger itinerary or cruise on the MV *Sepik Spirit* and it's possible to opt to stay at nearby villages (though they're far less luxurious).

Island Provinces

POP 1.1 MILLION / AREA 28,450 SQ KM

Best Places to Stay

➡ Walindi Plantation Resort (p162)

➡ Rapopo Plantation Resort (p154)

➡ Nusa Island Retreat (p167)

➡ Kabaira Beach Hideaway (p161)

➡ Clem's Place (p169)

Best Activities

➡ Kimbe's Walindi Plantation Resort Dive Centre (p162)

➡ Cycling the Boluminski Hwy (p170)

➡ Surfing, snorkelling and diving off Kavieng (p164)

➡ Hiking up a volcano in Rabaul (p158)

Why Go?

Largely untamed and raw, the islands of Papua New Guinea are not your classic beach paradise. Here you'll live out your Indiana Jones fantasies, blazing a trail of your own amid wild jungles. The adventure starts by climbing the volcanoes near Rabaul, looking for WWII relics on the Gazelle Peninsula, paddling through lagoons mottled with pristine reefs near Kavieng, exploring the rugged beauty of Bougainville or escaping to an island off Lavongai (New Hanover).

The islands' bounty goes beneath the surface, with its unbeatable repertoire of diving adventures. Shipwrecks, fish life in abundance and thriving reefs are the rewards of diving here. Surfers rave about the uncrowded waves off New Ireland.

Be ready for a culture shock, too. These islands are home to tiny villages where people lead lives that have changed little over centuries. If you plan a visit in July, try to make it coincide with the authentic Warwagira Festival of masked dance.

When to Go
Rabaul

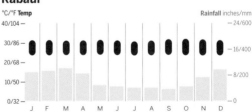

Dec–Mar Cyclone season, which can bring high winds and rough seas.

Nov–Apr The wet season; ideal surfing, with decent swell.

May–Oct The dry season, with slightly cooler temperatures.

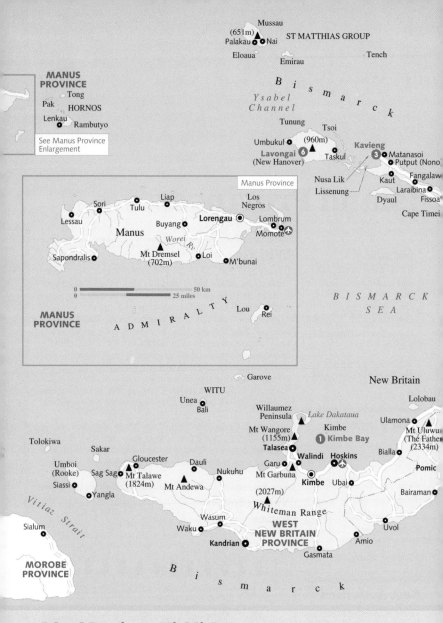

Island Provinces Highlights

1 Diving or snorkelling among some of the world's most diverse and colourful coral reefs in **Kimbe Bay** (p161).

2 Scaling **Kombiu** (p160), aka Mt Mother, and feasting your eyes on the 360-degree views of Rabaul, Gazelle Peninsula and the steaming vent of Tavurvur.

3 Taking a banana boat to an isolated surf break or uncrowded dive site near **Kavieng** (p164).

4 Experiencing tropical-island bliss and uncomplicated

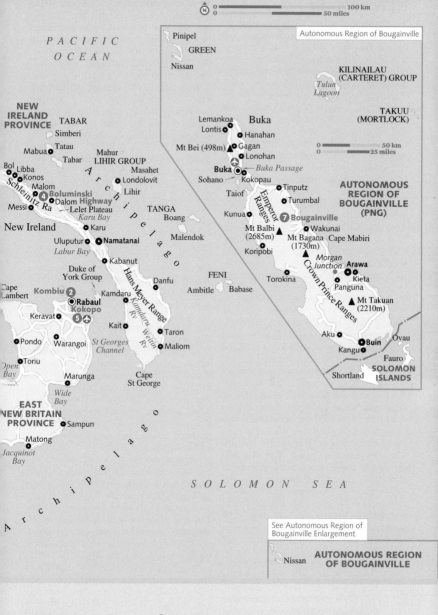

PACIFIC OCEAN

Autonomous Region of Bougainville

Pinipel
GREEN
Nissan

KILINAILAU (CARTERET) GROUP
Tulun Lagoon

TAKUU (MORTLOCK)

NEW IRELAND PROVINCE

TABAR
Simberi
Tatau
Mabua
Tabar
Mahur
LIHIR GROUP
Masahet
Londolovit
Lihir

Bol
Libba
Konos
Malom
Schleinitz Ra
Messi
4 **Boluminski**
Dalom Highway
Lelet Plateau
Karu Bay

Lemankoa
Lontis
Mt Bei (498m)
Hanahan
Gagan
Lonohan
Buka
Sohano
Kokopau
Buka Passage
Taiof
Tinputz
Turumbal

AUTONOMOUS REGION OF BOUGAINVILLE (PNG)

New Ireland
Uluputur
Namatanai
Labur Bay
Karu
TANGA
Boang
Malendok

Kunua
Emperor Ranges
7 **Bougainville**
Wakunai
Mt Balbi (2685m)
Mt Bagana (1730m)
Cape Mabiri
Koripobi
Morgan Junction
Arawa
Kieta
Panguna

Kabanut
Duke of York Group
Danfu
FENI
Ambile
Babase

Cape Lambert
Kombiu **2**
Rabaul
Kokopo
5
Keravat
Kamdaru
Kait
Taron
Maliom

Torokina
Crown Prince Ranges
Mt Takuan (2210m)

Pondo
Warangoi
St Georges Channel
Kamdaru Rv
Welm Rv

Aku
Buin
Ovau
Kangu
Fauro
Shortland
SOLOMON ISLANDS

Toriu
Open Bay
Marunga
Cape St George
Hans Meyer Range

EAST NEW BRITAIN PROVINCE
Sampun
Matong
Jacquinot Bay
Wide Bay

SOLOMON SEA

See Autonomous Region of Bougainville Enlargement

Nissan
AUTONOMOUS REGION OF BOUGAINVILLE

0 ____ 100 km
0 ____ 50 miles

0 ____ 50 km
0 ____ 25 miles

village life along the **Boluminski Highway** (p170).

5 Browsing the lively market and enjoying the volcanic scenery across Blanche Bay from **Kokopo** (p151).

6 Relaxing with a book and a fresh coconut on a blow-your-mind tropical island off **Lavongai** (p168), aka New Hanover.

7 Exploring mountain trails,

lush jungles and smiling villagers in rarely visited **Bougainville** (p175).

NEW BRITAIN

New Britain is stunning. PNG's largest island, it has a bit of everything you've come to this country for – think colonial history, remarkable traditional cultures and pristine wilderness (despite areas where there are logging and mining). The *pièce de résistance*? Volcanoes. The whole region is a rumbling, billowing string of cones and craters cloaked with virgin tropical rainforest. Some are dormant and harmless while others are scrappy villains that periodically flex their muscles. In September 1994 Mt Tavurvur and Mt Vulcan erupted and destroyed most of Rabaul, one of PNG's biggest and most alluring cities, in a furious rain of ash and rock.

After exploring the striking landscapes, be sure to don a mask and fins to delve into New Britain's sensational aquatic environs. To say that Kimbe Bay offers world-class dive sites is an understatement, but snorkellers shouldn't be deterred either – numerous coral fringing reefs with wild drop-offs can be accessed by boat. Rabaul's harbour and the various bays that carve out the Gazelle Peninsula also host superlative sites, including WWII wrecks and psychedelic coral reefs. There is one proviso, though: don't expect to find lots of secluded white-sand beaches – it's not New Britain's strong point.

New Britain is divided into two provinces; each has its distinctive feel. East New Britain (ENB) Province ends in the Gazelle Peninsula, where there has been lengthy contact with Europeans, education levels are high and the people are among the most economically advantaged in the country. The other end of the island, West New Britain (WNB) Province, is sparsely populated, little developed and did not come into serious contact with Europeans until the 1960s. The migrant workers from the Highlands, the colourful expats, army-like rows of oil palms and the dense bush give WNB a frontier flavour that the colonies might have had mid–20th century.

The most easily accessible areas for travellers include the Gazelle Peninsula and Kimbe Bay. If you want to explore the rest of the island, you'll have to cut a path of your own, which means a lot of gumption, time and money.

History

The island of New Britain was settled around 30,000 years ago. The Lapita people, the world's first true ocean navigators, arrived about 4500 years ago, bringing pottery and trade with them. Several hundred years ago, the Tolai people came from southern New Ireland and invaded the Gazelle Peninsula in northernmost New Britain, driving the Baining, Sulka and Taulil people south into the mountains.

From 1874 to 1876 German traders established settlements in the Duke of York Islands and Blanche Bay. The area was renowned for cannibalism. In some districts, more missionaries were eaten than heathens converted.

On 3 November 1884 a German protectorate was declared and the German New Guinea Company assumed authority, which it held until 1914 when Australian troops landed at Kabakaul, east of Kokopo. At the end of WWI, the German planters had their plantations expropriated and were shipped back to Germany.

In 1937 the Vulcan and Tavurvur volcanoes erupted, killing 507 people and causing enormous damage. Before this eruption, Vulcan had been a low, flat island hundreds of metres offshore. It had appeared from nowhere during an 1878 blast (and had been immediately planted with coconuts). When the 1937 eruptions ceased, Vulcan was a massive mountain attached to the coast.

In 1941 Rabaul was completely crushed by the advancing Japanese. At the peak of the WWII, 97,000 Japanese troops were stationed on the Gazelle Peninsula. But the Allies never came. More than 20,000 tonnes of Allied bombs rained down upon the peninsula, keeping the remaining Japanese forces underground and impotent. When the war ended, they were still there.

On 19 September 1994 Tavurvur and Vulcan re-awoke with relatively little warning, utterly destroying Rabaul. Only two people died but 50,000 people lost their homes and one of PNG's most developed and picturesque cities was flattened again. In the following weeks buildings creaked under the weight of the falling ash and collapsed. There was widespread looting.

Today the region's seismic activity is measured more conscientiously than ever and the vulcanology observatory posts regular bulletins. Tavurvur's occasionally spectacular emissions of smoke and noise are not presently considered dangerous.

Geography & Rainfall

New Britain is a long, narrow, mountainous island. The interior is rugged, split by gorges and fast-flowing rivers, and blanketed in thick rainforest. The Pomio and Jacquinot Bay area receives more than 6500mm of rainfall each year, while annual rainfall in the Blanche Bay and Simpson Harbour area is about 2000mm.

Culture

Most of the 184,000 people in ENB are Tolai, who share many cultural similarities with southern New Irelanders. Traditional enemies of the Tolai, the semi-nomadic Baining people of the mountains perform fire dances, which are a spectacular event. Gigantic bark-cloth masks with emphasised eyes and features are worn by dancers who walk on – and *eat* – red-hot coals.

Secret male societies play an important role in village life, organising ceremonies and maintaining customary laws. Tolai ceremonies feature leaf-draped, anonymous figures topped by masks – *tumbuans* and *dukduks*, which are constructed deep in the bush under tremendous taboo. He who dances in the mask is no longer himself, but rather the collective *kastom* (custom) of the tribe's long history. The most feared spirits are the *masalais*, which are spirits of the bush and water that live in certain rock pools and *dewel pleses* (thickets).

Shell money retains its cultural significance for the Tolai and is used mostly for bride price. Little shells are strung on lengths of cane and bound together in great rolls called *loloi*.

East New Britain Province

A basic network of coastal roads and two towns make this the most developed province in the New Guinea islands. With the once-beautiful city of Rabaul levelled by the volcanic eruptions of 1994, Kokopo is now the main centre. Between the two, a strip of villages hug the shore of Blanche Bay. Behind them, beyond the copra plantations and the occasional town, the Baining Mountains give way to a green expanse of bush and volcanic peaks.

Kokopo

Kokopo is an opportunistic town. It has literally risen from ashes. Kokopo started to develop just after Rabaul was flattened by the volcanic eruptions of 1994. While you can sense a palpable helplessness in Rabaul,

Kokopo feels more optimistic. The town emanates a sense of confidence and pride. But it lacks Rabaul's mysterious aura.

Kokopo is serviceable, with a range of well-organised accommodation options, banks, government services and lots of businesses, but there are no big-ticket sights.

If you come from mainland PNG, Kokopo is a good base to set your body clock to island time, get your bearings and make the most of the infrastructure before heading out to rougher areas found in the New Guinea islands.

◉ Sights & Activities

The beaches around Kokopo are nothing to write home about. If you're after that perfect beach or a good snorkelling spot, it's worth considering taking a day trip to the Duke of York Islands. The best place to soak up the atmosphere is the waterfront, where banana boats (speed boats) pull up on the east end of the beach and their drivers wait for a fare or go fishing. These boats come and go from all over the province, the Duke of Yorks and New Ireland.

East New Britain Historical & Cultural Centre　　　　MUSEUM
(Map p154; ☑982 8453; Makau Esplanade; admission K5; ⊙9am-5pm) The interesting East New Britain Historical & Cultural Centre has a fine if deteriorating collection of historical objects. There are fading photographs and numerous WWII relics, including massive guns, torpedoes and a corroding Zero fighter.

Queen Emma's Steps　　　　RUIN
(Map p154) From the Historical & Cultural Centre it's a short walk to the site of Queen Emma's house, Gunantambu, now occupied by of the Gazelle International Hotel and the Ralum Country Club. There's not much to see other than an old gate and the crumbling steps that hint at the once-grand colonial home that was ruined in WWII.

Emma Forsayth, from Samoa, started a trading business at Mioko in the Duke of York Islands in 1878 before extending her empire to include plantations, trade stores and ships.

Kokopo Market　　　　MARKET
(Map p154; Williams Rd; ⊙closed Sun) The buzzing Kokopo market is also well worth a stroll. It's best on Saturday. *Buai* (betel nut) and its condiments, *daka* (mustard stick) and *cum-*

Gazelle Peninsula

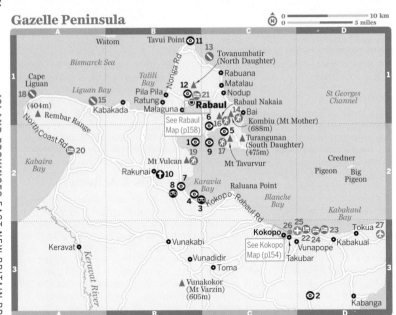

bung (mineral lime, which looks rather like cocaine in its little plastic wraps) account for half of the stalls, with produce such as fruit, vegetables, smoked fish and crabs accounting for the remainder. At the rear, tobacco growers sell dried leaves; home-made cigars wrapped with sticky tape at the mouth end.

Bita Paka War Cemetery CEMETERY
(Map p152; ⊙ dawn-dusk) This poignant war cemetery contains the graves of more than 1000 Allied war dead, many of them Indian slaves. The gardens are lovely. It's 8km off the main road towards the airport; the turn-off (signposted) is about 2km east of Rapopo Plantation Resort. Take PMV 9 and ask the driver to drop you there (K2). The return trip is a bit more tricky; you'll have to wait for the bus or walk to the main coastal road. Start early.

Kabaira Dive DIVING
(Map p152; ☑ 7191 6830; http://diveandtours rabaul.com; Rapopo Plantation Resort; shore dive K110, 1/2 boat dives K240/350) Kabaira Dive, with an office at Rapopo Plantation Resort and family connections at Kabaira Beach Hideaway, offers a range of day trips to reefs and wrecks. Equipment rental is K55. It's an excellent centre with professional staff.

🔄 Tours

You can arrange tours at Kokopo Beach Bungalow Resort, Taklam Lodge, Rapopo Plantation Resort, Gazelle International Hotel and Kokopo Village Resort. Popular excursions (half/full day from K240/360 for one; less per person as group size increases) travel from Kokopo to Rabaul, taking in all the sights along the way, including Mt Vulcan and the Submarine Base and tunnels. Harbour cruises are also available.

✨ Festivals & Events

Warwagira & Mask Festival FESTIVAL
(⊙ Jul) This is a great occasion, the last three days of which *dukduks* and *tumbuans* (masked forest spirits; *dukduks* are the taller ones) come out of the sea from canoes at dawn to dance. Check www.papuanew guinea.travel or one of the hotels to confirm the date and location (it takes place in either Kokopo or in Rabaul).

At night Baining fire dancers perform, fire walking in huge masks, with a live snake.

🛏 Sleeping

Vavagil GUESTHOUSE $
(Map p154; ☑ 982 8833; vavagil@global.net.pg; Williams Rd; s & d K243-286, s/d without bathroom K172/186; ✴) Vavagil has a medley of rooms,

Gazelle Peninsula

from dark budget quarters with spongy beds, low ceilings and lino floors to brighter doubles with clean private bathrooms. Light sleepers should avoid rooms fronting noisy Williams Rd. There is free airport transfer and a free shuttle service to the associated Vavagil Restaurant (though it is only a short walk).

Reception is in a separate building, two doors down the hill on the side road.

Seaview Beach Resort   GUESTHOUSE $
(Map p152; ☑ 982 8447; seaview.beachresort@gmail.com; r K198-297, without bathroom K160; ✷✸) The rooms are rather institutional (cinderblock walls and fluorescent lighting) and there aren't any amenities (aside from laundry service and kitchen access), though it is just steps to a pebbly beach, where you can stroll to Rapopo Plantation Resort for a bang-up meal. Free pick-up from the airport.

The beach out front is the Kokopo base for Solwara Meri (p156) boats to the Duke of Yorks and New Ireland.

Taklam Lodge   HOTEL $$
(Map p154; ☑ 982 8870; www.taklam.com.pg; Williams Rd; s K278-419, d K358-459, s/d without bathroom K188/268; ✷) Taklam is a rambling place with rooms ranging from small and windowless (those near reception) to sun-

nier quarters upstairs. All rooms show wear and tear and have thin walls. It's run by the same management as Kokopo Beach Bungalow Resort, meaning you can catch a free lift there for a meal with free wi-fi or to lounge by the pool or on the beach.

Room rates include breakfast. You can arrange tours here, but you will need a group to make the prices reasonable.

Queen Emma Lodge   HOTEL $$
(Map p152; ☑ 7178 2649; qel_reservations@swtpng.net; r K400-420, without bathroom K300, bungalow K550; ✷) Located 1km east of the town centre, Queen Emma has attractively designed wood-panelled rooms that open on to a common deck with garden or waterfront views plus a fully self-contained bungalow. The 'budget' rooms are pricey but comfortable and clean. There's a good restaurant, an outdoor thatch-roof bar and a tour desk with car hire. Free airport transfers.

Kokopo Village Resort   RESORT $$
(Map p154; ☑ 982 9096; www.kokoporesort.com.pg; off Williams Rd; r K242-550, without bathroom K176-198; ✷) This ageing resort consists of a series of two-storey buildings with red corrugated roofs, plus an on-site restaurant and a tour desk. All could do with some brightening up.

Kokopo

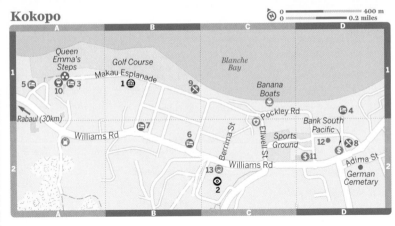

Kokopo

The cheaper, boxy rooms beside the reception are best avoided, though the more appealing deluxe rooms cost a premium.

★ Rapopo Plantation Resort — RESORT $$$
(Map p152; ☎982 9944; www.rapopo.com; s/d from K495/550; ☀@☎) This beautifully designed resort is set amid fig and coconut trees, with immaculate lawns, a large pool and a postcard beach. Expect tasteful, amply sized rooms with cultural tones and all mod cons, plus the added lure of sweeping views of the bay and Tavurvur volcano. Other perks include a stylish open-sided restaurant and a dive centre (p152). It's a mellow and comfortable place to stay, close to the airport and well away from the noisy town centre.

Gazelle International Hotel — HOTEL $$$
(Map p154; ☎982 5600; www.gazelleinternationalhotel.com; Makau Esplanade; r incl breakfast K520-572; ☀@☎☎) The Gazelle has comfy, contemporary rooms with small balconies, the best (and most expensive) with waterfront views. Though it's a rather soulless, modern place it could proffer just the sort of pampering you have been looking for, with ample amenities including complimentary laundry and the excellent Emma's restaurant. Heavily discounted weekend rates (from K330 per night).

Kokopo Beach Bungalow Resort — BUNGALOW $$$
(Map p154; ☎982 8788; www.kbb.com.pg; r incl breakfast K560-699; ☀@☎☎) This well-run establishment is a peaceful oasis in a mature tropical garden, with a pretty pool and steps leading down to a lovely beach. The handsome wood-carved bungalows scattered in the lush garden are attractive,

as are the more spacious suites. Most units have vistas over the bay. There's an excellent outdoor bar-restaurant with good food and water views. Check the website for weekend specials.

✕ Eating

Kokopo Market   MARKET $
(Map p154; Williams Rd; ⊘ closed Sun) The place to head to if you want to stock up on fruit and vegetables. You can buy sausage and rice, or fish, pumpkin and banana (with lots of tasty greens) wrapped in a banana leaf.

Andersons Foodland   SUPERMARKET $
(Map p154; Williams Rd; mains K5-12; ⊘ 8am-6pm Mon-Sat, 9am-2pm Sun) This higher-end super-market is well stocked, with a selection of Australian imports. There's a *kai* (fast-food) bar near the entrance, as well as a bakery with some of the best house-made savoury pies in PNG (steak and mushroom, egg and bacon), plus muffins and cakes (try the fluffy banana cake).

Haus Win   ASIAN $$
(Map p154; ✐ 982 8788; www.kbb.com.pg; Kokopo Beach Bungalow Resort; mains K28-98; ⊘ break-fast, lunch & dinner) Inside the Kokopo Beach Bungalow Resort, Haus Win serves up some of the city's best dishes. The Asian-influenced menu showcases regional del-icacies such as Kavieng chilli crab, New Ireland lobster and Ulaveo steak. Other hits include coconut-coated prawns, sweet-and-sour pork and Thai chilli prawns. The open-sided, thatch-roof restaurant with orchids on the tables has lovely bay views.

Vavagil Restaurant   PUB FOOD $$
(Map p154; ✐ 982 9417; Makau Esplanade; mains K32-52; ⊘ 7am-7pm) This small, boxy eatery and drinking spot offers filling meals (ke-babs, fish and chips, barbecue ribs and piz-za) best enjoyed on the thatch-roof terrace overlooking the coast.

Breezeway Restaurant   INTERNATIONAL $$
(Map p154; ✐ 982 9096; Kokopo Village Resort; mains K40-58; ⊘ breakfast, lunch & dinner) Kokopo Village Resort's restaurant has an uninspiring interior, but if you dine out on the veranda you can enjoy superb views over the bay. Highlights include *hap kararuk* (roast half-chicken and veggies), stir-fries, grilled steak or fish, garlic prawns and Kara-nus mud crab.

★ Emma's Restaurant   INTERNATIONAL $$$
(Map p154; www.gazelleinternationalhotel.com; Gazelle International Hotel; mains K45-75; ⊘ 6am-10pm) The Gazelle International's restaurant may not win any design awards but the food is top notch. There are tropical seafood dish-es: start with Peruvian ceviche and move onto grilled lobster or reef fish. There's also chicken and steaks and an excellent Indian menu – we recommend the fish Chettinad. The daily lunch special (four to five options) at K20 is great value.

Rapopo Plantation Resort   INTERNATIONAL $$$
(Map p152; ✐ 982 9944; mains K30-75; ⊘ break-fast, lunch & dinner) One of Kokopo's best dining options is a beautifully designed, open-sided affair serving an array of expert-ly prepared dishes using fresh ingredients, including mud crab, grills, lobster, daily specials and pasta. Lighter lunches are also available.

🍷 Drinking & Nightlife

If all you need is a cold beer and a chilled-out vibe, the bars at Rapopo Plantation Resort, Gazelle International, Queen Emma Lodge, Kokopo Village Resort and Kokopo Beach Bungalow Resort are worth investigating.

Ralum Country Club   CLUB
(Map p154; ⊘ 9am-2pm & 5-9pm) A mix of ex-pats and nationals come to this laid-back spot with sea-fronting veranda. In addition to cold drinks (and darts!), Ralum has Chi-nese and steak and chicken pub-style meals (mains K30 to K40) at its unglamorous Gurias restaurant. For a slice of island life, don't miss the weekly Joker Draw on Friday evening.

Vavagil Restaurant   LIVE MUSIC
(Map p154) Check the blackboard out front for live music and DJs, which occasionally rock into the night.

ⓘ Information

ANZ (Map p154; Williams Rd; ⊘ 9am-3pm Mon-Thu, to 4pm Fri) Has a guarded ATM (Visa and MasterCard), open from 7am to 7pm. Take your passport with you if you are changing cash or cheques.
Bank South Pacific (Map p154; Williams Rd; ⊘ 9am-3pm Mon-Thu, to 4pm Fri) Has four guarded ATMs open from 6am to 7pm. Central.
ENB Tourist Bureau (Map p154; ✐ 982 8697; ⊘ 8am-4pm Mon-Fri) Located at the ENB Historical & Cultural Centre.

Police (Map p154; ☑ 982 8222)

Post Office (Map p154; ⊙ 8.30am-4pm Mon-Fri)

Zoma Medical Clinic (Map p152; ☑ 982 9356, after hours 982 9718; Williams Rd; ⊙ 8am-5pm Mon-Fri, to 1pm Sat) Private clinic, east of the town centre.

❶ Getting There & Away

AIR

The Kokopo–Rabaul area is serviced by **Tokua Airport** (Map p152), 10km east of Kokopo.

Air Niugini (Map p154; ☑ Kokopo office 983 9325, Tokua Airport 983 9821; www.airniugini.com.pg; ⊙ 9am-4pm Mon-Fri, to noon Sat) Air Niugini schedules two flights daily to/from Port Moresby (K830, two hours) and one flight daily to/from Hoskins (K456, 35 minutes) and Kavieng (K412, 40 minutes). There are also flights to/from Buka (K450, 45 minutes, four weekly) and to/from Kieta (K485, 55 minutes).

PNG Air (Map p152; ☑ Kokopo 982 8852, Rabaul Hotel 982 1999; www.pngair.com.pg; Williams Rd) PNG Air flies to/from Port Moresby (K610, Monday, Wednesday, Thursday and Friday), Hoskins (K370), Lae daily (K550), Kavieng daily except Monday (K360) and Buka thrice weekly (K460). There are sales offices above the City Pharmacy about 500m east of the turn-ff to Kokopo Beach Bungalows and at the Rabaul Hotel.

Travel Air (Map p152; ☑ Kokopo 7373 4129, Tokua Airport 7264 0022; Queen Emma Lodge) Travel Air has flights to/from Lae (K656, Monday, Thursday and Friday), Buka (K500, Monday and Friday) and Hoskins (K380, Tuesday, Thursday and Sunday).

BOAT

Banana boats tie up on the beach near the post office and make regular departures to New Ireland (K70, two to three hours) from about 10am to 3pm.

Solwara Meri (Map p152; ☑ 7002 3712; Seaview Beach Resort) Solwara Meri is among the most reliable banana boat operators and has a larger boat and life jackets. His Kokopo base is at the Seaview Beach Resort.

❶ Getting Around

CAR

Daily 4WD hire (K320, plus K2 per kilometre) is costly. Add another K50 per day for insurance. More again for a driver. A few companies have offices at Tokua airport.

Avis (Map p152; ☑ 982 8179; Tokua Airport; ⊙ 8am-5pm Mon-Fri, 9am-4pm Sat)

Budget (Map p152; ☑ 983 9391; Tokua Airport; ⊙ 8am-5pm Mon-Fri)

Hertz (Map p152; ☑ 982 9153; Tokua Airport; ⊙ 8am-5pm Mon-Fri)

Travelcar (Map p152; ☑ 7092 1433; reservations@swt.com.pg) Also at Queen Emma Lodge.

PMV

The main **PMV stop** (Map p154) is just in front of the market. PMV 9, signed 'Tokua' on the windscreen, runs to the airport (K2, infrequent). This bus tends to meet the larger Air Niugini flights. Many guesthouses and hotels provide transfers (free to K44).

PMV 1 runs along the coast road past the Karavia barge tunnel (K2) to Rabaul (K4). Take PMV 2 to Warangoi (K3). PMV 3 goes to Vunadidir (K3) and Toma (K5), offering the chance to see the inland of the Gazelle Peninsula and perhaps a glimpse of the Baining mountains. PMV 5 goes to Keravat (K4) and Kabaira Bay (K5). PMV 8 goes to Vunapope and Takubar (K1).

TAXI

For metered taxis, call **Ark** (☑ 940 8693) or **Citylink** (☑ 7368 0185).

Kokopo to Rabaul

The coast road to Rabaul goes past Raluana Point, around Karavia Bay before squeezing between Vulcan and the hills, and then around Simpson Harbour to Rabaul.

Starting from Kokopo, you'll first drive past **Blue Lagoon Lookout** (Map p152), from where you can enjoy wonderful views of Blanche Bay with Tavurvur volcano as a fantastic backdrop. About 500m to the west, you'll come across a rusty Japanese **Floating Crane** (Map p152), which was bombed by the Allies.

Along this stretch of road are countless Japanese tunnels, including **Karavia Bay Tunnels** (Map p152), which were used as a hospital, and nearby **Japanese Barge Tunnels** (Map p152; admission K5), built to hold the barges out of sight from the Allies. They were hauled to the water along rails by Indian slaves (now buried at Bita Paka War Cemetery) in order to load shipping cargo. The main tunnel contains five rusty barges, lined up nose to tail; bring a torch (flashlight) and K5 *kastom* (custom) price. You'll also find a small **Chinese Cemetery** (Map p152) beside the Karavia Bay Tunnels.

The huge form of Vulcan (p160) rises from the roadside. The last eruption occurred in 1994. It's possible to climb up it, for a guide, ask at Rabaul Hotel (p158).

The **Burma** (Vuruga) Rd leaves the Kokopo–Rabaul Rd and climbs up to the

Malmaluan Lookout (Map p152; Burma Rd), at the Telikom tower. The views are OK, and there's an anti-aircraft gun and howitzer.

As the Burma Rd begins to dip towards the coast, it passes through the Rakunai site of **Peter ToRot's cemetery and memorial church** (Map p152; Burma Rd). Peter ToRot was a village priest who was killed by the Japanese in July 1945. His remains were beatified by John Paul II in 1995. It's moving to see a multitude of families in pressed shirts, print dresses and bare feet walk many kilometres to Sunday church.

Rabaul

Walking the forlorn streets of eastern Rabaul is like stepping into an apocalyptic film. On 19 September 1994 Mt Tavurvur, which looms ominously to the southeast, erupted, spewing huge amounts of ash over Rabaul and the Simpson Harbour and Karavia Bay area. It buried much of this once-lovely city in a desert-like landscape of black and brown ash. It's still active; it announced its latent potency with a sizeable eruption in 2014, and although it was ominously quiet throughout 2015, you can see it steaming gently or occasionally belching huge plumes of smoke into the sky.

Rabaul is not dead, though. Thanks to the deep water (and Kokopo's shallow water),

Rabaul's port facilities and associated industries will keep the town alive. There's quite a bit of life still buzzing around the market and nearby streets. East of here, however, Rabaul is still mostly abandoned, bar a couple of hotels that survived the Tavurvur eruption.

It's definitely worth staying a day or two in Rabaul to soak up the surreal atmosphere and explore the nearby sights.

◉ Sights

New Guinea Club & Rabaul Museum   MUSEUM

(Map p158; Clarke St; admission K5) Established in 1933, the New Guinea Club was a businessmen's club with strict guidelines for membership, although that didn't prevent a young Errol Flynn from charming his way in. It was badly damaged in WWII and rebuilt in the 1940s to its former glory, only to be destroyed again by fire in 1993. It has been partly restored and is now home to a small and interesting museum.

There's often a fee collector or local historian in attendance; otherwise ask at the Rabaul Hotel for the key.

Admiral Yamamoto's Bunker   HISTORIC SITE

(Map p158; Clarke St; admission K5) There are Japanese tunnels and caverns in the hillsides around Rabaul, though nearby to the Rabaul Museum is Admiral Yamamoto's

---

VOLCANO TOWN

Pre-1990s Rabaul had a certain hustle and bustle, but it also possessed that typical laid-back tropical air that was very friendly. It had the biggest market in the South Pacific, an orchid park, playgrounds and swimming pools.

There was a great music scene in Rabaul and PNG's thriving local music industry originated there. Rabaul's Pacific Gold Studios was the South Pacific's first recording studio. Now much of Rabaul is flattened or buried; in 1994 it collapsed under the weight of 1m to 2m of Tavurvur's volcanic ash load.

For several days after the eruption, there were severe earthquakes (known locally as *gurias*) as Tavurvur and Vulcan went at it, and Rabaul was evacuated. The dead of night would be broken by the sound of a building groaning as it eventually succumbed to the weight of ash on its roof.

However, the Rabaul Hotel is standing proof that most of the town could have been saved. Over several days the staff made a concerted effort to clear the flat roof of the piling ash. Rabaul was never swamped by lava, only by slowly piling ash that weighed as much as concrete. Rabaul might have been dusted off without being very damaged with a round-the-clock shovelling effort and a bit of protection from the hundreds of looters who paraded around with new clothes and stereos immediately after the blast.

Take a walk down Mango Ave, past the Rabaul Museum and you can barely imagine the town of old under the soft dust scuffed up by your steps – neat side roads, sewage systems, schools, theatres, parks and sporting ovals. Look up and you can see the rim of the old caldera with its five volcanoes, one still occasionally smoking, and acknowledge the power of Mother Nature.

Rabaul

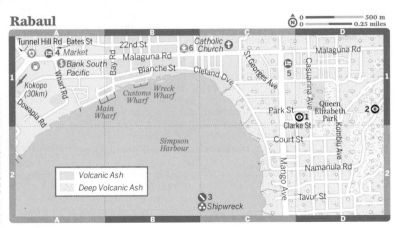

Volcanic Ash
Deep Volcanic Ash

Rabaul

Bunker. It is rather austere but nonetheless interesting and the placards near it are informative. Look for the map on the ceiling for plotting world domination.

Vulcanology Observatory   OBSERVATORY
(Haus Guria; Map p152; ⊘ 8am-4pm Mon-Fri, to 11am Sat & Sun) **FREE** A worthwhile site is the Vulcanology Observatory, about 900m off Tunnel Hill Rd, from where you can enjoy million-dollar views over the bay and the volcanoes. Ask to see inside where numerous informative posters explain the shakiness of the land; and even if you can't feel the small *gurias* (tremors) you can watch them tickle the seismographs, mostly digital screens these days but one old paper recorder still has a stylus and ink.

Japanese Peace Memorial   MEMORIAL
(Map p158) The Japanese Peace Memorial, the main Japanese memorial in the Pacific, is dignified and testament to the forgiveness of the local people. There's another wonderful view from here.

🏃 Activities

Simpson Harbour offers several first-class **wreck dives**, while the reefs off the western tip of Gazelle Peninsula are totally unspoiled and full of healthy hard and soft corals, sponges, gorgonians and a dizzying array of tropical fish: a perfect combination. For diving and snorkeling contact Kabaira Dive (p152) in Kokopo. For details on diving in the area, see the Diving chapter (p32).

For land lubbers, there are various hiking (p160) options around Rabaul.

👉 Tours

Albert Kuni   TOUR
(☑ 7987 0710) The organiser for the local guides from Matupit Island.

Rabaul Hotel   TOUR
(Map p158; ☑ 982 1999; www.rabaulhotel.com. pg; Mango Ave) Rabaul Hotel offers great and affordable possibilities, including local WWII heritage trips, hikes to the top of Kombiu (Mother Volcano), hot-spring dips, village stays, canoe/walking trips to see the megapode colonies on Matupit Island (K70 per person) and Indiana Jones–style multiday jungle treks across the Baining Mountains, through incredibly biodiverse forests.

🎇 Festivals & Events

Warwagira & Mask Festival FESTIVAL
(☺Jul) The location alternates between Kokopo (p152) and Rabaul.

Frangipani Festival PARADE
(☺Sep) Held in September, this festival celebrates the survival of Rabaul after the 1994 eruptions and is named after the glorious trees that still perfume the streets of Rabaul. There are floats (complete with belching volcanoes) that noisily ply the road between Kokopo and Rabaul, cultural dances, rock bands, fireworks (manufactured unless Tavurvur joins in) and a canoe race.

🛏 Sleeping & Eating

This is ground zero; staying here rather than Kokopo gives you that 'I was there' feeling. That said, services are limited, with dining restricted to the Rabaul Hotel, the market, or the food shops and *kai* bars facing the market.

Mesu Lodge GUESTHOUSE $
(Map p152; ☎7235 3355, 982 2090; Wanless St; r without bathroom with fan/air-con K100/150, self-contained flat K200; ❄) This guesthouse is a rambling place in the back streets of Rabaul with simple rooms and worn mattresses. All rooms air-conditioned apart from the K100 budget rooms. Meals available on request.

Barike Lodge GUESTHOUSE $
(Map p158; ☎982 1034; Malaguna Rd; s without bathroom with fan/air-con K80/130, d K150/200; ❄) A betel nut's throw from the market, Barike has cramped rooms with thin, battered mattresses and basic shared bathrooms. But it's tolerable and cheap (at least for PNG). There's a small beer shop at the front.

★ Rabaul Hotel HOTEL $$
(Map p158; ☎7189 3571, 982 1999; www.rabaul hotel.com.pg; Mango Ave; r budget K165, r K308-440; ❄ @ ⛱) Rabaul Hotel is Australian-run and has a wide array of prices; the budget rooms are comfortable and air-conditioned with a private bathroom, while the larger units sport flat-screen TVs and all the mod cons. Other strong points include the wide array of tours on offer, very good meals at the on-site restaurant (mains K35 to K60) and a convivial bar. Airport transfers cost K85 each way.

🛍 Shopping

PNG Diabetic Centre HANDICRAFTS
(Map p152; McNichol St; ☺8am-5pm Mon-Fri, to noon Sat) This place is a treasure trove for artefact hunters, with masks, necklaces, shells, carvings and other souvenirs.

ℹ Information

Bank South Pacific (Map p158; ☎982 1744; ☺8.45am-3pm Mon-Thu, to 4pm Fri) Changes cash and travellers cheques and can do cash advances on your credit card.

ℹ Getting There & Away

Rabaul is serviced by Tokua airport (p156).
PNG Air (Map p158; ☎982 1962) Has an office at Rabaul Hotel.
Chebu Shipping (Map p158; Malaguna Rd) The MV *Chebu* plies the Solomon and Bismark seas between Lae (departing every Sunday at 11am) and Rabaul (arrives Tuesday, returns Thursday, seat/upper deck seat/1st class K320/340/420 one way) via Kimbe. Every fortnight the ferry continues on to Buka before returning to Rabaul, Kimbe and Lae. Expect the schedule to change. The ticket office is on Malaguna Rd.

ℹ Getting Around

Tokua airport is about 45km from the town. PMVs run out to Tokua, and Rabaul Hotel can also provide transfers.

There aren't many PMVs on Sunday. PMV 1 goes from Rabaul to Kokopo (K4) and back. PMV 6 goes to the Vulcanology Observatory (inform the driver), Submarine Base and Nonga Hospital. PMV 5 goes to Rakunai (Peter ToRot's memorial church) and PMV 4 goes to Malmaluan Lookout.

Around Rabaul

The easiest way to visit the sights around Rabaul if you're pressed for time is to take a day tour. Your hotel in Kokopo or Rabaul can arrange a vehicle and a guide.

◎ Sights

Matupit Island ISLAND
(Map p152) The 1994 eruption should have destroyed little Matupit Island but the prevailing winds brought Tavurvur's load over Rabaul and left this connected island almost unscathed thanks, villagers say, to the local *dukduks.* (forest spirits) The thousand-strong village community still chooses to reside right beside the belching monster. You can hire a canoeist to get you around to see Tavurvur's southern slopes, which have

giant lava flows. The megapode-egg hunters are here, burrowing almost 2m into the black sand to retrieve the eggs.

Japanese Aircraft Wrecks　HISTORIC SITE
(Map p152; kastom fee K5) In the same area at Matupit Island, there's quite a smattering of Japanese aircraft wreckage scattered among the palm trees and now semi-buried in earth, including a **Japanese Betty Bomber** and a **helicopter**. They are close to the Old Rakunai Airport. The airport was completely destroyed during the 1994 eruption.

Hot Springs　SPRING
(Map p152) These hot springs are an impressive sight amid an eerie landscape where locals cook and devour their megapode eggs.

Beehives　LANDMARK
(Dawapia Rocks; Map p152) The two rocky pinnacles rising from the centre of Simpson Harbour are called the Beehives and are said to be the hard core of the original old volcano. You can visit them by boat and there is some good diving and swimming. Taklam Lodge and Rabaul Hotel can organise harbour boat trips that take in the Beehives.

Submarine Base　HISTORIC SITE
(Map p152; admission K15) For a picnic spot, nothing can beat the Submarine Base at Tavui Point. The Japanese used to provision submarines here during the war. There are tunnel and rail track remnants below and **guns and relics** in the hills. The Japanese pulled their submarines up to the reef and then surfaced, allowing soldiers to walk off over the reef.

There is great **snorkelling**; the coral bed is flat and almost horizontal until it drops down the 75m vertical wall. To get here, catch PMV 6 from the central PMV stop opposite Rabaul's new market on Malaguna Rd.

🏃 Activities

For the energetic, hiking up the volcanoes can be fun and thrilling, though it's potentially suicidal to climb Mt Tavurvur. They're mostly tracked, but there's often a good chance of getting lost – your best bet is to organise a guide from Matupit Island or the Rabaul Hotel. Guides from Matupit ask for K50 plus K5 *(kastom)*.

Tavurvur　HIKING
(Map p152) At the time of writing it was possible, if quite silly and risky, to hike to the top of Tavurvur and peer into the hissing

and spitting collapsed crater (two hours return). It's a hot, steep, and exposed scramble so leave early, take plenty of water and wear gloves and good shoes. We do not recommend this activity and your travel insurance probably forbids it, but the local guides are keen and knowledgable.

The newly born black rocks are loose, crumbly and razor sharp. The Vulcanology Observatory (p158) issues warnings when they observe subterranean disturbances, and these are posted up at the Rabaul Hotel, but they would never claim to be fool-proof. The direct route from the Hot Springs is steep, while the southern slopes, reached by canoe from Matupit, provide a gentler climb.

Kombiu　HIKING
(Mt Mother; Map p152) If you want a recommendation for a dormant volcano to climb, go for the 688m Kombiu. You'll be up and down in 2½ hours if you're reasonably fit and leave early in the morning. The views from the top are superb.

Rabaul Nakaia　HIKING
(Map p152) Like Kombiu, the adjacent Rabaul Nakaia is a good option for climbing a dormant volcano, featuring the shortest climb (about 30 minutes from the base of the volcano); beware once you've reached the narrow rim of the caldera – it's easy to feel dizzy and lose your balance.

Vulcan　HIKING
(Map p152) The slopes of Mt Vulcan are a bit tricky; they are scored with deep cracks from mud-ash drying and contracting, and can be 4m to 5m deep. They can be hard to spot now they're vegetated.

Local Walks
There are excellent walking routes around Rabaul, and you can spend hours just walking around the town overawed by its complete annihilation.

You can hike down to Matupit Island (p159) and back (although someone will probably offer you a lift) and the views from the Vulcanology Observatory (p158) also make it a rewarding walk.

If you're fit, you can climb Namanula Rd to meet the north coast road near Matalau. From here you can head north along the coast road, which rises over a pass and meets the Nonga–Submarine Base Rd. PMV 6 runs regularly to Nonga Hospital and sometimes beyond. Or you could walk the whole loop over Tunnel Hill Rd and take in the Vulcanology Observatory along the way. This would take about a day.

🍴 Sleeping & Eating

★**Kabaira Beach Hideaway** BUNGALOW $$
(Map p152; ☑983 9266; www.kabairabeach hideaway.com.pg; Kabaira Bay; s/d with full board K250/500, bungalow K300/600; ☎) This laid-back resort on the waterfront radiates a ramshackle air, and combines friendly informality and a picturesque setting. Lodgers can stay in one of four simple all-wood rooms with shared bathrooms or in one of the roomier bungalows, each with a private bathroom. There's excellent kayaking, swimming and snorkelling on the house reef and the homestyle cooking receives high marks.

A host of activities can be arranged, including diving with the associated Kabaira Dive (p152) in Kokopo, plus Robinson Crusoe–style picnics (or overnights) on nearby islands. It's about 60 minutes from Rabaul on PMV 5 (infrequent especially on Sundays), though you may have to transfer at Basis. From Kokopo take PMV 4 to Keravat and change to PMV 5 to Kabaira. Airport transfers are K50 one way. Free laundry. Reserve ahead.

West New Britain Province

If you're reading this, there's a great chance that you're a diver heading to Kimbe Bay. Kimbe Bay has become a byword for underwater action, with an amazing array of marine life and sensational reefs brushing the surface. However, there is life above the water as well, with some spectacular volcanoes brooding in the background and a handful of WWII relics. WNB has the country's greatest proliferation of volcanoes – five active and 16 dormant – and you can literally smell the sulphur in the air. It's also PNG's highest timber and palm-oil exporter with consequent tension between the province's villagers and settlers.

❶ Getting There & Away

Air Niugini (☑983 5077; www.airniugini.com.pg; Hoskins Airport) From Hoskins, Air Niugini flies to and from Port Moresby (K455, once or twice daily) and Lae (K430). It also flies to Rabaul/Kokopo (K410, Monday, Wednesday, Thursday and Friday) with flights returning Monday, Tuesday, Thursday and Friday). To

reach Kavieng, you'll have to transit through Rabaul/Kokopo.

PNG Air (Pacific Trade Travel; ☑983 5177; www.pngair.com.pg; Megamart Bldg, San Remo Dr, Kimbe) From Hoskins, PNG Air flies to and from Lae (K430, daily) and Rabaul (K360, daily). To reach Kavieng, you'll have to transit through Rabaul/Kokopo, and to reach Port Moresby transit through Lae.

Travel Air (☑983 5225, 7109 7994; www.travel airpng.com; Hoskins Airport) From Hoskins, Travel Air flies to Rabaul/Kokopo (K350, Tuesday, Thursday and Sunday) and returns on Tuesday and Sunday. Travel Air also flies to Lae (K415, Tuesday and Sunday) and flies the return route on Tuesday, Thursday and Sunday.

Chebu Shipping (Kimbe Wharf) The MV *Chebu* ferries passengers between Lae (departing every Sunday at 11am) to Kimbe (seat/upper deck seat/1st class K210/222/315 one way; arrives Monday at 1pm, departs Monday 5pm) and continues on to Rabaul (K160/170/240 one way; arrives Tuesday, returns Thursday). Every fortnight the ferry continues on to Buka from Rabaul. Expect the schedule to change.

❶ Getting Around

There are a few 4WD logging roads (in the dry season) leading towards the rugged and virtually unexplored mountains of the interior. PMVs go from Hoskins to Kimbe (K8, 40 minutes), where you can then transfer to a PMV towards Talasea.

Kimbe Bay & Around

The main attraction here is the unsurpassable diving and snorkelling in Kimbe Bay. The town of Kimbe itself is the provincial headquarters and a major centre for palm-oil production, and has no real interest for travellers.

◉ Sights & Activities

On a **dive** around Kimbe Bay you might see anything from a tiny glass prawn to a pod of killer whales. The marine biodiversity is stunning, with more than 413 types of hard coral and 860 species of fish vying for your attention. Drift along the reefs and enjoy the ultimate underwater drama. For details on diving in the area, see the Diving chapter (p33).

Nearby **Talasea** is an active volcanic region set in a dramatic landscape. **Lake Dakataua**, at the tip, was formed in a colossal eruption in 1884. It's worth seeing two **WWII plane wrecks** that lie partially disintegrated in the jungle near Talasea. There's a Mitchell

B-25 Bomber and a Lockheed Vega Ventura – an impressive sight.

Outdoorsy types might consider **trekking** up the active Mt Garbuna. The area also offers excellent **birdwatching** possibilities with several rare species.

Mahonia Na Dari
Conservation Centre   CONSERVATION CENTRE
(✍ 983 4241; www.mahonianadari.org; Kimbe Bay; ⊙ 8am-4pm Mon-Sat) **FREE** Everything you need to know about Kimbe Bay's marine environment and coral reef habitats should become clear at the Mahonia Na Dari Conservation Centre, next door to the Walindi Plantation Resort. This marine research centre is open to the public.

Garu Hot River   HOT SPRING
If you need to relax, it's well worth dipping your toes in the Garu Hot River. Waters are comfortably warm and there's a mini-waterfall.

Walindi Plantation Resort Dive
Centre   DIVING
(✍ 983 5441; www.walindi.com) The Walindi Plantation Resort has land and water tours for birdwatchers, trekkers and divers. It has a very professional dive centre. Expect to pay K395 for two dives on a day-dive boat. A multiday open-water course costs K1890. It also operates the MV *FeBrina,* a 22m liveaboard vessel that sleeps 12 passengers.

🛏 Sleeping & Eating

Mahonia Na Dari   BUNGALOW $
(✍ 7370 5699, 983 4241; www.mahonianadari.org; Kimbe Bay; dm/r K95/195) Next door to Walindi Plantation Resort, this place has simple but clean rooms and self-contained bungalows – when it's not booked out by scientists or school groups (rarely). There are no restaurant – either BYO and use the common kitchen, or plan to dine at Walindi. Airport pick-up can be arranged.

Manaia Guesthouse   GUESTHOUSE $$
(✍ 7204 4700, 983 5944; manaia.guesthouse@ gmail.com; Kimbe; r K200; ❄) This very friendly family-run guesthouse can be found at the western end of Kimbe town opposite the Department of Works. Currently there's seven supremely clean rooms with shared bathrooms and a couple of self-contained rooms under construction. Home-cooked breakfast/lunch/dinner costs K15/30/45. Airport transfer is K50.

★ Walindi Plantation Resort   RESORT $$$
(✍ 983 5441; www.walindi.com; s/d with full board K420/600, bungalow K516/730; ❄) ✎ This beautifully designed resort run by Cheyne and Ema Benjamin is highly recommended for divers due to its full-service on-site dive centre and easy access to the famous reefs of Kimbe Bay. The 12 traditional-style bungalows and eight smaller but equally attractive 'plantation house' rooms are surrounded by jungle-like gardens thick with birdsong. Excellent service and food, too.

Aside from diving, Walindi offers excellent birdwatching tours as well as trips to a volcano, a local village and WWII plane wrecks, among other activities. Airport transfers available (US$90 per person return). The resort has an energy-efficient design and was constructed from sustainable materials.

Liamo Reef Resort   HOTEL $$$
(✍ 983 4368; www.liamoreefresort.com; Kimbe; r K361-770; ❄ 🅿 ❄ ⊠) At the eastern end of town, Liamo is a good deal if you're after some cosseting in a serene environment. Liamo offers a range of air-con accommodation from functional rooms in a concrete building to larger stand-alone bungalows. The open-air restaurant overlooks the picturesque beach. Liamo also runs tours and manages a remote fishing lodge accessible only by boat.

San Remo Club   PACIFIC $
(✍ 983 4600; Kimbe; mains K18-45; ⊙ 11am-2pm & 4pm-late) We love this place – it feels so anachronistic. It's the most 'happening' spot in town, not far from Liamo Reef Resort. A mix of locals and expats gather here to catch the breeze from the terrace, sip a cold beer while gazing on smouldering Mt Garbuna in the distance, or enjoy a well-prepared steak or chicken with chips.

It really only buzzes on Wednesday night when indoor cricket is played outdoors on the tennis court!

🛍 Shopping

Le Riche Colours   ARTS
(✍ 983 4990; www.picturetrail.com/leriche) It's worth stopping at Le Riche Colours if you are after some original souvenirs. Artist Nathalie Le Riche has very colourful hand-painted T-shirts, gift cards, paintings, and other gifts that feature tribal portraits, market scenes and underwater compositions. Call ahead, as the shop keeps irregular hours.

ℹ️ Information

The Bank South Pacific and Westpac are one block south (inland) of Kmart supermarket in Kimbe. Both are equipped with ATMs (Visa and MasterCard). East of there are the post office and daily market.

NEW IRELAND PROVINCE

Few other places in PNG can boast such an interesting and accessible pick 'n' mix of nature, culture and landscapes. Sure, New Ireland doesn't offer the thrill of puffing volcanoes (in this respect, New Britain steals the show), but it boasts broad white-sand beaches and rivers of clear water tumbling down from the thickly forested central Schleinitz Range and a clutch of secluded islands off the 'mainland'.

For fans of traditional cultures, New Ireland is an unmissable destination. In the rugged south is the spiritual home of *tumbuan* culture. The north is home to Malagan, while Kabai culture dominates in the central areas.

And there's the wonderfully down-to-earth, unfussy atmosphere. New Ireland is far less developed than New Britain. Once you cross St Georges Channel, which separates the islands, you'll notice the laid-back vibe, the more sedate pace of life and a greater emphasis on the old ways. Outside Kavieng and Namatanai, the only towns of consequence, there are coastal communities on each side of the island but no real settlements bigger than a trade store or two.

The good thing is that you can mix slow-paced sun-and-sand holidays with action-packed experiences. For outdoorsy types, the pursuit of choice is scuba diving, on an equal footing with surfing. Kayaking, sport fishing, snorkelling and even cycling (yes!) are available.

History

The remains of rock shelters found near Namatanai suggest that New Ireland was inhabited 30,000 years ago. Missionaries began arriving in 1875 along with blackbirders who forcibly removed many New Irelanders to work on the plantations and cane fields of Queensland (Australia) and Fiji.

A villainous crew, blackbirders often posed as missionaries to coax men aboard, killing them offhand if they revolted. One slaver even impersonated the bishop of Melanesia; the real incumbent, believed to be an imposter, was later killed in vengeance! Meanwhile, the shortage of males devastated village life in places.

Cannibalism and head-hunting were rife. Even a death from disease was often attributed, from certain 'signs', to the actions of another tribe, which might be mercilessly attacked in revenge. In some communities, relatives smeared themselves with the blood of their deceased loved ones as part of their funeral rites.

During the German reign, large copra plantations made New Ireland one of the most profitable parts of the colony. The tyrannical Baron Boluminski became district

---

MALAGAN DEATH RITES

For centuries, it has been *kastom* (custom) for the Malagan to carve wooden masks and sacred figures for their mortuary rites. There are a few dedicated regular carvers on Tabar Island and Libba village near Konos; otherwise, carvings are done only by secret men's societies for mortuary ceremonies or rites of passage in the villages.

Different clans have different funerary traditions, including interment, cremation and burial at sea. The *tatanu* or *tanuatu* (soul) remains close to the body after death and it cannot go to the ancestors' world until the mortuary rites are performed. The spirit of a dead person enters the ancestors' world through the places that *masalais* (spirits of the bush and water) inhabit.

Feasts are often performed for more than one person as they are terribly expensive. Those deceased long ago can be included in the rite, which includes chanting, masked dancing, clouds of lime and a huge feast.

Masks may depict the totem animal of a specific tribe in stages of metamorphosis. Such was the fearful power of the mask that, in the past, they were burned after the ceremony. Designs are strictly 'patented' according to clan rites, and a complex ritual payment must be made to pass a design on to another carver. The problem is there are simply not enough young apprentices.

officer of Kavieng in 1910 and built the highway that bears his name by forcing each village along the coast to construct and maintain a section. He made villagers push his carriage over any deteriorated sections.

New Ireland fell to the Japanese in 1942 and Kavieng was developed into a major Japanese military base. Most of the Australians in Kavieng managed to escape, but some chose to stay behind as coastwatchers (spies).

The Allies made no attempt to retake New Ireland but rather bombed it into oblivion. The Japanese surrendered in Namatanai on 19 September 1945.

Geography & Climate

New Ireland is mountainous and riddled with huge, flooded caves. Midway down the island, the Lelet Plateau rises to 1481m and further south, near Taron, the Hans Meyer Range reaches 2399m. A fault line provides passage for the Weitin and Kamdaru rivers.

The area between Namatanai and Kavieng receives about 3m of annual rainfall and has a dry season between May and November. December to March is the cyclone season and can bring high seas.

Culture

The people of New Ireland are Melanesian and speak 19 local languages. The north embodies the complex system of spiritual traditions of Malagan cultures. 'Malagan' also refers to the northern New Irelanders' carvings.

In the island's south are the *tumbuan* traditions. The people from the south invaded the Gazelle Peninsula and settled the Duke of York Group several hundred years ago. *Dukduks* and *tumbuans* (forest spirits) are common to all three cultures. Around Namatanai and central New Ireland are the Kabai traditions, which are not yet as well understood.

As in most PNG islands, traditional clan power is wielded by chiefs or *bigmen* (important men or leaders), but clan rites and land claims are passed on in a matrilineal system.

Kavieng

Being the capital of New Ireland, Kavieng is the only town of any size in the province, but we're hardly talking Shanghai – the tallest construction is the telecommunication tower, and the busiest shops operate very much on Melanesian time. If you proceed from Kokopo, you'll find it remarkably quiet, with few cars in the streets. The seaside ambience, with its fisheries wharf and bustling market in the shade of huge trees, is a taste of genuine island life.

Kavieng itself won't fulfil all your fantasies of a tropical paradise, but it's optimally situated as a springboard to neighbouring islands, including Nusa Lik Island and Lavongai (New Hanover), and for explorations down the coast. There's good snorkelling and kayaking offshore and there's plenty of great diving in the area – not to mention excellent surf breaks.

⊙ Sights

Pickings for sightseers are quite slim in spread-out Kavieng. The northern end of **Nusa Parade** provides the setting for a lovely waterfront walk; the huge fig trees almost meet overhead. If you keep heading north of the Malagan Beach Resort, you will reach the intimate surrounds of **Patailu village**.

The southern section of Nusa Pde continues past the **market** and further along on the left are the **provincial government buildings**, built on the site of Baron Boluminski's residence.

The closest thing Kavieng has to a regular 'sight' is the **Bagail Cemetery** (Nusa Pde), where Boluminski was buried. The tough guy's grave is right before you as you enter the cemetery.

Kavieng has a large and beautiful **harbour**. You can go down to the waterfront and catch a banana boat out to one of the many islands.

🏃 Activities

Surfing

Kavieng has an up-and-coming surf scene, with a good range of reef breaks, both lefts and rights, that are easily accessible. They vary in difficulty, depending on the size and direction of the swell. From November to late April, swells of up to 2.4m are not unheard of. Among the most thrilling spots are Pikinini, Karanas, Nago Island, Edmago Island, Long Longs and Ral Island. For more information, contact the guys at Nusa Island Retreat (p167), they are surf specialists and can arrange surf packages.

Niu Ailan Surfriders Alliance　　SURFING
(www.surfingpng-newireland.org.pg) Even if it's growing in popularity, the Niu Ailan Surfriders Alliance ensures that the number of surfers is kept at a sustainable level thanks to a surf quota system.

LIFE IN A (NEW) IRISH VILLAGE

You'll attract a lot of attention when you show up, but it'll trail off; there's a quiet respect for your privacy in most villages. Take something (preferably lasting and useful) for the kids if you can, but give it to the local school or *bigman* (leader) to redistribute. A football (there's no describing the joy), swimming goggles (you can carry quite a few and they're functional) and pens are all good gifts. Salt, sugar and tea will be appreciated by your hosts in the more remote places, but don't worry about this if you're on the tarmac road. If you're way off the beaten track, BYO rice or you'll eat your hosts out of house and home.

A torch (flashlight), sleeping sheet, mosquito net, hammock, thongs (flip-flops; coral is sharp), book and roll of toilet paper are useful items to take along. Most villages have pit toilets these days, but if not, ask about the customary spot in the river or sea.

If you can, stay for Sunday. Whether you're religious or not, you can't fail to be moved by the whole community dressing up and heading off to church, then returning to discuss the sermon.

raw form, devoid of luxurious trappings (not a TV or hot shower in sight), look no further than this fascinating archipelago. Lavongai is a truly wild island, complete with dense rainforest, mountains, waterfalls and rivers. With just a handful of modest, homespun guesthouses, tourism in Lavongai and East Islands remains on a refreshingly humble scale.

🛏 Sleeping & Eating

There is no formal accommodation on Lavongai. Most guesthouses are on nearby islands, from where you can easily access Lavongai by dinghy. There's no phone, no electricity (except the odd generator, if you're lucky) and no shops (but you wanted a Robinson Crusoe experience, right?).

Lumeuas Cove GUESTHOUSE $
(📞 7213 6861; leahusurup@gmail.com; Tsoi Island; r with full board K80, bungalow per person from K160) Leah and Jethro Usurup provide a friendly welcome at this familial and charming spot near the waterfront. Accommodation is either in one of four private bungalows or one of the backpacker rooms, set in a long, thatched building decorated with *bilums* (string bags), weavings and baskets.

Attractions include snorkelling (BYO gear), surfing and hanging out with the friendly islanders who live nearby. Access by boat is charged at K420 return.

Clem's Place BUNGALOW $$
(📞 7022 2776; clementanton24@gmail.com; Tunung Island; r per person with full board K350) 🐟 On tiny Tunung Island, Clem's has six simple but charming bungalows made from woven sago leaves, and a clean ablution block (with flush toilets), amid a lovely property

a few steps from the beach. There are no public boats from Kavieng; contact Clem to arrange transport, which takes three hours and costs K700 each way, split evenly among the travellers.

Clem's Place is a magnificent getaway – 'end of the world, beginning of paradise' is how Clem Anton, the friendly and travel-savvy owner, describes it. Days are spent surfing, snorkelling (there's a nearby WWII wreck) and blissing out amid the tropical verdure of this island village. Snorkelling, fishing and river trips are included in the tariff. Fishing or river trips to Lavongai can also be arranged.

Tsoi Lik Lagoon Guesthouse GUESTHOUSE $$
(📞 7150 6386; Tsoi Island; s/d per person with full board K200/250) A good place to kick off your shoes for a few days. This little morsel of paradise is owned by the provincial administrator and has a lovely beachfront location. The two rooms and the ablution block are in good nick. One proviso: there's not much shade on the property (don't forget your sunscreen).

❶ Getting There & Away

To Tsoi Island, banana boats usually head off in the morning (around 8am to 10am Monday to Friday) from the market wharf in Kavieng (one way K30). It takes about two hours.

East Coast

Outside Kavieng, the plunge into a more traditional world is immediate. Though the east coast feels more 'developed' than the west, with the Boluminski Hwy running most of its length, it retains its aesthetic appeal, shown in its numerous beaches, limestone pinnacles jutting out of the ocean and lagoons of surpassing beauty.

Adventure and nature may stir your blood, but what will really sweep you off your feet are the stimulating people that live here. The coast is liberally sprinkled with communities where locals retain subsistence traditions. It's a great idea to ditch your guidebook, remain for a few days and experience a village stay. Digs are in basic bush-material huts, with no electricity and no running water. Meals are simple but nourishing (we hope you like taro). Otherwise there are small trade stores around but they sell mostly *tinpis* (tinned fish) and rice.

Now it's your turn to delve in, but take your time: you won't get to more than one, maybe two, places a day by public transport, and none on Sunday.

Boluminski Highway

Yes, New Ireland has a highway, which runs the 263km from Kavieng to Namatanai, making east-coast exploration easy. It is surfaced for much of the way and road work is ongoing. There are a number of villages along the way where you can break up your journey.

Leaving Kavieng, the first major settlement is **Matanasoi** (or Liga) village, about 5km along the highway from Kavieng airport. There's a limestone cave filled with crystal-clear water. The Japanese used this grotto for drinking water. Twenty-three kilometres further is **Putput** and the trippy Treehouse Village Resort.

At Km 90 you'll find **Cathy Hiob's Eels** (Boluminski Hwy; per person K10) at **Laraibina** (ask for Munawai village). Here you can see the hand-feeding of huge eels in the river, which slither right over your toes. Be warned that you'll need to buy a tin of fish (K8) at the village store. Fancy a dip? Try the crystal-clear,

natural **swimming pool** (Fissoa Vocational Centre, Boluminski Hwy; per vehicle K10-20) upstream from the bridge at **Fissoa** (Km 100).

At the village of **Bol**, about 120km from Kavieng, you can bunk down in the Panatalis Dodor Beach Peles. Located 4km south of Bol, **Libba** village is a great place to look at **Malagan art** and stock up on handicrafts. The village was home to the late master carver Ben Sisia. Ben's sons, Robin, David and Simon continue the tradition and charge K10 to see the Malagan house where a piece might sell for upwards of K300. Even the village church is carved in the local style.

In **Malom** village, 25km south of Konos, Laxasilong Guesthouse is a good place to rest your head, as are the village guesthouse at **Dalom** and Rubio Guesthouse, 42km further down.

At Km 263, you reach **Namatanai**, a ramshackle town with a few simple guesthouses and a supermarket. Most folks come here just to transit by boat to or from Kokopo in New Britain.

🛏 Sleeping

Panatalis Dodor Beach Peles GUESTHOUSE $
(Bol's Guesthouse; Bol Village; s/d with full board K100/120) Bunk down in the spacious Panatalis Dodor Beach Peles, which is a good place to see community life. It's run by Demas Kavavu, who's an interesting character who knows anything and everything on Malagan culture. The three rooms are very simple but overlook the beach, with Tabar Island looming on the horizon. The weak points are the toilets (pit) and the showers (nonexistent; prepare to bathe in the river). There's a nice wave here in surf season (November to March).

Laxasilong Guesthouse GUESTHOUSE $
(Malom Guesthouse; ☑ 7920 9052; Malom village; r per person with full board K160) In Malom

---

BOLUMINSKI HIGHWAY FROM THE SADDLE

Feel like enjoying the scenery and atmosphere from the saddle instead of a seat in a car or PMV? Cycling is an ecofriendly and cheap way to discover New Ireland's east coast along the cycle-friendly Boluminski Hwy. You can pick your own pace and become intimate with local communities. The Boluminski Hwy seems to have been purpose-built for cycling, with very little traffic, no pollution, a mostly surfaced road that's also largely perfectly flat and a number of guesthouses and villages conveniently located along the way. You can cover the whole stretch in four to five days.

Guided cycling tours and cycle hire around Kavieng and down the Boluminski Hwy can be organised through the New Ireland Tourist Bureau (p168), Noxie's Tours (p166), Tabo Meli's Rainbow Tours (p166) and Nusa Island Retreat (p167).

village, 181km from Kavieng, the well-run Malom Guesthouse has an enchanting setting, with lots of greenery, and it's a short stagger from the beach. Your gracious host, Cathy Nason, is a good cook too.

Dalom Guesthouse   GUESTHOUSE **$**
(☑ 7220 4031; Dalom village; r K80, daily meals K65) A serious contender for the title of best place to stay on the east coast, it boasts a modernish ablution block (flush toilets, hooray!) and four tidy rooms (think decent mattresses and mosquito nets). We fell for the setting, right on a gorgeous beach by a turquoise stream. Surfers take note: this is a good surfing spot. Try not to turn up on Friday evening or Saturday (the Adventists' Sabbath). BYO food supplies and use the kitchen.

Treehouse Village Resort   GUESTHOUSE **$$**
(☑ 7264 4433; www.treehouse.com.pg; Putput; bungalow s/d K185/260, daily meals per person from K138) The Treehouse Village Resort has a series of traditional-style, fan-cooled bungalows on stilts overlooking the beach. Two units are perched up a 200-year-old *Calophyllum* tree, above the dining room. A host of tours can be arranged, including village visits, rainforest walks, canoe trips in the mangroves and snorkelling excursions. This quirky venture is owned by Alun Beck, a Kiwi, who has become a local chief. Overall it's rustic and a tad overpriced (try to get a discount), but amusing.

Rubio Guesthouse   GUESTHOUSE **$$**
(☑ 984 1305, 7216 6566; www.newirelandsurf.com/rubio.html; Rubio Plantation, Karu; r with/without bathroom per person with full board from K265/255) Rubio is surf-loving spot with the most amenities (including refrigeration) on the east coast. Attractive bungalows with verandas all face the sea, and the cooking is good and varied. It's run by Shane Clark, a savvy surfer with American roots. BYO beer. Transfers from Kavieng/Namatanai cost K180/75.

Namatanai Lodge   HOTEL **$$**
(☑ 7162 6409; nti_lodge@yahoo.com; Namatanai; r without/with air-con K250/380; ❄) The Namatanai Hotel is right on the site of the old German station house by the waterfront. The six fusty rooms will suffice at a stretch, and there's a restaurant (set dinner K54).

Solwara Meri Guesthouse   GUESTHOUSE **$$**
(☑ 7136 3764, 7044 2254; Namatana; r with air-con K300, r without bathroom K150-250 ; ❄) This functional guesthouse with clean if plain rooms isn't great value but is obviously convenient if you are travelling to/from Kokopo on one of Solwara Meri's banana boats.

❶ Getting There & Away

PMVs for Kavieng leave from Namatanai at 9am to 10am and arrive from Kavieng at about 5pm (K40 to K45).

Banana boats travel between New Britain and New Ireland. The well-organised **Solwara Meri** (☑ 7253 8592) runs a truck (K2) from Namatanai down to Uluputur on the west coast, where it connects with boats making the crossing to Kokopo (K70). Trucks leave Namatanai at 6am, 11am, 1pm and 3pm Monday to Saturday. Returning boats depart from Kokopo to Uluputur from 10am until about 3pm. Go early for the calmest seas.

AUTONOMOUS REGION OF BOUGAINVILLE

In many ways, the islands that comprise the erstwhile North Solomons Province (Buka, Bougainville and a scattering of smaller atolls) feel different, and the influence of the PNG mainland is a distant memory. Look at a map, and you'll see why: the islands are closer to the neighbouring Solomon Islands than they are to PNG. The international border between the two countries passes just a few kilometres south of Bougainville Island. The Shortland and Choiseul islanders in the Solomons are very close to Bougainvilleans, culturally and ethnically – both have jet-black skin. Around PNG, Bougainvilleans are known as 'blackskins' or 'bukas'.

This region is best known for its tumultuous history. Until the secessionist rebellion, it had the most productive economy, best education and a well-run government. Between 1972 and its 1989 closure, the Panguna mine (see p173) made 45% of PNG's export earnings. But 'the Crisis' shattered all progress and much infrastructure was devastated.

After years of conflict, life has largely returned to normal. There is no longer any fighting and most of the region is safe to explore, even if the civil war still looms large in the psyche of many islanders. Bougainville is now poised for a great regeneration, thanks to a wealth of natural resources, including gold and cocoa, and its status within PNG – it has brokered a special autonomy status to control its own destiny. There's huge potential for ecotourism, diving, surfing, trekking, caving, cycling, kayaking, birdwatching and fishing, but there's little in the way of infrastructure and organised activities (for now).

Wherever you go in this province, you're unlikely to cross paths with other travellers. All the better for you: this less-visited part of the country remains something of a 'secret', adding to the sense of adventure. Note that in 2014 the Autonomous Bougainville Government (ABG) altered the time zone (forward one hour) to match the Solomon Islands.

History

There's evidence that humans settled on Bougainville at least 28,000 years ago.

Spanish mariner Luis Vaez de Torres passed through in 1606, and Bougainville acquired its name from French explorer Captain Louis-Antoine de Bougainville, who sailed up the east coast in 1768.

European settlements were established as the German New Guinea Company began trading in the late 1890s. Bougainville and Buka were considered part of the Solomons group, a British possession, until 1898 when they were traded to Germany. Australia seized the North Solomons, with the rest of New Guinea, at the start of WWI.

The Japanese arrived in 1942, swiftly defeating the Australians and holding most of the island until the end of the war. Buka became an important air base, and Buin, at the southern tip of Bougainville, was a base for ground troops. In 1943 American troops captured the port of Torokina and Australian forces fought their way south towards Buin. Of 80,000 Japanese troops only 23,000 were taken prisoner; 20,000 are thought to have been killed in action and the remaining 37,000 died of disease and starvation in the jungles. There's a moving monument to the Japanese dead atop Sohano Island's cliff.

In the 1960s and early '70s the North Solomons began a push to break away from Australian colonial control, climaxing in land disputes over the proposed Panguna mine. Before PNG independence, Bougainville pushed for an independent grouping of the Bismarck Archipelago. In 1974 the secessionist movement sprang into the picture.

Geography

Bougainville is volcanic, about 200km long and covered in jungle. The Crown Prince, Emperor and Deuro ranges make up the central spine and Mt Bagana frequently erupts.

Mt Balbi, the island's highest point at 2685m, is a dormant volcano; Benua Cave is perhaps the world's largest at 4.5 million cubic metres. The island has many natural harbours, and large swamps on its western edge.

Buka Island is formed almost entirely of raised coral. It's separated from Bougainville Island by Buka Passage, a tidal channel only 300m wide and a kilometre long. Buka Island is generally low-lying, apart from a southern hilly region. Another 166 islands spread over 450,000 sq km of sea. It's the most earthquake-prone area of the country.

Culture

Intricately woven *bukaware* baskets are made all over the country except here, it seems, where they originated. The baskets are made from jungle vine, and the variation in colour is achieved by scraping the skin off the vine. They can be simple drink coasters or giant laundry baskets, and they're the most skilfully made, solid and durable baskets in the Pacific. They were originally made by the Siwai and Telei people of southwest Buka Island.

There are 23 languages in the Autonomous Region of Bougainville; Tok Pisin is the second main language but most people speak English well. The people of Takuu (Mortlock) and Nukumani islands are Polynesian.

Bougainvilleans have a matrilineal system of clan membership and inheritance rights. Most still live in bush-material housing in villages and grow cash crops.

Buka Island

Buka Island is mostly covered with copra plantations. To the southern tip of the island, Buka is the centre of activity in the province and the main gateway to the islands.

Buka

An ambitious town, Buka used to be a tiny place but it has boomed in the last 20 years, during the war and afterwards, and now has many new buildings and residents. Although tourist sights are as scarce as hen's teeth, it's worth spending a day or two soaking up the atmosphere and chatting with the locals. Most of the shops and services are on, or just off, the main waterfront strip of Buka.

Buka remains an important port for copra and cocoa; but for travellers, it serves primarily as a point of departure to Bougainville.

At the time of writing, the Buka service was only fortnightly; the ferry turning back from Rabaul to Kimbe and Lae, but keeping to the above schedule (which, of course, can change).

Bougainville

Once at the centre of PNG's worst regional armed conflict, Bougainville has put aside its troubled past and is slowly recovering.

Green, rugged and little developed, this large volcanic island has a dramatic setting, with thick forests, towering volcanoes, tumbling rivers, azure lagoons, plunging waterfalls, giant caves and impenetrable valleys that slither into the mountains. For now, visitors can have the island pretty much to themselves. There's huge potential for small-scale tourism, but little in the way of organised activities; it's DIY travel.

Starting from **Kokopau**, you'll head due south and traverse several coastal communities where time seems to have stood still. Why not pull over in picturesque **Tinputz**, a one-hour drive to the south? There's a friendly guesthouse; for guided hikes up to Namatoa Crater Lake get in touch with Osborne (☑7112 0637).

A good base, **Wakunai** is where you can arrange a three-day trek to **Mt Balbi** (2685m), or follow the **Nooma Nooma track** that crosses the island to Torokina, on the west coast (count on a three-day minimum). From Mt Balbi, you can see the active Mt Bagana (1730m).

Continuing south, you'll drive past the infamous **Morgan Junction**, where you can catch a glimpse of the former 'no-go zone' and **Panguna**. High in the centre of the island, this dormant mine is one of the world's largest artificial holes. Copper was discovered here in 1964, and Bougainville Copper Limited was the operator of the open-cut mine. The Arawa Women's Centre Lodge can help arrange visits to the mine.

About 10km south of Morgan Junction, you'll reach **Arawa** and **Kieta**, which are virtually contiguous. Both were severely damaged during the conflict, and whole neighbourhoods have been abandoned. In Arawa, **Bougainville Experience Tours** (Zhon Bosco Miriona; ☑626 3583, 7162 6393; www.bougtours.com) leads guided single- and multi-day tours of the area (birdwatching, trekking and village visits).

About 260km south of Buka, **Buin** really feels like the end of the line. It suffered less damage than Kieta and Arawa during the conflict. During WWII, Buin hosted a large Japanese army base and the area has many rusting relics. **Admiral Yamamoto's aircraft wreck** is the area's most historically interesting wreck. Admiral Isoroku Yamamoto, who planned the attack on Pearl Harbor, left Rabaul in a 'Betty Bomber' on 18 April 1943 with a protective group of Zeros, not realising that US fighters were waiting for him near Buin. The wreckage of the bomber still lies in the jungle a few kilometres off the Panguna–Buin road. It's signposted, near Aku, 24km before Buin.

🛏 Sleeping & Eating

Buin has a few basic guesthouses.

Sunrise Guest House GUESTHOUSE $$
(☑7272 6998, 7913 3430; Arawa; fan/air-con r with full board K200/270) A friendly and affordable (for Bougainville) option in Arawa with basic rooms and clean shared bathrooms. The kitchen cooks local meals of yam, taro and vegetables, which receive high praise.

Arawa Women's Centre Lodge GUESTHOUSE $$
(☑7197 6976; Arawa; s/tw K300/360; ❄) This long-standing choice in Arawa is a peaceful spot with tidy rooms, crisply dressed beds and well-maintained shared bathrooms. The wood-panelled restaurant serves tasty market-fresh fare (breakfast K25, lunch k30 and dinner K40). There's also a grassy lawn and a *haus win* (wooden open-air structure).

Buin Inn GUESTHOUSE $$
(☑7100 0227; Buin; s/tw with fan K180/360, with air-con K220/440; ❄) Probably the best of the meagre options in Buin. Don't expect luxury despite the tariff – only two of the 10 rooms have air-con. Meals cost extra (breakfast K15, lunch K25 and dinner K25).

ℹ Getting There & Around

The most convenient way to get around Bougainville Island is by PMV. There's only one main gravel road, running down the east coast to Arawa and Kieta, and on to Buin to the south.

Regular PMVs ply the route between Kokopau and Arawa (K50, 3½ hours), where you can continue on to Buin (K70, another four to five hours).

Air Niugini (www.airniugini.com.pg; Kieta Airport) Flies directly between Kieta and Port Moresby (K1007, two hours, three or four times a week) and Kokopo/Rabaul (K660, 55 minutes, three times a week).

Solomon Islands

♪677 / POP 538,000 / AREA 27,540 SQ KM

Best Historical Sites

➡ US War Memorial (p177)

➡ Tetere Beach & WWII Museum (p189)

➡ Vilu War Museum (p190)

➡ Skull Island (p194)

Best Places to Stay

➡ Rekona Flourish (p181)

➡ Tavanipupu Private Island Resort (p190)

➡ Urilolo Lodge (p198)

➡ Uepi Island Resort (p193)

➡ Sanbis Resort (p199)

Why Go?

Forget what travelling the Pacific *used* to be like – around the Solomon Islands it's still that way. These islands are laid-back, welcoming and often surprisingly untouched. From WWII relics scattered in the jungle to leaf-hut villages where traditional culture is alive, there's so much on offer. Then there's the visual appeal, with scenery reminiscent of a Discovery Channel documentary: volcanic islands, croc-infested mangroves, huge lagoons, tropical islets and emerald forests.

Don't expect white-sand beaches and ritzy resorts. With only a smattering of traditional guesthouses and comfortable hideaways, it's tailor-made for ecotourists. For outdoorsy types, lots of action-packed experiences await: climb an extinct volcano, surf uncrowded waves, snorkel pristine reefs or kayak across a lagoon. Beneath the ocean's surface, awesome WWII wrecks and dizzying drop-offs will enthral divers. The best part is that there'll be no crowds to mar the experience.

When to Go
Honiara

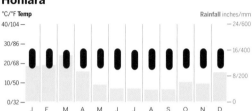

Dec–Mar Intervals of calm weather broken by storms, making for good reef breaks and diving.

Jun–Sep High season's mild weather (but rough seas) is good for hiking, but less ideal for diving.

Apr–May & Oct–Nov The shoulder seasons are relatively dry and aren't a bad time to visit.

GUADALCANAL

POP 109,000

The largest island in the Solomons, Guadalcanal hosts the national capital, Honiara. There's no iconic calling card but a smattering of cultural sights, including well-preserved WWII relics along the northern coast, as well as a few modest beaches. There's also fantastic diving at Iron Bottom Sound, the famous graveyard of WWII's Battle for Guadalcanal, just off the north coast. Outside the northern coast, the island has the genuine look of a lost world. The hills behind the capital eventually become a mighty mountain range rising to 2400m, which remains untamed and raw.

Honiara

POP 68,000

The first port of call for most visitors, due to its position at the hub of all activity within the archipelago, it's hard not to spend some time in Honiara, the closest thing you'll find to a city in the Solomons. Just over a decade ago it was little more than a sleepy South Seas port, but over the last few years it has undergone an urban boom, and traffic snarl-ups at peak hours are now increasingly common in the centre.

It's rarely love at first sight – the architecture wins no prizes and sights are sparse. But get under the city's skin and the place just might start to grow on you. Hang around the atmospheric wharf, wade through the shambolic market, grab a few gifts in the well-stocked souvenir shops and get your first taste of Melanesian culture by visiting the museum.

Honiara is also the optimal launching pad for exploring Guadalcanal's outdoor offerings and the various WWII battlefields around the city.

◎ Sights

★ Central Market   MARKET

(Map p184; Mendana Ave; ⊙6am-5pm Mon-Sat) While Honiara won't be mistaken for Lagos, the country's bubbling principal food market covers a whole block between Mendana Ave and the seafront. It has a huge selection of fresh produce, especially fruits and vegetables, that come from outlying villages along the northern coast and from Savo Island. Also on sale are traditional crafts. The fish market is at the back. There's no hassling to buy anything, but beware of pickpockets.

Holy Cross Catholic Cathedral   CATHEDRAL

(Map p184; Mendana Ave) Honiara's most prominent religious building is this cathedral perched on a hill to the east of the centre. Visitors are welcome to attend, but make sure you dress modestly.

National Parliament   BUILDING

(Map p186; Lower Vayvaya Rd; ⊙8am-4pm Mon-Fri) The conical-shaped concrete building that's perched on the hill above Hibiscus Ave is the National Parliament. Inside, the dome boasts a rich tapestry of traditional art, including arching frescoes.

National Museum   MUSEUM

(Map p186; ☑24896; Mendana Ave; admission by donation; ⊙9am-4pm Mon-Fri, 10am-2pm Sat) This modest museum (it has only one room) features interesting displays and old photographs on traditional dance, body ornamentation, currency, weaponry and archaeology. It also covers the role of the coastwatchers during WWII and the influence of missionaries.

US War Memorial   HISTORIC SITE

(Map p184; Skyline Dr) This superb memorial is a five-minute taxi ride from the centre. The well-maintained compound has marble slabs bearing detailed descriptions of battles fought during the Guadalcanal campaign. It was unveiled on 7 August 1992, the 50th anniversary of the US beach landings. There are also great views of the northern coast.

✦ Activities

Diving is Honiara's trump card; a fantastic collection of WWII wrecks lie offshore in an area known as Iron Bottom Sound, including Bonegi I and Bonegi II to the west, and USS *John Penn* to the east. For more, see p33.

Solomon Islands

Diving – Tulagi Dive   DIVING, SNORKELLING

(Map p186; ☑25700; www.tulagidive.com; Mendana Ave; single/double dive from S$900/1200; ⊙9am-5pm Mon-Fri, 8am-5.30pm Sat & Sun) This highly professional dive shop run by Australian Neil Yates adheres to strict safety procedures for deep dives. It specialises in dive sites along the northern coast but also organises day trips to the Florida Islands (S$1700 including two dives, equipment and lunch; minimum six divers) and snorkel trips (S$400) to Bonegi. It's beside Point Cruz Yacht Club.

Ko Kama Rafting   RAFTING

(☑7494788; aemmett04@gmail.com; trips S$700; ⊙Sat & Sun by reservation) East of Honiara, the

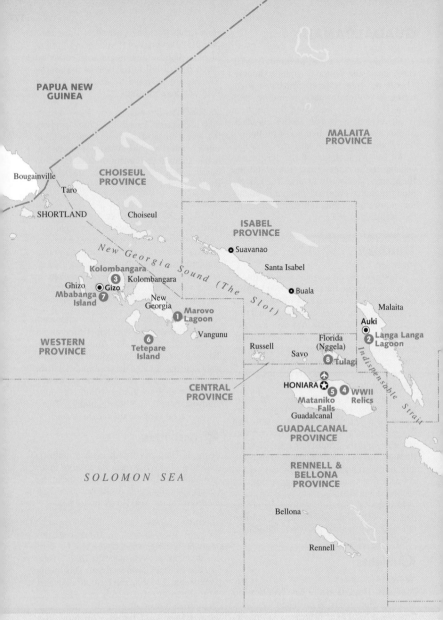

Solomon Islands Highlights

1 Diving and snorkelling in fish soup in **Marovo Lagoon** (p190).

2 Feeling free in an intimate lodge at **Langa Langa Lagoon** (p203).

3 Huffing to the top of the mount on **Kolombangara** (p200).

4 Spending the day spotting rusty **WWII relics** (p188) around Honiara.

5 Taking a dip in a natural pool at **Mataniko Falls** (p188).

6 Assisting rangers in tagging marine turtles on ecofriendly **Tetepare Island** (p194).

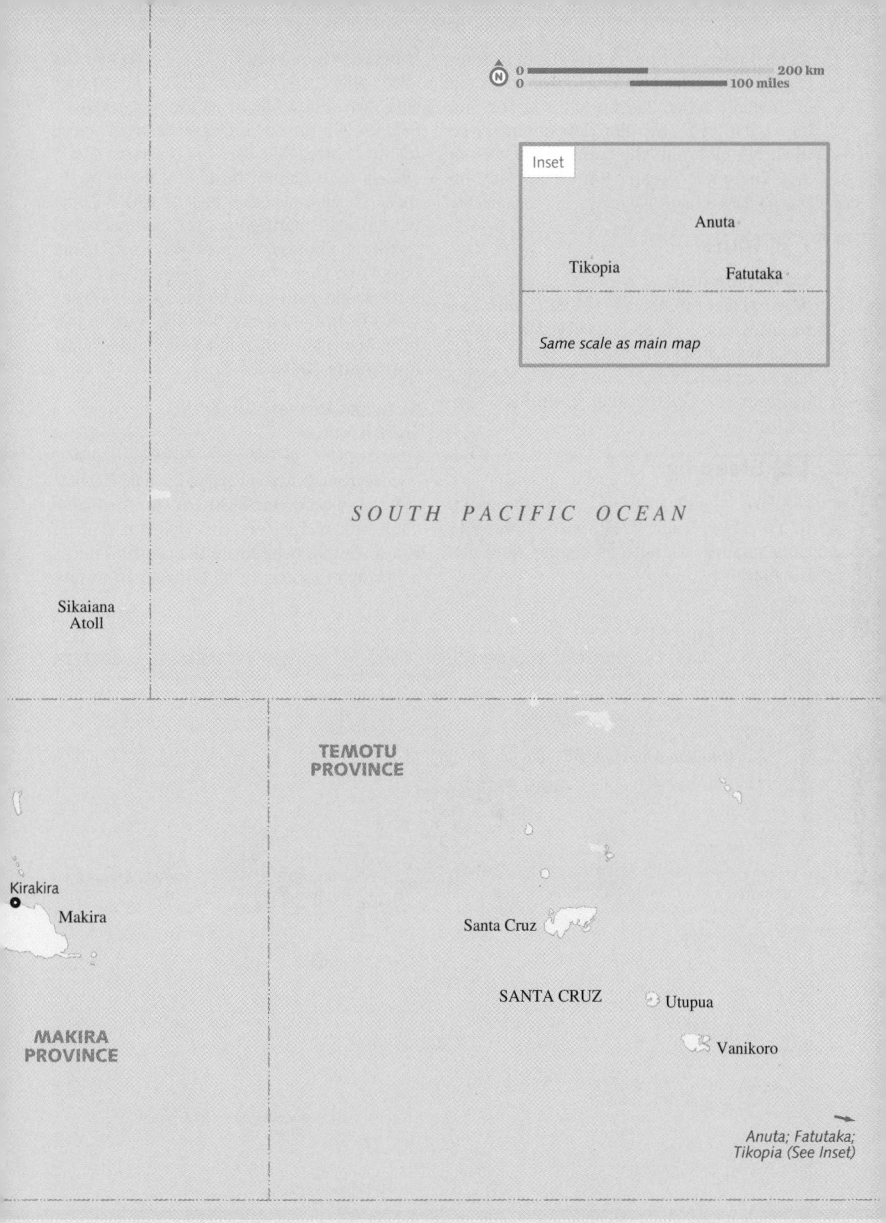

SOUTH PACIFIC OCEAN

0 ——————————— 200 km
0 ——————————— 100 miles

Anuta; Fatutaka;
Tikopia (See Inset)

Inset

Anuta

Tikopia   Fatutaka

Same scale as main map

Sikaiana
Atoll

TEMOTU
PROVINCE

Kirakira
Makira

Santa Cruz

SANTA CRUZ   Utupua

Vanikoro

MAKIRA
PROVINCE

⑦ Chilling out at a laid-back
resort on **Mbabanga Island**
(p198).

⑧ Flipper-kicking into
sunken WWII wrecks off **Tulagi**
(p189).

scenic Lunga river offers superb white-water experiences. Trips last four to five hours and are usually scheduled on Saturday or Sunday, but they're weather dependent. Prices include lunch and the transfer from Honiara. The outfit doesn't have a website, but there's a Facebook page.

☞ Tours

Travel Solomons CULTURAL TOUR
(Map p186; ☑ 7489974, 24081; www.travel solomons.com; 1st fl, Sol Plaza Bldg, Mendana Ave; ⊙ 8.30am-4.30pm Mon-Fri) This travel agency can arrange half- and full-day WWII historical tours on Guadalcanal (from S$350 per person).

🛏 Sleeping

Honiara is expensive and, with the exception of a few simple guesthouses, hotels that cater mainly to businesspeople dominate the market.

Hibiscus Homestay GUESTHOUSE $
(Map p184; ☑ 7762960, 22121; kwendy64@ gmail.com; Kukutu St; d with/without bathroom S$500/400) On a quiet backstreet close to the centre, this B&B-like oasis is a safe choice, with helpful hosts and good amenities. The four rooms, two of which come with private bathrooms, are compact and simply laid out but neat and serviceable, and have fans. There's a spacious lounge area, an impeccable communal kitchen and good sea views from the terrace. Wendy, your affable host, has plans to build two more rooms downstairs. No wi-fi.

St Agnes Mother's Union Transit House GUESTHOUSE $
(Map p184; ☑ 7485532, 27785; stagnes@ solomon.com.sb; Lower Vayvaya Rd; d S$450-600, with shared bathroom S$330-370; ❄) A reliable choice for budgeteers, this well-run venture is a 10-minute walk from the centre. There's a variety of rooms for all budgets, from fan-

Guadalcanal

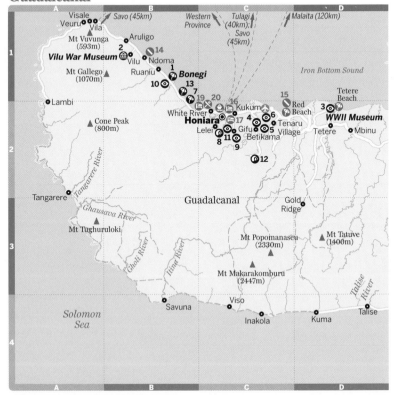

flower coverage, this sprawling hotel has seen better days but the deluxe rooms in the more recent wings are light-filled and come with good sea views and a private terrace. The cheaper rooms feel gloomy and uninspiring in comparison. Amenities include a bar, three restaurants and, best of all, a large pool.

Caveat: there's no lift and the walk up to the highest units may leave you short of breath. It's a short taxi ride from the centre.

Coral Sea Resort
RESORT $$$

(Map p184; ☑26288; www.coral-sea-resort.com; Mendana Ave; P ❋ ☎) Honiara's most recent hotel, the Coral Sea Resort was built in 2016 and features a casino, a restaurant and a series of buildings that shelter rooms with sea views.

✖ Eating

Sky Horse
FAST FOOD $

(Map p186; ☑25552; Mendana Ave; mains S$15-45; ☺6am-5pm) This sprightly little joint is the ideal pit stop for a midday nibble. It churns out delicious rotis ($15) as well as ready-made meals.

The Bakery
CAFETERIA $

(Map p186; Sol Plaza Bldg, Mendana Ave; mains S$10-30; ☺7.30am-7.30pm Mon-Sat) Located inside the Sol Plaza building, this offbeat cafeteria is a handy spot for an affordable, uncomplicated, walk-in bite. Choose from rotis, doughnuts, pizza slices and buns, all delicious and moderately priced. It also has excellent coffee drinks and first-rate smoothies (S$35).

Honiara Hot Bread Kitchen
BAKERY $

(Map p186; Mendana Ave; buns S$3-6; ☺6am-7pm) For the most flavoursome buns and scones in town, take your sticky fingers to this unassuming outlet on the main drag. Come early: by 10am they're sold out. Bread also available.

Frangipani Ice
ICE CREAM $

(Map p186; Mendana Ave; ice cream from S$4; ☺8am-6pm) This unassuming ice-cream parlour on the main drag is very popular with locals. It also has waffles, milkshakes and smoothies.

★Mambo Juice
CAFETERIA $$

(Map p180; ☑28811; Mendana Ave; mains S$35-90; ☺7am-6pm Mon-Fri, 8am-5pm Sat & Sun) Just off Mendana Ave, this easy-to-miss cafeteria is a surprise, with its enticing outdoor seating area, super-fresh fare and explosively fruity juices and smoothies. It offers an appetising selection of gourmet sandwiches, salads, omelettes and homemade yoghurt. It's about 1km west of the centre.

Bamboo Bar & Cafe
CAFETERIA $$

(Map p186; ☑21205; Hibiscus Ave; mains S$50-190; ☺7am-3.30pm Mon-Fri; ☎) This cheerful

SOLOMON ISLANDS HONIARA

ITINERARIES

One Week

In a week you'll be able to explore Guadalcanal and either Savo or Tulagi. Base yourself in **Honiara** (p177) and spend three days (four if you're a diver) visiting the capital and the historic sites dotted along the northern coast. Then catch a boat to **Savo** (p189) and settle in for a couple of days of relaxation. If you're keen on diving, opt for **Tulagi** (p189), which features superb wreck dives. Another option, if your budget permits, is to skip Savo and Tulagi in favour of Tavanipupu Private Island Resort (p190) – a luxurious yet laid-back hideaway tucked in a sweet eastern corner of Guadalcanal.

Two Weeks

With two weeks, you can easily include the Western Province in your itinerary. Start with your one-week itinerary, then hop west to **Munda** (p194), which offers great diving and snorkelling options and good day tours to some must-see WWII relics. Afterwards, grab a flight or catch a boat to **Gizo** (p196) where three to four days can easily be spent messing around in and on the water. You might also make time for a hike on **Kolombangara** (p200). Fly back to Honiara the day before your international flight out.

Three Weeks

With three weeks, fly to Seghe and devote a few days to **Marovo Lagoon** (p190), where all sorts of water activities and adventures await. Thanks to fairly reliable inter-island boat services, a trip to **Malaita** (p200) could even be on the cards – fly back to Honiara and catch a boat to **Auki** (p200) and chill out in **Langa Langa Lagoon** (p203) for a couple of days.

Greater Honiara

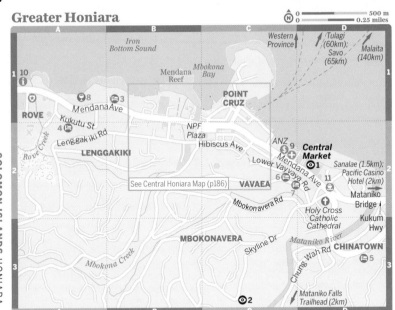

See Central Honiara Map (p186)

place is perfect for a comforting breakfast (fab banana pancakes!), lunch or a snack attack any time of the day. The menu is straightforward but scrummy and features tasty dishes such as chicken curry, vegetarian omelette and focaccia. Healthy smoothies, great coffee and sweet treats are also on offer, and there's outdoor seating. Free wi-fi.

Lime Lounge   CAFETERIA **$$**
(Map p186; ☑23064; www.limelounge.com.sb; off Mendana Ave; mains S$40-100; ☼7am-4pm Mon-Fri, 8am-3pm Sat & Sun; ☎) Funky little Lime Lounge is highly popular with expats. There's everything from satisfying breakfasts to palate-pleasing salads, well-made sandwiches, burgers and yummy pastries (hmmm, the banana cakes). No view and no terrace, but the walls are adorned with paintings by local artists, which gives the place a splash of style. Free wi-fi.

Breakwater Cafe   CAFE **$$**
(Map p186; ☑23442; Mendana Ave; breakfast S$80-110, pastries S$25-40; ☼7am-4pm Mon-Fri, from 7.30am Sat & Sun) This slick venture that seems to have been imported direct from Oz is the meeting point for expats who are yearning for a satisfying breakfast. Desserts like carrot cake, cheesecake, doughnuts, brownies,

banana muffins and other pastries from the bakery window are not to be missed.

The Ofis   PIZZERIA, CAFE **$$**
(Map p180; ☑7355620, 20334; White River; mains S$60-180; ☼5-9pm Wed-Fri, from 8am Sat & Sun) A very relaxing spot. Picture a lovely waterfront location, ample views of Savo, and good thin-crust pizza, wraps and salads. It also offers lovely coffee, juices and smoothies. For dessert, try the belt-bustingly good brownie with homemade chocolate sauce. Copious all-day breakfasts are available on weekends. It's in White River, about 3km west of the centre. Go by taxi as the area is a bit dodgy after dark.

Taj Mahal   INDIAN **$$**
(Map p186; ☑7478550; www.tajsolomon.com; Point Cruz Yacht Club, Mendana Ave; mains S$60-120; ☼11am-3pm & 5-9pm Mon-Sat, 5-9pm Sun) The dining room is nothing fancy (think plastic chairs) but Taj Mahal serves authentic, richly flavoured Indian and Sri Lankan specialities at puny prices. Tandooris, tikkas, biryanis and masalas are all here plus a good selection of veggie options. Brilliant value. Also does takeaway.

Hong Kong Palace   CHINESE **$$**
(Map p186; ☑23338; Hibiscus Ave; mains S$50-200; ☼11am-2pm & 5.30-9.30pm) This unmissa-

Greater Honiara

◉ Top Sights
1 Central Market D2

◉ Sights
2 US War Memorial.................................C3

⊜ Sleeping
3 Coral Sea Resort B1
4 Hibiscus Homestay A2
5 Honiara Hotel D3
6 Rekona Flourish C2
7 St Agnes Mother's Union
   Transit House C2

⊗ Eating
Club Havanah .... (see 5)
Oasis Restaurant .... (see 5)

⊜ Drinking & Nightlife
8 Monarch Bar & Grill A1

ⓘ Information
9 Honiara Private Medical Centre..........C2
10 Nature Conservancy A1

ⓘ Transport
11 MV Fair Glory...D2

ble reddish pagoda on Hibiscus Ave brings an unexpected dash of orientalism in an otherwise dull area. Inside, it's much more sterile, with neons and tiles, but you'll be too busy choosing from the mile-long menu to bother.

Hakubai   JAPANESE $$$
(Map p186; ☑ 20071; Solomon Kitano Mendana Hotel, Mendana Ave; mains S$100-250; ⊙noon-2pm & 6.30-9pm Mon-Fri, 6.30-9pm Sat & Sun) If you have a sashimi or yakitori craving that must be met, head to Hakubai inside the Mendana Hotel for authentic Japanese food. On top of the classics, tuck into seductive offerings like *nikomi* noodles (udon noodles with half-cooked poached egg) or beef teppanyaki. Don't miss the sushi buffet on Saturday.

Club Havanah   FRENCH $$$
(Map p184; ☑ 21737; Honiara Hotel, Chinatown; mains S$110-300; ⊙6.30-9pm) Inside Honiara Hotel, Club Havanah's adept French chef cooks up ambitious dishes with a strong French accent – think wild pigeon cooked in red-wine sauce or snails in garlic butter. Just one grumble: the big fake fish and siren at the back are ludicrous.

Capitana   INTERNATIONAL $$$
(Map p186; ☑ 20071; Solomon Kitano Mendana Hotel, Mendana Ave; mains S$100-250; ⊙noon-2pm

& 6-9pm) This popular restaurant inside the Mendana Hotel serves classic Western dishes and boasts a terrace overlooking the sea. Its Wednesday dinner buffet (S$260) draws the crowds.

Oasis Restaurant   INTERNATIONAL $$$
(Map p184; ☑ 21737; Honiara Hotel, Chinatown; lunch mains S$100-120, dinner S$220-300; ⊙11.30am-2pm & 6.30-10pm) Part of the Honiara Hotel, the Oasis enjoys a great location next to the pool. The food is nothing spectacular, but there's a good choice ranging from burgers and salads to meat dishes and fish fillet. Catch the Melanesian dance show and dinner buffet Sunday nights at 7pm.

⚲ Drinking & Entertainment

If you've just arrived in the Solomon Islands, you'll find Honiara's bar scene pretty dull. But if you've just spent several weeks in the provinces you'll feel like you're in Ibiza! Hotel bars open to nonguests and are a good place to hook up with expats. Sometimes they offer live entertainment – bamboo bands, Micronesian hula dancers and karaoke. Many restaurants also double as bars.

Monarch Bar & Grill   BAR
(Map p184; Mendana Ave; ⊙9am-10.30pm Mon-Thu, to 2am Fri & Sat) Skip the food; it's only so-so. The bar is definitely the main focus, and can get tremendously lively on a Friday or Saturday night when there's usually a live band. There's a pleasant deck that overlooks the water.

Disco Heritage Park   CLUB
(Map p186; Heritage Park Hotel, Mendana Ave; cover S$30; ⊙6pm-2am Wed-Sat) Honiara's sole decent club is the elegant Disco Heritage Park, inside Heritage Park Hotel.

⌂ Shopping

Honiara is a good place to pick up souvenirs. On top of the souvenir shops, it's also worth considering the gift shops at top-end hotels and the stalls at the central market.

King Solomon Arts & Craft Centre   HANDICRAFTS
(Map p186; Mendana Ave; ⊙8.30am-noon & 1-4.30pm Mon-Fri, 8.30-11.30am Sat) Has a wide selection of masks, basketwork and skilfully crafted wooden carvings.

Museum Handicraft Shop   HANDICRAFTS
(Map p186; ☑ 20137; National Museum, Mendana Ave; ⊙9am-4.30pm Mon-Fri, 9am-3pm Sat) Next

SOLOMON ISLANDS HONIARA

Central Honiara

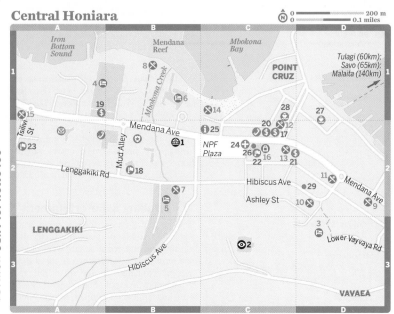

to the National Museum, this well-stocked store features a good selection of woodcarvings, basketwork, Malaitan shell money, souvenir shells and forehead ornaments made of fossilised clams.

ⓘ Information

DANGERS & ANNOYANCES

It's safe to stroll around the centre by day, provided you use your common sense and avoid walking alone in deserted streets. After dark, take a taxi. Beware of pickpockets at the market and in crowded areas.

INTERNET ACCESS

You'll find a couple of internet cafes in the NPF Plaza building. There's a small internet outlet at the post office, too. Rates average S$20 per hour. Wi-fi is available at most hotels as well as at some cafes and restaurants, but a fee usually applies.

MEDICAL SERVICES

Honiara Private Medical Centre (Map p184; ☑ 7492434, 24027; Hyundai Mall, Mendana Ave; ☺ 8am-5pm Mon-Fri, 9am-1pm Sat) A well-regarded clinic inside the Hyundai Mall. A consultation costs S$250.

Point Cruz Chemist (Map p186; ☑ 22911; Mendana Ave; ☺ 8am-5pm Mon-Fri, 8.30am-1.30pm Sat) A well-stocked pharmacy. Also sells locally made cosmetics and soaps.

MONEY

You'll find a good dozen 24-hour ATMs in the centre. There's a small bureau de change at the airport.

ANZ (Map p184; Hyundai Mall, Mendana Ave; ☺ 9am-4pm Mon-Fri) Changes major currencies and has one ATM inside.

Bank South Pacific (BSP; Map p186; Mendana Ave; ☺ 9am-4pm Mon-Fri) Changes major currencies. Has ATMs (Visa only). Other ATMs are in the main BSP office near Heritage Park Hotel; there's also one ATM beside the reception at Heritage Park Hotel.

Bank South Pacific (BSP; Map p186; Mendana Ave; ☺ 9am-4pm Mon-Fri) On the same side of the road as Sky Horse fast-food joint. Changes major currencies. Has two ATMs.

POST

Solomon Post (Map p186; Mendana Ave; ☺ 8am-4.30pm Mon-Fri) Also houses a Western Union counter and a small internet cafe.

TELEPHONE

Bmobile/Vodafone (Map p186; ☑ 8444101; www.bmobile.com.sb; Mendana Ave; ☺ 8am-5pm Mon-Fri, to noon Sat) Sells prepaid SIM cards.

Our Telekom (Map p186; ☑ 21164; www.ourtelekom.com.sb; Mendana Ave; ☺ 8.30am-4.30pm Mon-Fri, 9am-noon Sat) Sells prepaid mobile phonecards and prepaid wi-fi access cards. Has a couple of other branches in town.

Central Honiara

SOLOMON ISLANDS HONIARA

TOURIST INFORMATION

Solomon Islands Visitors Bureau (SIVB; Map p186; ☑ 22442; www.visitsolomons.com.sb; Mendana Ave; ⊙ 8am-4.30pm Mon-Fri) There's little printed material, but staff can provide advice and help with accommodation bookings. Also sells a map of the country (S$60).

ⓘ Getting There & Away

AIR

International flights land at Honiara's Henderson Airport, and all domestic routes begin and end in Honiara.

Guadalcanal Travel Services (GTS; Map p186; ☑ 22586; guadtrav@solomon.com.sb; Mendana Ave; ⊙ 8am-4.30pm Mon-Fri, 9am-noon Sat) This well-established travel agency represents most international and regional airlines.

Solomon Airlines (Map p186; ☑ 20152, 20031; www.flysolomons.com; Hibiscus Ave; ⊙ 8am-4pm Mon-Fri, 8.30-11.30am Sat) From Honiara, Solomon Airlines flies to most islands in the country.

BOAT

The cost and departure times are subject to change. All ferries and boats dock at Point Cruz.

To/From Tulagi and Malaita

MV 360 Flyer/Discovery (Map p186; ☑ 20555; Fera Pako Building, off Mendana Ave; ⊙ 8am-4.30pm Mon-Fri, to noon Sat) This passenger boat travels between Honiara and Auki (S$250 to S$350 one way, three to four hours) three times a week; two days a week it makes a stop at Tulagi (S$200). Tickets can be bought at the ticketing office or on board.

MV Express Pelican II (Map p186; ☑ 28104; Fera Pako Building, off Mendana Ave; ⊙ 8am-noon & 1-4pm Mon-Fri, 8-11am Sat) This passenger boat operates twice weekly between Honiara and Auki (S$200 to S$250 one way, three to four hours). The ticketing office is in a building close to Lime Lounge but tickets can also be bought on board.

To/From the Western Province

MV Anjeanette (Anolpha Shipping Services; Map p186; ☑ 22719; Point Cruz) This cargo

---

ⓘ **GETTING AROUND THE NORTH COAST**

Exploring the north coast by public transport is not really an option. Most sights are not signed and are not easy to find. Your best bet is to hire a taxi in Honiara; count on S$100 to S$120 per hour.

boat offers a weekly service between Honiara and Gizo via Marovo Lagoon (Mbunikalo, Nggasini, Chea and Seghe). The Honiara–Gizo trip costs S$460 (S$500 in 'first class') and takes about 27 hours (10 to 13 hours to Marovo Lagoon). To Mbunikalo it costs S$380. It leaves Honiara on Saturday evening (return on Tuesday). The ticketing office is at Point Cruz but tickets can be bought on board.

MV Fair Glory (Fairwest Shipping; Map p184; ✆22899; Mendana Ave) This cargo boat offers a weekly service between Honiara and Gizo via Marovo Lagoon (Mbunikalo, Batuna, Chea and Seghe). The Honiara–Gizo trip costs S$480 on the deck (S$1490 per cabin) and takes about 27 hours (10 to 13 hours to Marovo Lagoon). Deck passage to Mbunikalo is S$380. It generally leaves Honiara on Sunday morning (return on Tuesday); check while you're there.

The ticketing office is across the road from the cathedral but tickets are also sold on board.

To/From Other Provinces

Island hopping on the cargo boats that sail between Guadalcanal and other provinces is an inexpensive but adventurous and rough way to travel. Departure times and dates are unscheduled and the best way to find out what's available is to ask around at the docks.

⊙ Getting Around

From the airport, the standard taxi fare into town is S$100.

Honiara's minibuses are cheap, frequent (in daylight hours) and relatively safe. The flat S$3 fare will take you anywhere on the route, which is written on a placard behind the windscreen of the bus.

There are taxis everywhere in Honiara. They don't have meters, so agree on a fare before hopping in – S$10 per kilometre is reasonable.

East of Honiara

You'll need a day to take in the sights.

◉ Sights & Activities

Solomon Peace Memorial Park MEMORIAL
(Map p180; Mt Austen Rd; S$50) The road to Mt Austen begins in Kukum and climbs up to the historical sites where Japanese troops doggedly resisted the US advance. About 3.5km from the main coastal road, this large, white memorial was built by Japanese war veterans in 1981 to commemorate all who died in the WWII Guadalcanal campaign.

Mt Austen MOUNTAIN
(Map p180) The clearing at the summit of Mt Austen (410m) offers a marvellous view northeast over Henderson. Americans in WWII dubbed this spot Grassy Knoll. There's a plaque that explains the strategic importance of the hilltop during WWII.

Betikama SDA Mission HISTORIC SITE
(Map p180; Betikama; museum S$25; ⊗8am-noon & 1-5pm Sun-Thu, 8am-noon Fri) In Betikama village, this sprawling property comprises a small WWII museum with an outdoor collection of salvaged material (mostly US aircraft) as well as two small Japanese anti-tank guns. There's a handicraft shop, specialising in Western Province products and stylish modern copperware.

DON'T MISS

TAKE A DIP!

Short of dreamy expanses of white sand on Guadalcanal, you can take a dip in lovely natural pools.

Mataniko Falls (Map p180; guided walk S$200-250) One of the star attractions in Honiara's hinterlands is Mataniko Falls, which feature a spectacular thundering of water down a cliff straight into a canyon below. The hike to these waterfalls starts in **Lelei** village with a steep ascent to a ridge, followed by an easier stretch amid mildly undulating hills. Then you'll tackle a gruelling descent on a muddy path to reach the floor of the little canyon where the Mataniko flows. It's roughly two hours return.

A guide from Lelei is required – the tourist office in Honiara (p187) can make arrangements on your behalf.

Tenaru Waterfalls (Map p180; guided walk S$150) At 63m, these waterfalls are spectacular. They are a fairly easy four-hour walk (return) from a tiny settlement about 2km south of **Tenaru Village**. It's flat and shady all the way. The path follows the floor of the river valley and cuts across the river's many bends, crossing and recrossing a dozen times before reaching the falls.

Guides are available at Tenaru Village – contact the tourist office in Honiara.

WORTH A TRIP

TULAGI & SAVO

Another world awaits just a two-hour boat ride from Honiara, either on Tulagi or Savo.

In the middle of the Florida Islands, **Tulagi** was the Solomons' former capital; it was also a Japanese base during WWII. It's now a renowned playground for divers, with a series of fabulous wrecks lying just offshore. **Raiders Hotel** (☑ 7938017, 7494185, 32070; www.raidershotel.com; Tulagi; s S$550-990, d S$825-1265; ❊ ☎), right on the waterfront (no beach), features tip-top rooms and has a professional dive shop that caters mainly to certified divers (no courses are offered). A single dive costs S$550 and diving-gear hire is S$450 per day. Wreck buffs will need a few days to explore the huge **WWII wrecks** lying just offshore, including the monster-sized USS *Kanawha*, the USS *Aaron Ward* and the *Moa*. Raiders Hotel can organise private transfers, or you can take an outboard-powered dinghy from the little beach next to Point Cruz Yacht Club in Honiara (about S$200 one way, or S$1800 if it's chartered). The passenger boat **MV 360 Flyer/Discovery** (p187) also travels between Honiara and Tulagi (S$200 one way, two hours) twice a week. For more details on dive sites in the area, see p33.

Though lying just 14km north of Guadalcanal, **Savo** is another great escape. Imagine an active **volcano** with a pair of dormant craters, coconut groves, a narrow strip of grey-sand beach and a few **hot springs** that are accessible by foot. The island also features a **megapode field** where hundreds of female birds lay their eggs in holes scratched into the hot sand. If you're lucky, you'll also spot pods of dolphins just offshore. **Sunset Lodge** (☑ 7498347; Kuila; full board per person S$450) has basic rooms and can arrange various tours as well as transfers from Honiara (S$400 per person return).

Henderson Airport Memorial Gardens   HISTORIC SITE
(Map p180; Henderson Airport) A small memorial outside the airport entrance honours US forces and their Pacific Islander allies. In front is a Japanese anti-aircraft gun. About 100m to the west of the terminal is the scaffold-style US WWII control tower, disused since the early 1950s.

Bloody Ridge   HISTORIC SITE
(Map p180) From Henderson airport, a track leads south to this area that's also called Edson's Ridge, after Edson's Raiders. Commanded by Colonel Merritt Edson, they defended the ridge against the Japanese in 1942 in their determined but unsuccessful attempts to seize the airfield. There's a humble pyramid-shaped US war memorial on the ridge. About 1km beyond Bloody Ridge, you'll come across a **Japanese war memorial** that honours the 2000 or more Japanese killed during these actions. There are great views of Mt Austen, the surrounding valleys and villages dotted around the hills.

★ WWII Museum   HISTORIC SITE
(Map p180; Tetere; admission S$100) A few metres before reaching the shore of **Tetere Beach**, a dirt track to the west leads to 30 or more abandoned amtracks (amphibious troop carriers). Many of these rusty relics are shielded by prickly thorns, adding to the poignancy of the site.

USS John Penn   DIVING
(Map p180) This large US-troop ship was bombed and sunk about 4km offshore, east of Honiara. For experienced divers only.

West of Honiara

Life becomes very sedate as one heads west through some of the north coast's divine scenery. Urban existence is left behind once the road traverses White River and crawls its way along the scenic coastline.

The area boasts a high historical significance. The seas between Guadalcanal's north-western coast and Savo Island were the site of constant naval battles between August 1942 and February 1943. By the time the Japanese finally withdrew, so many ships had been sunk it became known as Iron Bottom Sound.

◉ Sights

Lela Beach   BEACH
(Map p180; admission S$30) Popular with locals and expats at weekends, this beach has black sand and is OK for swimming and bathing.

Turtle Beach   BEACH
(Map p180; admission S$30) Turtle Beach is an appealing strip of white coral sand fringed with coconut trees.

★**Bonegi** BEACH
(Map p180; admission S$30) About 12km west from Honiara, Bonegi is music to the ears of divers, snorkellers and sunbathers. Two large Japanese freighters sank just offshore on the night of 13 November 1942, and make for a magnificent playground for scuba divers, who call them Bonegi I and Bonegi II (p33). As the upper works of Bonegi II break the surface, it can also be snorkelled. There's also a black-sand beach that is suitable for a picnic.

Sherman Tank HISTORIC SITE
(Map p180; admission S$25) Just across the road from Bonegi beach, there's a bush track that heads inland and runs about 400m to a rusty US Sherman tank called *Jezebel,* which was used for wartime target practice once the Guadalcanal campaign was over.

★**Vilu War Museum** MUSEUM
(Map p180; admission S$100) About 25km from Honiara, a turn to the south from the coastal road brings you to this great open-air museum. Here there are US, Japanese, Australian, Fijian and New Zealand memorials, four large Japanese field guns and the remains of several US and Japanese aircraft, including a Betty bomber, a Lightning fighter and a Wildcat fighter whose wings can still be folded as they were for naval carrier-borne operations.

WORTH A TRIP

TAVANIPUPU ISLAND

If you've ever dreamed of having your own island paradise, the idyllic **Tavanipupu Private Island Resort** (Map p180; ☑ 7378317; www.tavanipupu.com; d A$190-300), on a small island off Guadalcanal's eastern tip, has all the key ingredients: exclusivity, seclusion and atmosphere. Digs are in six spacious bungalows, scattered in a well-tended coconut grove that overlooks the beach. The restaurant uses only the freshest seafood (meals cost A$121 per person per day).

Snorkelling is excellent (gear provided), as is fishing, and you can work your tan on sandy beaches. Solomon Airlines flies two to three times a week from Honiara to Marau (S$1700 return, 30 minutes), from where it's a 15-minute boat ride to the resort.

Visale VILLAGE
About 40km from Honiara is this timeless hamlet blessed with a majestic setting – it's wedged between the sea and a soaring, velvet-green hill. Soak up the rural atmosphere and make the most of the beach lapped by clear waters.

WESTERN PROVINCE

POP 76,600

Marovo Lagoon, Munda and Ghizo Island are the three unmissable destinations in the Western Province. Thanks to reliable inter-island boat and plane services, they can easily be combined and toured at a comfortable, leisurely pace.

Marovo Lagoon

On New Georgia's eastern side, Marovo Lagoon is the world's finest double-barrier-enclosed lagoon, bordered by the large New Georgia and Vangunu Islands on one side and a double line of long barrier islands on the other. It contains hundreds of beautiful small islands, most of which are covered by coconut palms and rainforest and surrounded by coral.

Don't expect sweeping expanses of silky sands, though. Although Marovo Lagoon boasts aquamarine water, it's not a beach-holiday destination. You come here to dive in fish soup, visit laid-back villages, picnic on deserted islands, take a lagoon tour, meet master carvers, kayak across the lagoon or take a walk through the rainforest or up awesome summits.

🏃 Activities

Diving & Snorkelling
Marovo Lagoon offers plenty of exhilarating dives for both experts and novices. Here's the menu: channels, caves, drop-offs, coral gardens, clouds of technicolour fish and a few wrecks thrown in for good measure. A few iconic sites include Uepi Point, General Store and Lumalihe Passage.

With dozens of lovely sites scattered throughout the lagoon, snorkelling is equally impressive. Lodges can organise lagoon tours and snorkelling trips, which cost anything from S$100 to S$300 per person depending on distance and duration. Bring your own gear.

For more on diving in the area, see p34.

Western Province

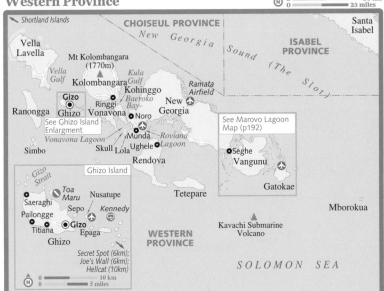

Solomon Dive Adventures
DIVING

(☑7469007; www.solomondiveadventures.com; Kahaini Island; 1-/2-tank dives S$600/1200) This small outfit is based at Kahaini Guesthouse near Chea (North Marovo). The ebullient American owner, Lisa Roquette, runs dive trips to nearby islands, passages and reefs. Two-tank outings include a picnic lunch on a deserted island. Rental gear is available (S$300 per day). Cash only.

Uepi Island Resort
DIVING, SNORKELLING

(www.uepi.com; Uepi island; single dive A$75; ⊙by reservation) This outfit has a great reputation for service and professionalism and offers stunning dives for all levels of proficiency throughout Marovo Lagoon. It's also renowned for its certification courses and dedicated snorkelling trips. It caters mainly to the resort's guests; nonguests may be accepted, space permitting and by prior arrangement.

Dive Wilderness
DIVING

(☑in Australia +61 2 9299 4633; www.diveadventures.com.au; Peava, Gatokae Island; single dive A$75) This modest operation caters to guests staying at the Wilderness Lodge and runs dive trips to Mbulo and Male Male Islands.

Kayaking

Diving is king in Marovo, but sea kayaking can be very rewarding, too.

Kayak Solomons
KAYAKING

(☑in Australia +61 3 9787 7904; www.kayaksolomons.com; per person per night A$255) Based at Uepi Island Resort, this reputable outfit can arrange multiday kayaking trips, overnighting in villages along the way – an excellent way to discover the lagoon at a leisurely pace.

Walking

If you've got itchy feet, don't forget your walking shoes. Consider scaling Mt Mariu (887m) on Gatokae (two days), climbing the hill that lords over Chea village on Marovo Island (two hours) or tackling Mt Reku (520m) on Vanganu (half a day).

⚲ Tours

All kinds of tours and activities, including village visits, guided walks, picnic trips and lagoon excursions, can be arranged through the region's lodges.

🛏 Sleeping

There's a small network of ecolodges on the lagoon. These rustic, family-run establishments are great places to meet locals and offer an authentic cultural experience. If you want to pamper yourself, opt for Uepi Island Resort.

Marovo Lagoon

Matikuri Lodge BUNGALOW $

(☑7467177; Matikuri Island; dm with full board S$400, bungalow per person S$490) Matikuri Lodge's drawcard is its soothing sense of isolation, sitting on the western arc of Marovo Lagoon. Digs are in three island-style, basic bungalows that face the sea; the four dorm-style rooms in the main house are rudimentary. Toilets and showers (cold water) are shared. No electricity, but kerosene lamps are provided.

The dining area has a large deck on stilts. There's good swimming just offshore and some great snorkelling spots nearby. A host of guided walks, village visits and lagoon tours can be organised, and there are kayaks for hire. One-way boat transfers to Seghe airstrip (20 minutes) are S$250 per person. Cash only.

Kahaini Guesthouse GUESTHOUSE $$

(☑7469007; www.solomondiveadventures.com; Kahaini Island; per person with full board S$700-950) Run by American Lisa, this simple yet inviting guesthouse with a small on-site dive centre is on tiny Kahaini Island, just offshore from Chea village. Guests are accommodated in a large wooden house with three simply laid-out and clean rooms. There's a rudimentary outside shower and 24-hour electricity.

Aim for the slightly dearer East Room, which has its own toilet. Food is fresh and tasty, and there's excellent swimming and snorkelling around the islet. Although Kahaini Guesthouse mainly targets divers, it will also appeal to nature lovers – the atmosphere is delightfully chilled-out. Boat transfers to Seghe airstrip (30 minutes) are S$500 for two people one way. Cash only.

Ropiko Beach Resort BUNGALOW $$

(☑23226, 7495805; www.ropikobeachresort.com. sb; Gatokae Island; d bungalow A$135; 🖝) Entirely refurbished in 2015, this charming place grows on you quickly, with a clutch of well-proportioned bungalows nestled in a superb coconut grove. They're modern, well equipped

Marovo Lagoon

and comfy, but don't have terraces. Boat transfers to Mbunikalo wharf cost A$30 per boatload; to Seghe airstrip, it's A$300. Cash only.

Sunbathing is top-notch but swimming is not that enthralling, with very shallow waters; there's a tiny cove with deeper water nearby. Village visits, snorkelling trips, spearfishing and diving can be organised.

★ Uepi Island Resort   RESORT $$$
(www.uepi.com; Uepi Island; s with full board A$245-330, d A$430-550; 🛜) This extremely well-run resort is very popular with Australian divers, who stay here to get thrilled by the sensational dive sites right on their doorstep. The best thing is that it also appeals to honeymooners, families and kayakers. The 10 spacious wooden bungalows are comfortable but not flash (no air-con and ordinary furnishings), and are scattered amid lovely bush gardens and coconut palms.

They're well spaced out and have large terraces. Snorkellers will get a buzz on the house reef that spreads from the end of the short jetty. And, joy of joys, there's a beach with safe swimming. The ethos here is laidback and activity-oriented. Perks include a bar, a breezy dining room with excellent meals, a full dive shop and a good excursion program. Boat transfers to Seghe are A$153 per person return. Three nights minimum.

Wilderness Lodge   BUNGALOW $$$
(🖉 in Australia +61 2 9299 4633; www.diveadventures.com.au; Peava, Gatokae Island; s/d with full board A$165/250, bungalow A$356/400) Nestled in a coconut grove right by the lagoon, this

'lodge' features a large leafhouse with two bedrooms that share a bathroom as well as two seafront bungalows with private facilities (cold-water showers). Meals incorporate locally grown fruit and vegetables.

Various sea- and land-related excursions are available, including diving (there's a small on-site dive centre), hiking, crocodile-spotting and snorkelling along the house reef. Take note that the nearest airstrip is Seghe, a two-hour boat ride away (A$260 per boatload one way). Check if Gatokae airfield, which is a mere 10-minute boat ride away, has reopened when you book.

ℹ Information

Marovo Lagoon is strongly Seventh Day Adventist, so you can't do much on Saturdays.

Marovo Lagoon has no ATMs and no banks, and credit cards are only accepted at Uepi Island Resort, so you'll need to bring a stash of cash to cover your entire bill (including accommodation, meals, activities and transport), plus some extra for surprise add-ons.

The mobile phone network doesn't cover Marovo Lagoon entirely; at the time of writing, South Marovo wasn't yet covered. Bookings for resorts and lodges can be made online or through SIVB in Honiara (p187).

ℹ Getting There & Away

AIR

There are two main gateways to Marovo: Seghe (for North Marovo Lagoon) and Gatokae Island (for South Marovo Lagoon). Because of land disputes, the Gatokae airfield was closed at the time of writing.

Solomon Airlines (www.flysolomons.com) Connects Seghe with Honiara (S$1300, daily), and Munda (S$820) and Gizo (S$950) once a week.

BOAT

The cargo boat **MV Fair Glory** (p187) offers a weekly service between Honiara and Gizo via Marovo Lagoon (Mbunikalo, Mbatuna, Chea and Seghe). The Honiara–Mbunikalo trip costs S$380 in deck class and takes about 10 hours. It generally leaves Honiara on Sunday morning (return on Tuesday).

The cargo boat **MV Anjeanette** (p187) also offers a weekly service between Honiara and Gizo via Marovo Lagoon (Mbunikalo, Nggasini, Chea and Seghe). The Honiara–Mbunikalo trip costs S$380 and takes about 10 hours. It leaves Honiara on Saturday evening (return on Tuesday).

ℹ Getting Around

If you've booked accommodation, your hosts will arrange airport transfers. Costs depend on distance travelled and number of passengers.

OFF THE BEATEN TRACK

TETEPARE ISLAND

The large rainforest-covered **Tetepare Island** (in Munda 62163; www.tetepare. org; full board per person S\$500) is one of the Solomons' conservation jewels. The Tetepare Descendants' Association, which manages the island, welcomes visitors in its rustic yet genuinely eco-friendly leafhouses (no air-con, solar power and shared facilities). What makes this place special is the host of environmentally friendly activities, including snorkelling with dugongs, spotting crocodiles, birdwatching and turtle-tagging.

Activities are free (except those that involve boat rides) and you'll be accompanied by trained guides. Food is fresh and organic. No alcohol is available, but it's BYO. Minuses: the cost and duration of transfers (S\$2000 per boatload one way, at least 2½ hours from Munda).

Public transport does not exist. To get from South Marovo to North Marovo (or vice versa), you'll need to charter a boat; a ride between Wilderness Lodge and Uepi should set you back around S\$2200.

West New Georgia

West New Georgia has its fair share of attractions as well as a few reliable accommodation options, a hatful of historic sites – from WWII relics to skull shrines – and thrilling dive sites.

It comprises the islands of Vonavona, Kohinggo, Rendova, Tetepare and New Georgia itself, together with many smaller neighbours. Given the lack of infrastructure, your best bet is to base yourself in Munda and take half- or full-day tours to nearby sights.

Munda & Around

The largest settlement, the little town of Munda on New Georgia, makes a convenient, if unglamorous, base for exploring the area's attractions. It's at its liveliest on Friday, which is market day.

◉ Sights

Peter Joseph WWII Museum   MUSEUM
(☑ 7432641, 7400387; Munda; admission S\$50; ⊙ 6am-5pm) History buffs should consider this excellent private 'museum' of WWII relics. Run by knowledgeable Alphy Barney Paulson, it features lots of utensils, ammu-

nition, machine guns, shells, crockery, helmets, shavers and knives, all left behind by the Japanese and Americans. It's behind the soccer field, a 20- to 30-minute walk from the market, to the east.

★ Skull Island   ISLAND
(admission S\$50) A 30-minute boat ride from Munda, this tiny islet on Vonavona Lagoon is the final resting place for the skulls of countless vanquished warriors, as well as a shrine for the skulls of Rendovan chiefs. They date from the 1920s. The skull house is a small, triangular-shaped casket that also contains the chiefs' clamshell-ring valuables.

Baeroko Bay   HISTORIC SITE
(New Georgia Island) The Japanese garrison stationed in Baeroko Bay held the besieging US forces off for five weeks before finally being overwhelmed in August 1943. A silent reminder of this period is the *Casi Maru,* a sunken Japanese freighter near the shore. Its rusty masts protrude from the water. Enoghae, at the jutting northern lip of the bay, has several large Japanese WWII anti-aircraft guns still hidden in the scrub.

Kohinggo Island   ISLAND
On Kohinggo Island, a wrecked US Sherman tank lies at Tahitu on the northern shore. It was lost in action in September 1943 when US marines overran a Japanese strongpoint.

✇ Activities

Munda is a destination of choice for demanding divers, with an exciting selection of wrecks, drop-offs, reefs and underwater caves. A few favourites include the atmospheric wrecks of the *Corsair* and a P-39 Airacobra. Top Shelf and Shark Point are awesome reef dives with plenty of fish life. For beginners, Susu Hite is a great spot, with a dense aggregation of reef species in less than 20m. For more on diving in the area, see p34.

Dive Munda   DIVING, SNORKELLING
(☑ 7400328, 62156; www.mundadive.com; Agnes Lodge; 1-/2-tank dive S\$650/1300; ⊙ by reservation) Based at Agnes Lodge, Dive Munda offers dive trips and certification courses. Snorkelling trips (S\$500) and excursions to Skull Island (S\$800) can also be arranged.

☞ Tours

The easiest way to get a broad look at the delights around West New Georgia is to take a half- or one-day tour.

Go West Tours TOUR
(✏ 62180; Agnes Lodge, Munda; ☺ by reservation)
Based at Agnes Lodge, this small venture offers a range of excursions around West New Georgia. Prices start at S$850 for two people.

🍴 Sleeping & Eating

Qua Roviana GUESTHOUSE $
(✏ 7472472, 62123; quaroviana@gmail.com; Munda; s/d with shared bathroom S$250/500, r S$800; ❄ 🛜) Just across the road from the market, this family-run abode is great value. The 15 rooms are simply furnished but serviceable, and the common lounge, bathrooms and kitchen are clean and well fitted out. The ground floor rooms are darker but come equipped with a kitchenette. Cash only.

Titiru Eco Lodge BUNGALOW $
(✏ 8593230; titiru.eco.resort@gmail.com; Rendova Island; full board per person S$500) After something well off the beaten track? This 'ecolodge' opened in 2014 on Rendova Island; it's a great place to sample authentic Melanesian life. Digs are in four rustic bungalows that share facilities, but that's part of the fun. It's close to Ughele village.

In a lovely setting, the property is filled with colourful flowers and it overlooks a scenic bay. Instead of sand at the front, it's mangrove, but your hosts will take you to a safe swimming area. Boat transfers to Munda airstrip (S$1600 per boatload return) take between 45 and 60 minutes and can be uncomfortable in bad weather.

Lolomo Eco Resort BUNGALOW $$
(✏ 7661222, 7495822; warren.paia@gmail.com; Kohinggo Island; d with shared bathroom S$450) Halfway between Munda and Gizo, this supremely relaxing place has three thatched-roof bungalows on stilts, but sadly it's not suitable for swimming; the shore is fringed with mangroves. The owners will happily take you to a nearby sandy island for a dip. The ablution block is squeaky clean and equipped with flush toilets and hot-water showers. The meals package costs S$310 per day.

Lolomo is very isolated but convenient nonetheless, as the shuttle operated by Rava stops here between Munda and Gizo. Private boat transfers to either Munda or Gizo cost S$1200 per boatload return. Cash only.

Agnes Lodge INN $$
(✏ 62133; www.agneslodge.com.sb; Munda; d S$770-1100, with shared bathroom S$440-550, ste S$1200-1400; ❄ 🛜) This long-established venture right on the waterfront (no beach) has seen better days – some say it rests on its laurels – but it has a variety of rooms for all budgets, from fan-cooled, two-bed rooms to spacious self-contained units with air-con and a private terrace. Downside: rooms are tightly packed together. Amenities include a bar, a restaurant (mains S$80 to S$300) and a dive shop. It's a short walk from the airstrip. Credit cards are accepted.

Zipolo Habu Resort RESORT $$$
(✏ 7471105, 62178; www.zipolohabu.com.sb; Lola Island; bungalow with shared bathroom A$140-190, deluxe bungalow A$230-340; 🛜) On Lola Island, about 20 minutes by boat from Munda, this small resort with a casual atmosphere satiates the white-sand beach, coconut-palm, azure-lagoon fantasy, with six spacious, fan-cooled bungalows scattered amid a nicely landscaped property. The cheaper ones are fairly basic leafhouses, while the two deluxe units boast private bathrooms and unobstructed views over the lagoon.

The restaurant (meals per day A$80) gets good reviews. This place offers village tours, lagoon excursions and sport-fishing charters, and there's a great beach with good swimming. Bonus: free kayaks. Return boat transfers to Munda cost A$120 per boatload. Divers can be picked up at the resort by the local dive centre. Credit cards are accepted.

Leaf Haus Cafe CAFETERIA $
(✏ 62136; Munda; mains S$30-60; ☺ 7.30am-4.30pm) Located right on the main street, Leaf Haus Cafe is a handy spot for a cheap, uncomplicated, walk-in bite – think chilli chicken, fish and chips or toasted sandwiches. Keep your fluids up with a zesty milkshake (S$30) or a thick smoothie (S$30).

ℹ️ Information

Bank South Pacific (BSP; Munda; ☺ 8.30am-3.30pm Mon-Fri) Changes currency and has an ATM (Visa only).

Our Telekom (Munda; per hr S$20; ☺ 8am-noon & 1-4.30pm Mon-Fri) Internet access.

ℹ️ Getting There & Away

AIR
Solomon Airlines (✏ 62152; www.flysolomons.com; Munda) Connects Munda with Honiara (S$1500, daily), Gizo (S$800, daily) and Seghe (S$820, once a week).

BOAT
Rava (✏ 62180) Based at Agnes Lodge, this outfit offers a shuttle service to Gizo (S$250,

two hours) stopping at various places en route, including Zipolo Habu Resort and Lolomo Eco Resort. It usually departs from Munda at 7.30am on Monday and Friday. It also operates on Wednesday if there's a minimum of six passengers.

The boat has a roof and rain jackets are provided, but expect to get wet if it's raining.

Ghizo

Little Ghizo Island is dwarfed by its neighbours, but it has the Solomons' second-biggest 'city', Gizo (pronounced the same, spelt differently), the most developed area outside the capital.

Gizo

POP 2900

Gizo is the hub around which the Western Province revolves. Sprawled along the waterfront with its steep hills behind, the town is not devoid of appeal, although its architecture is charmless. Apart from the bustling market on the waterfront, there are no specific sights, but there are some appealing lodgings a short boat ride away. Gizo is also a good base for divers, surfers and hikers.

🏃 Activities

Diving & Snorkelling

Most dive sites are less than a 20-minute boat ride from Gizo and include wrecks and reef dives that are suitable for all levels. A mere 15 minutes away north of Gizo, the *Toa Maru* is the best wreck dive around. There's fabulous snorkelling off Kennedy Island, just off Fatboys. Arrange a boat transfer to Fatboys (p199), hire snorkelling gear at the resort and snorkel to your heart's content. To the southeast of Kennedy Island, there's also a small Hellcat lying on a sandy floor in 9m. It's a fun dive that's usually combined with Secret Spot or Joe's Wall, two first-class dive sites famous for their schooling fish and atmospheric seascapes. For more on diving in the area, see p34.

Dive Gizo DIVING, SNORKELLING
(☑ 60253; www.divegizo.com; Middenway Rd; introductory/2-tank dive A$150/160; ⊙ 8am-5pm) This solid professional outfit at the western end of town leads a range of dives and can arrange dive certification courses and snorkelling trips. Their two-tank dive, which includes a picnic on a secluded island, is great. Gear rental is A$40 per day.

World Fish Centre SNORKELLING
(☑ 60022; Nusatupe Island; ⊙ by reservation) On Nusatupe Island (Gizo's airstrip), this clam farm and research centre is a good spot if you want to snorkel over giant clams of up to 1m long in the lagoon (bring your own gear). Boat transfers from Gizo cost about S$200, or you can take the Solomon Airlines shuttle (S$60 one way).

🛏 Sleeping

Cegily's Guesthouse GUESTHOUSE $
(☑ 60035, 7467982; r with shared bathroom S$290-420) This small guesthouse with five fan-cooled rooms is very simple but clean, calm and secure. There's a well-kept communal kitchen, a tidy lounge area and a terrace with good ocean views. Angle for room 3, which gets more natural light and has the best views. It's just past the hospital, on a hillside.

Nagua Resthouse GUESTHOUSE $
(☑ 60012; s with shared bathroom S$300, d with shared bathroom S$400-450, d S$500-600; ❄) A short (uphill) walk from town, this family-run guesthouse features plain, functional well-scrubbed rooms with air-con, and there's a nice communal kitchen. Upstairs bathrooms have hot showers. The place is well maintained, linen is fresh and the staff friendly, but quarters are a bit cramped. Rooms 8 to 11 afford dashing ocean views.

Rekona Moamoa Lodge GUESTHOUSE $$
(☑ 60368; rekona.lodge@gmail.com; dm S$160, d with shared bathroom S$320, d S$430-720; ❄🛜) This great option has something for all purse strings. The cheaper rooms are fairly spartan, but at these rates you know you're not getting the Ritz. The dearer ones – especially rooms 16 to 20, upstairs – occupy a separate building and are way more inviting. They come with private bathrooms (hot showers), balconies with unobstructed views and air-con. There's a kitchen area for common use. Credit cards are accepted with no surcharge.

Gizo Hotel HOTEL $$
(☑ 60199; www.gizohotel.com; Middenway Rd; d S$650-720; ❄🛜🏊) Gizo's only hotel has suffered in recent years from a lack of maintenance and TLC, and we've heard reports of poor service. That said, it's an acceptable fallback, with ordinary, motel-like rooms, a restaurant and a bar. Some rooms have sea views, while others open onto the garden. The pool at the back is a bit of a joke.

Gizo

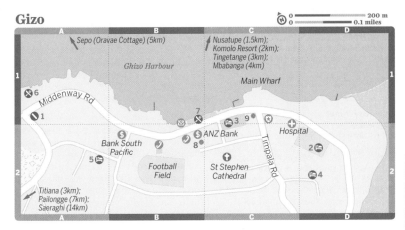

✗ Eating

Gizo has several well-stocked supermarkets, open Monday to Saturday.

Market MARKET **$**
(Middenway Rd; ⏱ 6am-5pm Mon-Sat) Villagers from neighbouring islands arrive each morning by boat to occupy their little stands under the shade of tall trees. Stock up on fruit and vegetables, as well as fresh fish and delicious buns and scones. It's at its liveliest Monday and Friday mornings.

PT 109 SEAFOOD **$$**
(✆ 60257; Middenway Rd; mains S$50-80; ⏱ 11.30am-1.30pm & 5-8pm Mon-Fri; 🐟) Named after John F Kennedy's WWII patrol boat that sank off Gizo, and situated in a great waterfront location, this place has a relaxed vibe. A blackboard displays a few simple dishes, such as fish and chips or burgers, as well as lobster.

Gizo Waterfront SEAFOOD **$$**
(Middenway Rd; mains S$50-80; ⏱ 11.30am-1.30pm & 6-9pm) There aren't too many options at this Gilbertese-run eatery, but the daily specials are well prepared and won't blow your budget. Best of all, the open-air dining room overlooks the water.

🍷 Drinking & Nightlife

The only drinking den in town is Gizo Waterfront, but it can get raucous in the evening – steer clear of inebriated patrons. During the day, nothing can beat a frothy tropical cocktail or a cold beer at SB Bar (p199) or Fatboys (p199) on Mbabanga Island.

Gizo

🛍 Shopping

Dive Gizo has a wide selection of stonework and woodcarvings from Marovo.

ⓘ Information

ANZ Bank (Middenway Rd; ⏱ 9am-4pm Mon-Fri) Currency exchange. Has an ATM (Visa and MasterCard).

Bank South Pacific (BSP; Middenway Rd; ⏱ 9am-4pm Mon-Fri) Currency exchange. Has an ATM (Visa only).

Bmobile/Vodaphone (www.bmobile.com.sb; Middenway Rd; ⏱ 8am-4.30pm Mon-Fri, to noon Sat) Sells SIM cards and prepaid wi-fi cards.

Hospital (✆ 60224; Middenway Rd; ⏱ 8am-4pm) Has reliable medical services.

Immigration Office (off Middenway Rd; ⏱ 8-11.30am & 1-4.30pm Mon-Fri) Behind ANZ Bank. Can issue a visitor's permit for yachties proceeding from PNG and the Shortland Islands. Opening hours are erratic.

Our Telekom (☑ 60127; www.ourtelekom. sb; Middenway Rd; ⊘ 8.30am-4pm Mon-Fri, 9am-noon Sat) Sells SIM cards and wi-fi prepaid cards.

❶ Getting There & Away

AIR

Solomon Airlines (☑ 60173; www.flysolomons. com; Middenway Rd; ⊘ 8am-5pm) Has up to three daily flights between Gizo and Honiara (from S$1380). There are also daily flights between Gizo and Munda (from S$685), and three weekly flights between Gizo and Seghe (from S$790). From Gizo you can also fly to the Shortland Islands and Choiseul. The airfield is on Nusatupe Island (boat transfer S$60).

BOAT

MV Fair Glory (p187) Cargo boat offering a weekly service between Honiara and Gizo via Marovo Lagoon. The Gizo–Honiara trip costs S$480 in deck class (S$1490 per cabin) and takes about 27 hours. For Seghe, it's S$270. It generally leaves Gizo on Tuesday morning; check while you're here.

MV Anjeanette (p187) Cargo boat offering a weekly service between Gizo and Honiara via Marovo Lagoon. The Gizo–Honiara trip costs S$460 (S$500 in 'first class'). It leaves Gizo on Monday afternoon.

Rava (p195) This shuttle boat connects Gizo to Munda (S$250, two hours), stopping at various places en route. It usually leaves Gizo at 1pm on Monday and Friday. It also operates on Wednesday if there's a minimum of six passengers.

Around Gizo

The main road out of Gizo skirts the shore to **Saeraghi** at the island's northwestern end, which has lovely beaches. There's excellent point surfing off **Pailongge**, on Ghizo's southern coast. The October-to-April swell rises to 2m or more. There's a great left-hander near **Titiana** village, with a long paddle out to the reef's edge, and a right at Pailongge. To get to these spots, take a taxi from Gizo (S$200 to S$300 depending on distance). Bring your own board.

🛏 Sleeping & Eating

Urilolo Lodge   BUNGALOW $$
(☑ 8624768; Saeraghi; bungalow s/d S$270/360) Saeraghi, at the northern tip of Ghizo, is a terrific place to kick off your shoes for a few days. This lovely haven consists of two charmingly simple bungalows that are right on a divine stretch of white sand, with Ranongga Island as a backdrop. Swimming,

snorkelling and sunbathing are top-notch, the atmosphere is delightfully chilled out and family-style meals are tasty.

A host of guided tours and visits can be organised. Transfers can be arranged from Gizo (S$415 per boatload one way) or you can take a taxi (S$300). No website, but there's a Facebook page.

Komolo Resort   BUNGALOW $$
(☑ 7463365; Epaga Island; d S$450) 'Resort' is a pompous description for three plank-wood bungalows with bucket showers, but this family-run abode on a secluded islet lying a 10-minute boat ride from Gizo has all you need to throw your cares away. All three units are ideally positioned on a skinny stretch of white sand and offer killer views over the turquoise water.

Your host, Grace, can cook hearty meals (from S$60). There's not a great deal to do on the island apart from spending time in the water, but it's a great place to get away from it all while still being close to town. Boat transfers from/to cost S$100 per person.

Imagination Island   BUNGALOW $$
(www.imaginationisland.com; Tingetange Island; r with shared bathroom A$60, bungalow d A$160-185, bungalow q A$190-225) This low-key resort, which opened in 2016, enjoys a great location on an islet lying a five-minute boat ride from Gizo. It comprises four sea-facing bungalows, a couple of miniscule budget rooms, a three-room house, a bar and an overwater restaurant. There's superb snorkelling offshore.

Oravae Cottage   BUNGALOW $$$
(☑ 7400774, 7690026; www.oravaecottage.com; Sepo Island; d cottage with full board A$300) Just 20 minutes from Gizo on an isolated island, this lovely retreat has three handsomely designed plank-wood bungalows, two of which have private facilities. This is not a place for those looking to be pampered – air-con and hot showers are unknown – but for those who appreciate tropical charm and a laid-back atmosphere, look no further. Swimming and snorkelling are excellent.

It can accommodate two to 10 people at a time; families or groups of friends are preferred. Add A$140 per person extra.

Mbabanga Island

A mere 10-minute boat ride south of Gizo, this island has a brochure-esque appeal, with an expansive lagoon and a string of white-sand beaches.

🛏 Sleeping

Sanbis Resort RESORT $$$

(☑ 7443109; www.sanbisresort.com; Mbabanga Island; d A$270; 🛜) A place of easy bliss. Relax in your creatively designed bungalow, snorkel over healthy reefs just offshore, snooze in a hammock, treat yourself to a tasty meal at the laid-back over-the-water restaurant or kayak over translucent waters. There are only six units, which ensures intimacy. No air-con, but the location benefits from cooling breezes. The beach is thin but attractive.

It's a good base for honeymooners, divers (there's a small on-site dive shop) and fisherfolk (professional equipment is available for rent). No kids under 12.

Fatboys RESORT $$$

(☑ 7443107, 60095; www.solomonislandsfatboys. com.au; Mbabanga Island; d A$255-275; 🛜) This small complex consists of five sea-facing bungalows that blend tropical hardwoods and traditional leaf. It's quite spread out so you can get a decent dose of privacy. The defining factor, however, is the lovely bar and restaurant directly over the exquisite waters

of the lagoon. The narrow beach is average, but the snorkelling is sensational.

Couples will opt for the snug Kusui bungalow, which is open-fronted and boasts an overwater terrace, while families will book the very spacious Haguma unit. Kayaks and snorkelling gear are free.

🍴 Eating

SB Bar INTERNATIONAL $$

(☑ 7443108; Sanbis Resort, Mbabanga Island; mains S$60-120; ⊙11am-4.30pm; 🛜) In a sublime location overlooking the turquoise lagoon, Sanbis Resort's overwater restaurant is an atmospheric place to sample a well-executed pizza, a burger or a plate of grilled fish at lunchtime. Call reception to arrange transfers from Gizo; there's generally a daily shuttle at 11.30am (with a return trip at 4.30pm).

Fatboys INTERNATIONAL $$$

(☑ 60095, 7443107; Mbabanga Island; mains S$120-200; ⊙noon-2pm; 🛜) What a sensational setting! The dining room is on a pier that hovers over the turquoise waters of Vonavona Lagoon – it can't get more mellow than

SOLOMON ISLANDS GHIZO

BEST OF THE REST

If, after visiting Guadalcanal, Malaita, Central and Western Provinces, you still feel the urge for more off-the-beaten-track adventures, and if time is really no object, consider travelling to the other provinces.

Shortland Islands Like Choiseul, the Shortland Islands are culturally closer to Bougainville in PNG, which lies only 9km to the north.

Choiseul One of the least-visited provinces in the Solomons. Choiseul has two airfields, on Taro Island and in Kagau.

Isabel This province is a castaway's dream come true, especially if you can make it to the Arnarvon Islands, off the northwestern tip of Isabel. It's a conservation area and one of the world's largest nesting grounds for the hawksbill turtle. There's one basic guesthouse run by the rangers. Trips to Arnarvon Islands can be arranged through **Nature Conservancy** (Map p184; ☑ in Honiara 20940; www.nature.org; Mendana Ave; ⊙8am-4.30pm Mon-Fri) in Honiara. On Isabel, **Papatura Island Retreat** (www.papatura.com) offers snorkelling, fishing and surfing outings. The gateways to Isabel are Buala and Suavanao.

Rennell & Bellona Both islands are Polynesia outliers, sharing similar languages and cultures. Geologically they're both rocky, uplifted-coral atolls. Rennell has **Lake Te'Nggano**, the South Pacific's largest expanse of fresh water.

Makira-Ulawa An untouched world only one hour from Honiara. Kirakira is the main gateway. Sensational surfing off **Star Harbour**.

Temotu Temotu Province lies at the Solomons' most easterly point. **Lata**, the provincial capital, on Santa Cruz Island, is the main launching pad for outlying islands, such as Reef Islands, Utupua and Vanikoro. One guesthouse on Pigeon Island (Reef Islands) is **Ngarando Faraway Resort** (☑7495914; tavakie@gmail.com; Pigeon Island, Temotu Province; bungalow s/d S$450/720), a two- to three-hour boat ride from Lata.

this. The choice is limited but the food is fresh and tasty. Good cocktails (from S$60), too. Call the reception to arrange transfers from Gizo (S$180/290 for one/two people).

After your meal, rent snorkelling gear (S$30) or a kayak (S$30) and explore the sandy shallows that extend to Kennedy Island.

Islands Around Ghizo

Natural attractions and a few war relics are the main drawcards of the islands surrounding Ghizo. Tourist infrastructure is minimal but all islands offer accommodation in the form of village stays.

The islands around Ghizo have no regular boat services. Your best bet is to find a shared ride at Gizo market. Dive Gizo (p196) can arrange excursions to Simbo and Kolombangara islands.

Simbo

Simbo is definitely worth a visit for its megapode hatcheries and its easily climbable volcano. There's also a sulphur-covered crater lake.

Kolombangara

A perfect cone-shaped volcano that rises to 1770m, Kolombangara looms majestically on the horizon, northeast of Ghizo Island. It rises from a 1km-wide coastal plain through flat-topped ridges and increasingly steep

---

DON'T MISS

HIKING IN KOLOMBANGARA

Growing weary of water activities? Consider climbing up to the crater's rim on Kolombangara (the big island facing Gizo). It's an exhilarating two-day/one-night hike. Take note that it's an arduous walk – it's wet and muddy all the way up, it's steep, and the path is irregular – so you'll need to be fit. But the atmosphere and views are surreal.

You'll need guides, porters and food. Dive Gizo (p196) and **Kolombangara Island Biodiversity Conservation Association** (KIBCA; ✆ 7401198, 60230; www.kolombangara.org) can arrange logistics. Plan on S$2000 per person, excluding boat transfers from Gizo (S$1700 per boatload return).

Kolombangara also has less challenging hikes, including crater walks and river walks.

---

escarpments to the rugged crater rim of Mt Veve. For history buffs, there are **WWII Japanese relics** scattered around the island.

MALAITA

POP 137,500

Easily reached from Guadalcanal, Malaita is a hauntingly beautiful island with narrow coastal plains, secluded bays and a rugged highland interior. As well as having a host of natural features to explore, Malaita has an equally fascinating ethnic heritage. It's a rare combination of being both an adventure island as well as a stronghold of ancient Melanesian traditions and cultures.

Unlike in Guadalcanal and the Western Province, the development of tourism is still in its infancy here. The main destinations (Auki and Langa Langa Lagoon) have enough infrastructure to travel safely on your own. Elsewhere it's virtually uncharted territory.

Auki & Around

POP 1600

Curled around a wonderfully shaped bay and surrounded by jungle-clad hills, Auki is the Solomons' third-largest town. It's a nondescript little port town, with a few low-slung buildings and a smattering of houses on stilts. Everything moves slowly except at the lively market and the bustling wharf, at the town's southern end.

◉ Sights & Activities

Lilisiana   VILLAGE

With its traditional-style houses raised on stilts over the shore, the friendly fishing village of Lilisiana, about 1.5km from Auki, is photogenic to boot. Lilisiana's peaceful **beach** is a narrow, long, golden sand spit beside coral shallows.

Riba Cave   CAVE

(admission S$50) East of Auki is this haunting cave, with stalagmites, several large subterranean chambers and an underground river. Caveat: it's very slippery – wear sturdy walking shoes. From Auki, you can take a taxi (S$100 return) then walk the final stretch (about five minutes) down to the entrance. It's best to go with a guide.

Kwaibala Waterfall   WATERFALL

If you need to refresh yourself, make a beeline for Kwaibala Waterfall, about 3km from Auki. This little waterfall drops into a few pools that

Malaita Province

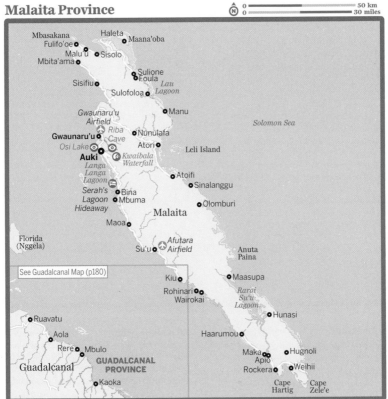

beg swimming. It's a 30-minute walk from town, or you can take a taxi (S$20) then walk the final stretch (about 20 minutes) along the Kwaibala River to the waterfall. It's not signposted; you'll need a guide to get there.

Osi Lake   LAKE

On the northern outskirts of Auki, this lake is a nature-lovers' paradise, home to colonies of seabirds. It can be explored in a dugout. You might be asked to pay a *kastom* (cultural) fee of S$50.

🖝 Tours

Discover Malaita Tours   TOUR

(☑ 7458201; silas.malai@yahoo.com) You'll need a guide to visit Riba Cave and Kwaibala Waterfall, which are difficult to find. Silas Diutee Malai is a freelance guide who charges S$200 for Riba Cave, S$200 for Kwaibala Waterfall and S$100 for Osi Lake. His prices are valid for a group of up to five people.

Kastom fees and taxi rides are not included in the prices he quotes. He can also arrange various village stays.

🛏 Sleeping

Auki Motel   HOTEL **$**

(☑ 7808884, 40014; aukimotel@solomon.com. sb; Loboi Ave; dm S$150, s with/without bathroom S$350/250, d S$450; ❄) This Auki stalwart caters to all budgets. On a shoestring? Opt for a bed in a neat three-bed dorm. In search of more privacy? Upgrade to a single. Want a few more creature comforts? The rooms with air-con and private facilities are your answer. It ain't fancy, but it's clean and there's an appealing terrace and communal kitchen.

Auki Lodge & Restaurant   LODGE **$$**

(☑ 40079; Batabu Rd; d S$620; ❄) Auki Lodge occupies a great location in the centre of town, near the post office. Rooms are plain and functional, with clean bathrooms; angle

Auki

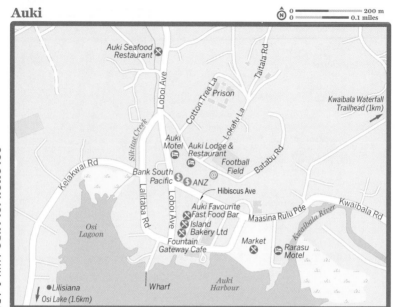

N 0 ——————— 200 m
   0 ——————— 0.1 miles

Map labels:
Auki Seafood Restaurant
Loboi Ave
Cotton Tree La
Taitala Rd
Prison
Lokafu La
Kwaibala Waterfall Trailhead (1km)
Sikitae Creek
Auki Motel
Auki Lodge & Restaurant
Batabu Rd
Kelakwai Rd
Bank South Pacific
ANZ
Football Field
@
Laitaba Rd
Hibiscus Ave
Loboi Ave
Auki Favourite Fast Food Bar
Maasina Rulu Pde
Kwaibala River
Kwaibala Rd
Island Bakery Ltd
Osi Lagoon
Fountain Gateway Cafe
Market
Rarasu Motel
Lilisiana
Osi Lake (1.6km)
Wharf
Auki Harbour

---

for rooms 1, 3, 5, 7 or 9, which have terraces overlooking a garden. The menu at the restaurant varies according to what's available.

Rarasu Motel
HOTEL **$$**

(☑40454; d S$610-790; ❋🤖) A betelnut's throw from the market, this two-storey hotel is a good surprise. The rectangular building is nothing flash, but it's calm, tidy and well managed, which is all that really matters. Rooms are ordinary but spacious; those upstairs come with parquet flooring and a terrace.

🍴 Eating

Auki Favourite Fast Food Bar
FAST FOOD **$**

(☑7369497; Hibiscus Ave; mains S$10-50; ⊙7.30am-5pm Mon-Fri) A very friendly bolt hole that's popular with locals any time of the day. Dig into budget savouries such as beef or chicken stews, omelettes or sweet-and-sour fish. In the morning, don't miss their freshly prepared roti (S$10).

Fountain Gateway Cafe
INTERNATIONAL **$**

(☑7791763; Hibiscus Ave; mains S$40-50; ⊙8am-5pm Mon-Sat) This well-run venture with a kitschy dining room is a good-value stomach filler for those in need of some honestly prepared stews, soups, sandwiches and fish and chips at puny prices. Good roast chicken, too.

Island Bakery Ltd
BAKERY **$**

(Hibiscus Ave; buns S$6; ⊙6am-8pm Mon-Sat, 6-8am Sun) The only bakery in town has fresh bread and excellent coconut buns from about 7am. It's pretty basic and super cheap.

Market
MARKET **$**

The place to stock up on fruit and vegetables. You can also buy cakes.

Auki Seafood Restaurant
SEAFOOD **$$**

(☑7540118; Loboi Ave; mains S$65-70; ⊙11am-2pm & 6.30-9.30pm Mon-Sat, 6.30-9.30pm Sun) The decor is bland but the food is tasty at this modest joint near the police station. The owner has worked as a cook for the Australian High Commission and serves up a mean garlic lobster accompanied with sweet potato chips. Enjoy.

ℹ️ Information

ANZ (Maasina Rulu Pde; ⊙9am-4pm Mon-Fri) Has one ATM (Visa and MasterCard) and changes major currencies.

Bank South Pacific (BSP; ☑40484; cnr Loboi Ave & Maasina Rulu Pde; ⊙8.30am-3pm Mon-Fri) Has one ATM (Visa only) and changes major currencies.

Our Telekom (Balabu Rd; per hr S$20; ⊙8.30am-4.30pm Mon-Fri, to 12.30pm Sat; 🤖) Has a few computers as well as wi-fi access.

ⓘ Getting There & Away

Because of land disputes, flights were indefinitely suspended between Honiara and Auki at the time of writing.

Passenger boats **MV Express Pelican II** and **MV 360 Flyer/Discovery** (p187) run regular services between Honiara and Auki (from S$250 one way, three to four hours). The MV *360 Flyer/Discovery* stops at Tulagi twice weekly.

Langa Langa Lagoon

Langa Langa Lagoon is indisputably one of Malaita's highlights. Extending from 7km to 32km south of Auki, the lagoon is famous for its artificial islands built of stones and dead corals. It's also a strong centre for traditional activities, especially shell-money making and shipbuilding.

One proviso: 'lagoon' is a bit misleading. If it has recently rained, waters may be more chocolate than bright turquoise, and you won't find stunning beaches to sun yourself on. People rather come here for the laidback tempo and the magical setting.

🛏 Sleeping & Eating

Serah's Lagoon Hideaway   BUNGALOW **$$**
(☑ 7472344; serah_kei@yahoo.com.au; full board r per person S$550, bungalow S$650-800) This relaxing retreat run with flair by Serah Kei consists of one tiny bungalow on stilts and a much larger unit with a superb terrace overlooking the lagoon. Both are simply built and as clean as a whistle. There's also a much simpler four-room house. The ablution block is tip-top, with a proper shower and flush toilets, and the meals are memorable.

WORTH A TRIP

GWAUNARU'U

If you want to get a taste of rural life and enjoy superb scenery without travelling too far from Auki, make a beeline for Gwaunaru'u on Malaita. This sweet little village near the airfield, about 10km north of Auki, abuts a huge bay fringed by a 2km-long expanse of volcanic sand. It's at the mouth of a river that offers great swimming opportunities. Be warned: there are plenty of sand flies. Get here by taxi or contact Discover Malaita Tours (p201).

Beyond the river, amid a coconut grove, you'll find the graveyards of two missionaries – very Indiana Jones.

There's no electricity but solar lighting is available. Your host can arrange lagoon tours as well as cultural shows, such as a demonstration of shell-money making (S$300). No beach but there's good swimming and snorkelling. Offers transfers from Auki (about S$500 per boatload one way, 45 minutes).

UNDERSTAND THE SOLOMON ISLANDS

Solomon Islands Today

The RAMSI (Regional Assistance Mission to Solomon Islands) drawdown is well under way. The army has left and all the civilian positions have been transitioned into bilateral aid project positions. The police are the only RAMSI left and it's hoped that all RAMSI police will have withdrawn by 2017 or 2018. It depends on the ability of the Royal Solomon Islands Police Force (RSIPF) to take over the full security role. A staged rearmament of the local police is also under way.

With restored security, increased stability and better air connections from Australia, tourism is slightly on the rise. That said, the country remains one of the poorest in the Pacific. The improvement of transport infrastructure is widely acknowledged as vital for boosting the fragile economy.

History

Papuan-speaking hunter-gatherers from New Guinea were the only inhabitants of the Solomons for thousands of years, until Austronesian-speaking proto-Melanesians began moving in around 4000 BC. The Lapita people appeared between 2000 and 1600 BC. Polynesians from the east settled the outer islands such as Rennell, Bellona and Ontong Java between AD 1200 and 1600.

The first European visitor was Spaniard Don Alvaro de Mendaña y Neyra in 1568, who returned in 1595 to establish a settlement on Santa Cruz. There was almost no further contact with Europeans until 1767, when the British Captain Philip Carteret came upon Santa Cruz and Malaita. British, French and American explorers followed, and whalers began arriving in 1798. Sandalwood traders visited from the 1840s to late 1860s.

On 6 October 1893, Britain proclaimed a protectorate over the archipelago's southern islands, which was extended in 1897 and again in 1898. In 1899 Britain relinquished claims to Western Samoa, and in return Germany ceded the Shortlands, Choiseul, Ontong Java and Santa Isabel to Britain.

Between 1871 and 1903 blackbirders (slave traders) took 30,000 men from the Solomons to work in the cane fields of northern Australia and Fiji.

The year 1942 marked a turning point: in April the Japanese seized the Shortland Islands. Three weeks later Tulagi was taken and the Japanese began building an airstrip on Guadalcanal. United States troops landed on Guadalcanal in August 1942, but were severely defeated by a Japanese naval force that had left Rabaul in New Guinea to attack the US transports. However, the US forces gradually gained the upper hand. During the Guadalcanal campaign, six naval battles were fought and 67 warships and transports sunk – so many ships were sunk off the northern coast of Guadalcanal that this area is now called Iron Bottom Sound. Around 7000 American and 30,000 Japanese lives were lost on land and at sea. The Allies recovered all islands after the official Japanese surrender in 1945. The town of Tulagi was gutted during the war and the Quonset-hut township of Honiara replaced it as the capital.

A proto-nationalist postwar movement called Marching Rule sprang up in Malaita, opposed to cooperation with the British authorities, whose rule had been restored after WWII. Britain began to see the need for local government, and a governing council was elected in 1970. The British Solomon Islands Protectorate was renamed the Solomon Islands five years later and independence was granted on 7 July 1978.

Ethnic tensions started to fester; the Gwale people (people from Guadalcanal) resented the fact that their traditional land was being settled by migrants from Malaita. Early in 1999, the inevitable happened. Civil war broke out, and hundreds died in the fighting.

Following mediation by Australia and New Zealand, the Townsville Peace Agreement was signed between the two factions in October 2000. However, what began as ethnic tension descended into general lawlessness. Though the conflict was confined to Guadalcanal, 'events' started happening elsewhere, including in the Western Province. The whole country was crippled and traumatised, and the fragile economy collapsed.

On 24 July 2003, the RAMSI, an Australian-led coalition of police from Pacific Island states, was deployed throughout the whole country to restore law and order. However, this progress was seriously undermined in April 2006, when the election of controversial Snyder Rini as prime minister resulted in two days of rioting in the streets of Honiara, despite the presence of RAMSI. Australia flew in reinforcements for the RAMSI personnel, which brought calm to the Solomons' capital.

In early April 2007, a tsunami struck Western and Choiseul provinces. Aid workers arrived en masse to help rebuild the local economy.

The Culture

Solomon Islanders' obligations to their clan and village *bigman* (chief) are eternal and enduring, whether they live in the same village all their lives or move to another country. As in most Melanesian cultures, the *wantok* (clan or kinfolk) system is observed here. All islanders are born with a set of obligations to their *wantok*, but they're also endowed with privileges that only *wantok* receive. For most Melanesian villagers it's an egalitarian way of sharing community assets. There's no social security system and very few people are in paid employment, but the clan provides economic support and a strong sense of identity.

Melanesian culture is rooted in ancestor worship, magic and oral traditions. Villagers often refer to their traditional ways, beliefs and land ownership as *kastom;* it's bound up in the Melanesian systems of lore and culture.

The Solomons' 2014 population was estimated at 610,000. Melanesians represent 94% and Polynesians 4%. The large Micronesian communities who were resettled from Kiribati by the British in the 1960s are still called Gilbertese. The remainder of the population is made up of Asians and expats, mainly Aussies and Kiwis. Most of the population lives in rural villages.

JFK

In 1960 John F Kennedy invited two Solomon Islanders to his presidential inauguration in Washington DC. They were turned away because they spoke no English. In 1943 these two islanders had rescued 26-year-old skipper JFK and 10 survivors after their boat was sunk by Japanese during WWII.

About 96% of the population is Christian. Of these, 35% are members of the Anglican-affiliated Church of Melanesia and 20% are Roman Catholics.

Islanders still practise pre-Christian religions in a few remote areas, particularly on Malaita; in other places traditional beliefs are observed alongside Christianity.

Arts

Solomon Islanders are incredibly musical people – it's a must to go to a local church service to listen to the singing. The Malaitan pipe bands (or bamboo bands) are amazing. In ensembles of 12 or so members, the band plays bamboo pipes in all sizes bundled together with bushvine. They're played as panpipe and flutes, and as long tubes whose openings are struck with rubber thongs to make an unusual plinketty-plonk sound. One of the most famous panpipe groups is Narasirato (www.narasirato.com), from Malaita; this group has gained international recognition. They mix classic Malaitan pan-pipe music with contemporary beats.

There are also strong carving traditions in the Solomons. Carvings incorporate human, bird, fish and other animal motifs, often in combination, and they frequently represent deities and spirits. Woodcarvings are inlaid with nautilus or trochus shell. Decorated bowls and masks are widely available, as are stone replicas of traditional shell money.

Shell money is used in Malaita, while in the Temotu Islands red-feather coils are still used.

Environment

The islands of the Solomons form a scattered double chain that extends 1667km southeast from Bougainville in Papua New Guinea. The country's highest peak, Mt Makarakombu (2447m), is located on Guadalcanal. There are active volcanoes, and earthquakes are common.

The country is largely covered by tropical rainforest, but much of it has been degraded by logging operations. Excessive logging threatens the rich diversity of flora and fauna as well as the traditional lifestyle of villagers. Other possible negative effects include erosion, climate change, loss of water resources and disruption to coral reefs. In Marovo Lagoon, Isabel and other islands, the effects of logging are clearly being felt. That said, there are plans to reduce logging and thus the pressure on the environment.

The spectacular marine environment is home to a rich variety of fish, corals, anemones and many other creatures, including eight species of venomous sea snakes. Several islands are breeding grounds for green and hawksbill turtles.

The Solomons has 173 bird species, with 40 endemic. Native reptiles include the 1.5m-long monitor lizard, freshwater crocodiles and the very dangerous saltwater crocodile.

SURVIVAL GUIDE

ℹ Directory A-Z

ACCOMMODATION

Tourist-class hotels are confined to Honiara, Tulago, Gizo and Munda. Although fairly basic by international standards, these hotels generally have rooms with or without private shower and air-con. Most have restaurants and bars, offer wi-fi service and take credit cards. There's also a handful of upmarket resorts in Honiara and the Western Province.

Elsewhere accommodation is offered in private houses, usually with only basic shared bathrooms, or in basic leafhouse-style lodges: traditional huts made from woven coconut thatch and other natural materials.

The visitor information centre in Honiara (p187) can make suggestions and help with bookings. You can also check out www.solomonislands-hotels.travel. This portal is a good source of information and offers online bookings, but its listings are not selective.

EMERGENCY

Police & Fire (☑ 999)

EMBASSIES & CONSULATES

Australian High Commission (Map p186; ☑ 21561; www.solomonislands.embassy.gov.au; Mud Alley, Honiara) In the centre of town.

French & German Consulates (☑ 7494820)

New Zealand High Commission (Map p186; ☑ 21502; www.nzembassy.com/solomon-islands; City Centre Bldg, Mendana Ave, Honiara; ☉ 8am-noon & 1-4.30pm Mon-Fri) On the main drag.

ℹ SLEEPING PRICE RANGES

The following price ranges refer to a double room with bathroom:

$ less than S$500

$$ S$500–1000

$$$ more than S$1000

Papua New Guinea High Commission (Map p186; ☑ 20561; www.pnghicom.com.sb; Tsilivi St; ⏰ 9am-noon & 1-4.30pm Mon-Thu) Off Mendana Ave.

UK High Commission (Map p186; ☑ 21705; www.gov.uk/government/world/solomon-islands; Heritage Park Hotel, Mendana Ave; ⏰ 8am-noon & 1-4pm Mon-Thu, to 3pm Fri) Inside the Heritage Park Hotel.

HOLIDAYS

New Year's Day 1 January

Easter March or April

Whit Monday May or June

Queen's Birthday First Monday in June

Independence Day 7 July

Christmas 25 December

National Thanksgiving Day 26 December

INTERNET ACCESS

➼ You'll find a few internet cafes in Honiara. Our Telekom (www.ourtelekom.com.sb) has public email facilities in Honiara, Gizo, Munda and Auki.

➼ Wi-fi is available at the better hotels and at a few cafes in Honiara, Auki, Munda and Gizo, but a fee usually applies. Our Telekom sells prepaid wi-fi access cards that can be used at hot spots around the country, including at some accommodation and a number of restaurants and cafes. These prepaid wi-fi cards are also available in some hotels.

➼ Most remote islands have no internet.

➼ Connections can be excruciatingly slow.

MONEY

ATMs There are ATMs at the ANZ bank and Bank South Pacific (BSP) in Honiara, and in Auki, Munda and Gizo. Note that ATMs at BSP only issue cash advances against Visa (not MasterCard). ANZ ATMs accept both Visa and MasterCard.

Credit cards The main tourist-oriented businesses, the Honiara branch of Solomon Airlines, a few dive shops and most upmarket hotels and resorts accept credit cards (usually with a 5% surcharge), but elsewhere it's strictly cash. The most commonly accepted cards are Visa and MasterCard.

Currency The local currency is the Solomon Islands' dollar (S$). A supply of coins and small-denomination notes will come in handy in rural areas, at markets, and for bus and boat rides.

Moneychangers The Bank South Pacific and ANZ will change money in most major currencies. There's also a bureau de change at the airport. Australian dollars are the best to carry, followed by US dollars. Euros are OK, but bank exchange rates are poor.

Taxes There's a 10% government tax on hotel and restaurant prices, but more basic places often don't charge it. All prices given include tax.

Tipping and bargaining Tipping and bargaining are not traditionally part of Melanesian culture.

OPENING HOURS

Banks 8.30am to 3pm Monday to Friday

Government offices 8am to noon and 1pm to 4pm Monday to Friday

Restaurants 11am to 9pm

Shops 8.30am to 5pm Monday to Saturday

TELEPHONE

Solomon Islands' country code is ☑ 677; there are no area codes. All landlines have five digits.

Mobile Phones

➼ Our Telekom (www.ourtelekom.com.sb) and Bmobile/Vodafone (www.bmobile.com.sb) offer GSM mobile phone service in most areas (but Marovo isn't entirely covered yet).

➼ Prepaid SIM cards are available for purchase. You can buy top-up cards in many outlets.

➼ Note that most foreign phones set up for global roaming won't work in the Solomons because the local providers don't have roaming agreements with foreign operators. That said, both operators have international roaming agreements with Telstra and Optus (Australia).

VISAS

Citizens from most Western countries don't need a visa to enter the Solomon Islands, just a valid passport, an onward ticket and sufficient funds for their stay. On arrival at the airport, you will be given an entry permit for up to six weeks.

WOMEN TRAVELLERS

➼ Exercise normal caution in Honiara – after dark, take a taxi and stay in busy areas.

➼ Melanesians are very sensitive about the display of female thighs, so shorts and skirts should be knee-length and swimwear should incorporate boardshorts rather than bikini bottoms.

❶ Getting There & Away

AIR

Most visitors arrive in the Solomons by air. All flights arrive at Henderson International Airport, 11km east of Honiara.

Access is easy from Australia, Fiji, Papua New Guinea and Vanuatu with direct flights. Coming

---

ⓘ EATING PRICE RANGES

Tipping is not expected in the Solomons and prices listed include tax. The following price ranges refer to standard mains:

$ less than S$60.

$$ S$60–120.

$$$ more than S$120.

from anywhere else, the easiest option is to travel to Brisbane, Sydney, Nadi, Vila or Port Moresby and connect with flights to Honiara.

Air Niugini (www.airniugini.com.pg) Flies from Port Moresby (Papua New Guinea) to Honiara three times a week. Also has a weekly flight from Honiara to Port Vila (Vanuatu) and a weekly flight from Honiara to Nadi (Fiji).

Fiji Airways (www.fijiairways.com) Has one weekly flight to Port Vila (Vanuatu) and two weekly flights to Nadi (Fiji) with onward connections to Auckland, Honolulu and Los Angeles.

Solomon Airlines (www.flysolomons.com) The national carrier has weekly flights between Honiara and Sydney and flies to Brisbane four times a week. Also has a weekly service between Honiara and Nadi (Fiji) via Port Vila (Vanuatu).

Virgin Australia (www.virginaustralia.com) Has three flights per week to/from Brisbane.

SEA

The Solomons is a favourite spot for yachties who take refuge in the lagoons during cyclone season. Along with Honiara, Korovou (Shortland Islands), Gizo, Ringgi and Tulagi are official ports of entry where you can clear customs and immigration.

Getting Around

AIR

Solomon Airlines services the country's 20-odd airstrips. Honiara is the main hub. From the capital there are frequent flights to the main tourist gateways, including Gizo, Seghe (for Marovo Lagoon) and Munda, but be sure to confirm your flight at least 24 hours before your departure. Baggage allowance is 16kg per passenger.

BOAT
Dinghies

Outboard-powered dinghies are the most common form of transport in the Solomons. People pay a fare to travel a sector. Charters cost around S$1500 per day for boat and a driver; fuel is often not included (S$22 per litre in remote areas).

Inter-Island Ships

➜ There are a couple of reliable passenger boats from Honiara. The MV *360 Flyer/Discovery* (p187) has regular services between Honiara, Tulagi and Auki (Malaita), while the MV *Express Pelican II* (p187) has a twice-weekly service between Honiara and Auki. In Western Province, *Rava* (p195) operates a twice-weekly shuttle between Munda and Gizo.

➜ On top of passenger boats, there are also freighters that take passengers, including the MV *Anjeanette* (p187) and the MV *Fair Glory* (p187), which both operate between Honiara and the Western Province.

➜ Most shipping companies have offices near Honiara's main wharf.

BUS

Public minibuses are found only in Honiara. Elsewhere, people pile into open-backed trucks or tractor-drawn trailers.

CAR & MOTORCYCLE

➜ The country has around 1300km of generally dreadful roads. International driving permits are accepted, as are most driving licences.

➜ Driving is on the left side of the road.

➜ Hire cars are available only in Honiara.

TAXI

Taxis are plentiful in Honiara and there are small fleets in Gizo and Auki. They are meterless, so agree on the price before you set off.

TOURS

Allways Dive Expeditions (www.allwaysdive.com.au) An Australian-based company that organises dive trips to the Solomons.

Battlefield Tours (www.battlefields.com.au) This Australian-based operator runs tours of important WWII battlefield sites and memorials around Honiara. All tours are led by historians.

Dive Adventures (www.diveadventures.com.au) Offers diving trips to the Solomons.

Diversion Dive Travel (www.diversionoz.com) This Australian-based company specialises in diving trips.

MV Bilikiki (www.bilikiki.com) This highly reputable live-aboard dive boat offers regular cruises around the Russell Islands and Marovo Lagoon.

Sol Surfing (www.surfingsolomonislands.com) Specialises in community-based surf tours to Guadalcanal, Malaita, Isabel and Makira Islands.

Solomon Islands Dive Expeditions (www.solomonsdiving.com) Live-aboard dive trips around the Central Province and the Western Province. Trip lengths vary from three to 15 days.

Surf Solomons (www.surfsolomons.com) This specialist outfit organises community-based surfaris to Guadalcanal, Malaita, Isabel and Makira Islands.

Understand
PNG

Papua New Guinea Today

Over recent years Papua New Guinea has transformed itself into a major energy exporter to Asia, with the latest in natural gas extraction technology materialising in remote primeval jungles. What's more, traditional landowners have found themselves in charge of millions of kina in royalties – almost overnight. In 2015 PNG celebrated 40 years of independence, and while governance has taken many a strange twist and turn during that period, parliamentary democracy endures.

Best in Print

Beyond the Coral Sea (Michael Moran; 2004) A fascinating portrait of PNG's island cultures.

Throwim Way Leg (Tim Flannery; 1998) Enjoyable account of Flannery's adventures as a biologist in remote New Guinea.

Into the Crocodile's Nest (Benedict Allen; 1987) A masochist-adventurer becomes the first Westerner initiated into a Sepik crocodile cult.

Four Corners: A Journey into the Heart of Papua New Guinea (Kira Salak; 2001) Chronicles a woman's intrepid journey across remote western PNG and into the Highlands.

The Last Men: Journey Among the Tribes of New Guinea (Iago Corazza; 2010) Photographic journey visiting PNG's most colourful and decorated tribes.

Best on Film

First Contact (1982) Extraordinary film about the 1933 first contact of Westerners with PNG's Highlanders.

Joe Leahy's Neighbours (1988) A traditional society coming to terms with the modern world.

Splinters (2011) The evolution of surfing in PNG.

Shark Callers of Kontu (1982) About the ancient art of shark-calling.

A Chaotic Political Atmosphere

Politics is a topsy-turvy affair in Papua New Guinea, with a parliament often mired in dysfunction. This is perhaps not surprising, given the nation's bewildering political complexities – where 111 MPs representing 820 languages regularly cross the floor to vote with the opposition, often showing little or no allegiance to their political party or coalition. As a consequence, since 1975 (when PNG became independent) only one prime minister has served a full five-year term without being brought down in a no-confidence vote. Survival, not policy, tends to be the focus of PNG politics.

The chaotic political scene sometimes takes a turn for the absurd, as happened in late 2011, when two men each claimed to be the legitimate prime minister.

A New Path?

Peter O'Neill, who replaced Michael Somare as prime minister during the latter's absence on medical grounds, cemented his grip on power in the 2012 elections. But even these elections had to be postponed when the ghosts of PNG's mysterial past took on a ghastly modern form. A bizarre cult sprang up near Madang that allegedly killed and ate witch-doctors accused of abusing the local community. The gang leaders were arrested and soon the election was back on track.

On a brighter note, the newly elected O'Neill promised a new era in PNG government: better education and health care, major investment in infrastructure and a more inclusive environment for women. He also aimed to clean up corrupt government practices.

In 2014 the anti-corruption team, Taskforce Sweep, began to show interest in the prime minster himself, to the point of serving an arrest warrant over allegations of fraud. O'Neill denied the allegations and shut down the watchdog.

On 8th June 2016, ongoing anticorruption protests erupted into violence when police opened fire on a group of students who were calling for O'Neill to step down. Several were seriously injured.

Testing Times

PNG has suffered natural disasters such as volcanic eruptions, earthquakes, landslides and tsunamis over the years, but more recent misfortunes have been of the human-made variety.

In February 2012 the *Rabaul Queen* sunk in heavy seas on its voyage from Kimbe to Lae, taking the lives of more than 100 passengers. Allegations of poor maintenance and overcrowding added to the distress of the victims' families. In a widely applauded nation-building gesture in 2014, the Autonomous Bougainville Government and a prominent PNG business family replaced the *Rabaul Queen* with the MV *Chebu*.

Meanwhile, the Australian Immigration Detention Centre on Manus Island lurched back into the headlines with the death of a 23-year-old detainee in 2014. The centre is part of Australia's controversial 'Pacific Solution' for asylum seekers who have been intercepted by authorities on their way to Australia. In early 2016, the PNG Supreme Court declared the centre illegal, and the Australian and PNG governments were negotiating a resettlement plan.

Being Meri

It's tough being a woman (*meri* in Tok Pisin) in PNG. Statistics provided by organisations such as Human Rights Watch make grim reading. More than two-thirds of women have suffered domestic violence and, on the other side of the story, more than 80% of men have admitted perpetrating family or partner violence. Tradition plays a part, with women regarded as a man's property, and with accusations of sorcery used to justify abuse.

Yet there is also progress to report, with increased funding for campaigns to prevent violence, and for support services for victims, as well as new laws introduced to protect women. PNG's women are also finding their own voice across the media, including empowering women's magazines, *Stella* and *Lily*.

Gas-Powered Economy

On the economic front, the letters on everyone's lips are LNG. The US$19 billion resource-extraction project – run by the US company Exxon Mobil – is PNG's biggest commercial endeavour ever. Centring on the Hides, Angore and Juha gas fields in Hela and Southern Highlands Provinces, and including pipelines in the Gulf Province, the project is expected to contribute at least US$1 billion every year to PNG's revenue for up to 30 years. The first shipment to Asia left PNG in 2014, ahead of schedule. Whether this massive extraction project ends up benefiting the masses or the few is the multibillion-dollar question.

POPULATION: **7.74 MILLION**

AREA: **462,840 SQ KM**

GDP: **US$16.9 BILLION**

GDP GROWTH: **8.5%**

LANGUAGES SPOKEN: **820**

POLITICAL PARTIES: **46**

if Papua New Guinea were 100 people

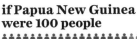

87 would live in a rural area
13 would live in an urban area

belief systems
(% of population)

69
Protestant

27
Roman Catholic

3.5
Indigenous religions

0.5
Baha'i

population per sq km

PNG   AUSTRALIA   USA

👤 ≈ 3 people

History

Papua New Guinea's history is strewn with stories of struggle in paradise. Beyond the picturesque yet malaria-prone coast, the magnificent mountains have long challenged human migration. Later arrivals had to contest with hardened pioneers: these idyllic islands and emerald forests were notoriously tainted with tales of cannibalism. Europeans first arrived in the 16th century, though the hostile territory and fierce natives tempered any colonial enthusiasm – until, that is, missionaries and industrialists saw the region as a rich repository of unclaimed souls and wealth.

The First Arrivals

Archaeological evidence suggests humans first reached New Guinea, and then the Solomon Islands and Australia, by island-hopping across the Indonesian archipelago from Asia at least 60,000 years ago. The migrations were made easier by a fall in the sea level during the Pleistocene period, or Great Ice Age, and by a land bridge that linked PNG with northern Australia. The descendants of these people speak non-Austronesian (or Papuan) languages and are today called Melanesians.

Top PNG History Reads

....

A Bastard of a Place, by Peter Brune (2003)

....

Fortress Rabaul, by Bruce Gamble (2010)

....

The Bone Man of Kokoda, by Charles Happell (2008)

....

The Sandline Affair, by Sean Dorney (1998)

World's First Agriculturalists

Evidence of early New Guinea coastal settlements includes 40,000-year-old stone axes found in Morobe Province. Humans probably climbed up to settle in the Highlands about 30,000 years ago. At Kuk (or Kup) Swamp in the Wahgi Valley in Western Highlands Province, archaeologists have found evidence of human habitation going back 20,000 years and there is evidence of gardening beginning 9000 years ago. They cultivated breadfruit, sago, coconuts, yams and sugar cane (which originated in New Guinea). New Ireland, Buka and the Solomon Islands were probably inhabited around 30,000 years ago and Manus Island 10,000 years ago.

Elsewhere in the world, the development of agriculture resulted in the establishment of cities and an elite class, but this did not happen in New Guinea or the Solomon Islands. Perhaps this was because basic food crops could not be stored for long, so food couldn't be stockpiled.

TIMELINE ⟩	60,000 BC ⟩	30,000 BC ⟩	7000 BC ⟩
	The Ice Age of the Pleistocene period allows the first humans to island-hop their way from Asia across the Indonesian archipelago to New Guinea and the Solomon Islands.	Papuan-speaking hunter-gatherers from New Guinea settle islands in the eastern Solomons before the sea levels rise with the end of the Ice Age in 10,000 BC.	The use of food gardens – breadfruit, sago, coconuts, yams and sugar cane – and domesticated pigs makes New Guineans among the world's first agriculturalists.

It's not known when pigs and more productive starch crops (Asian yams, taro and bananas) were introduced, but New Guineans have had domesticated pigs for at least 10,000 years. People lived in small villages on well-established tribal lands practising shifting cultivation, fishing and hunting. Coastal people built canoes, and feasting and dancing were regular activities. Each settlement comprised just one extended family as well as the captives from raiding neighbouring settlements – ritual head-hunting, slave-raiding and cannibalism were common. People worshipped ancestors, not gods.

Polynesians & Malay Traders

Between AD 1200 and 1600 some Polynesians started heading westward and, finding most of the islands of New Guinea already inhabited, settled some of the remaining isolated islands and atolls. They travelled vast distances in small canoes.

By the mid-16th century, sweet potatoes were being taken from South America into southeast Asia by the Portuguese and Spanish, and Malay traders brought them to the western part of the New Guinea island. The high yield of sweet potatoes in cold climes allowed for the colonisation of still higher altitudes in the Highlands and the domestication of many more pigs. Around this time steel axe-heads were traded into the Highlands from the coast. These developments saw huge rises in population, and an increase in war, slave-trading and head-hunting.

First European Contact

The first definite European sighting of the New Guinea island was in 1512, when Portuguese sailor Antonio d'Abreu sighted the coast. However, it wasn't until 1526 that another Portuguese, Jorge de Menezes, became the first European to set foot on the main island – he named it Ilha dos Papuas. But New Guinea was regarded as a large, daunting place with no obvious wealth to exploit and very hostile natives, so it was largely left alone while European colonists plundered the Americas.

European Exploration

Eager to prevent incursions into the eastern end of their fabulously profitable Dutch East Indies Empire (modern-day Indonesia), the Dutch East Indies Company claimed sovereignty over unexplored New Guinea in 1660. And so it remained for more than a century.

In 1768 Louis-Antoine de Bougainville explored Buka, Bougainville and Choiseul islands. Many British, French and American explorers followed and from 1798 whalers sailed through the islands. Sandalwood and *bêche-de-mer* (sea cucumber) traders brought iron and steel tools, calico and fish hooks, but ultimately it was treachery and resentment

Sixteenth-century Portuguese explorers named New Guinea Ilhas dos Papuas (Islands of the Fuzzy-Hairs) from the Malay word *papuwah*. Later, Spanish navigator Ynigo Ortis de Retez likened it to West Africa's Guinea and named it New Guinea. The names were combined at independence in 1975.

AD 1526	mid-1500s	1660	1699
Jorge de Menezes, Portuguese explorer and governor of Ternate in present-day Indonesia, becomes the first European to land on the New Guinea mainland; he names the region Ilhas dos Papuas.	Malay traders introduce sweet potatoes into western New Guinea (present-day Indonesian Papua), sourced from the Spanish and Portuguese exploits in South America.	The Dutch East India Company claims Dutch sovereignty over still-unexplored New Guinea in order to protect its profitable business interests in modern-day Indonesia. It remains Dutch-owned for the next century.	Swashbuckling Englishman William Dampier charts the southeastern coasts of New Britain and New Ireland and names the Dampier Strait between the New Britain and the New Guinea mainland.

that they left. European diseases were devastating in New Guinea, and the guns the traders brought resulted in an explosion of warfare and head-hunting.

The British East India Company explored parts of western New Guinea in 1793 and even made a tentative claim on the island, but in 1824 Britain and the Netherlands agreed the latter's colonial claim to the western half of the New Guinea island should stand (and it did until 1963). A series of British 'claims' followed, which were repudiated each time by Queen Victoria's government.

By the late 1860s the sandalwood had been exhausted and resentment towards Europeans led to the murder of several missionaries. The islands quickly became notorious as the most dangerous place in the Pacific, inhabited by head-hunters and cannibals. There were violent and unpredictable attacks on foreigners, and several savage massacres.

Colonialism

German interest in New Guinea's northeast coast finally spurred Great Britain to get serious about its own colonial ambitions. In September 1884, when the British announced that they intended to claim part of New Guinea, the Germans quickly raised the flag on the north coast. A compromise was reached – an arbitrary line was drawn east–west through the 'uninhabited' Highlands between German and British New Guinea.

New Guinea was now divided into three sections: a Dutch half protecting the eastern edge of the Dutch East Indies; a British quarter to keep the Germans (and everybody else) away from Australia; and a German quarter that would ultimately become a highly profitable outpost of German plantation agriculture. The Germans eventually decamped to New Britain, where German-initiated plantations still operate today.

Government by Patrol

In 1888, when Sir William MacGregor became British New Guinea's administrator, he established a native police force to spread the benefits of British government. He instituted the policy of 'government by patrol', which continued through the Australian period. In 1906 British New Guinea became the Territory of Papua and its administration was taken over by newly independent Australia.

Despite being in decline elsewhere, slavery was thriving in New Guinea during the late 19th and early 20th centuries. Known as 'blackbirding', men were carted off to provide plantation labour in northern Australia and Fiji.

In 1880 French nobleman the Marquis de Ray, having never been to New Guinea, sent 340 would-be settlers to his New France 'colony' near Cape St George in New Ireland. Instead of fertile land and friendly natives, emigrants confronted impenetrable jungle, malaria, starvation and cannibals. Only 217 survived.

1768	1876	1884	1906
Louis-Antoine de Bougainville sails through the Solomon Islands and names Bougainville after himself; Choiseul after French diplomat Étienne-François duc de Choiseul; and Buka after an Islander word.	Italian adventurer Luigi d'Albertis charts the Fly River in a tiny steamer, the Neva, taking eight weeks to travel 930km upriver and using fireworks to scare off menacing-looking locals.	Germany hoists the flag on the north coast of the New Guinea mainland and establishes the German Neuguinea Kompanie at Finschhafen. An arbitrary line divides German and British New Guinea.	British New Guinea becomes the Territory of Papua and its administration is taken over by newly independent Australia. Progressive Sir Hubert Murray is governor from 1907 until 1940.

THE LAND THAT TIME FORGOT

When Mick Leahy ventured inland in 1930 he was looking for gold. Instead, on that and nine subsequent expeditions over the next five years, Leahy, his brother Dan and Jim Taylor 'discovered' about a million people living in the secluded valleys of the New Guinea Highlands.

New Guinea's white colonialists had thought the area uninhabited, but it was the most densely populated part of the country. In an age of aeroplanes, radio and international telecommunications, the discovery was stunning. It didn't take long for the 'land that time forgot' to be dragged into the 20th century. The Leahy brothers introduced coffee, and before long missionaries and aircraft were also arriving. The Highlanders, who had only known a barter economy, were quick to adapt to cash.

Mick Leahy's meticulous recording of events – in his diary, several hours of 16mm film and more than 5000 photographs – can be seen in the 1983 documentary *First Contact*.

1914–41

When WWI broke out in 1914, Australian troops quickly overran the German headquarters at Rabaul and for the next seven years German New Guinea was run by the Australian military. In 1920 German New Guinea was officially handed over to Australia as a mandated territory.

Australia was quick to eradicate the German commercial and plantation presence, baulking only at the German missions. Australia enacted legislation aimed at restricting the commercial exploitation of Eastern New Guinea to British nationals and, more particularly, Australians. Copra, rubber, coffee and cocoa were the main earners.

The discovery of large deposits of gold at Edie Creek and the Bulolo Valley in the 1920s brought men and wealth to the north coast. After 400 years of coastal contact, some of those white men finally made it into the interior.

Under the Australian administration, *kiaps* (patrol officers) were usually the first Europeans to venture into previously 'uncontacted' areas, and were also responsible for making the government's presence felt on a regular basis. This situation continued until independence.

WWII & the Birth of the Kokoda Legend

Having raced south through Asia and the Pacific, the Japanese occupied Rabaul in New Guinea in January 1942. However, Japanese successes in New Guinea were short-lived. Australian troops fought back an advance along the rugged Kokoda Track (p224), which the Japanese were using in an attempt to reach and take Port Moresby, the only remaining Australian stronghold on the island. In a flanking move, the Japanese

In 1927 an 18-year-old Errol Flynn arrived in New Guinea. He worked as a cadet patrol officer, gold prospector, slaver, plantation manager, copra trader, charter-boat captain, pearl diver and a diamond smuggler for six years. He called New Guinea one of the great loves of his life.

1914	1930	1942	1957
Australia seizes German New Guinea at the outbreak of WWI and is officially given German New Guinea in 1920 as a mandated territory by the League of Nations.	The Australian Leahy brothers walk into and 'discover' the Highlands – and about one million people living completely unaware of the outside world. It's a monumental anthropological breakthrough.	The invading Japanese establish a base in Rabaul in January; by April they've taken most of New Guinea and the Solomons and by September they've begun their retreat along the Kokoda Track.	Kiaps (Australian patrol officers) organise the first Goroka Show. It grows to become one of the largest and best-known *singsings* (festivals) in the country, attracting scores of participating tribes.

landed at Milne Bay but were repulsed after a bloody 10-day battle with Australian troops.

The Japanese came within 50km of Port Moresby, but an unsustainably extended supply line and heroic resistance by Australian soldiers with local help turned the course of the whole Pacific war. By September 1942 the previously undefeated Japanese were in a slow and bloody retreat. Over the next 16 months, Australian and US forces battled their way towards the Japanese strongholds along the north coast at a cost of thousands of lives.

The Japanese refused to surrender. It took until 1945 to regain all the mainland from the Japanese, but New Ireland, New Britain and Bougainville were not relieved until the official Japanese surrender. For years after the end of WWII there were stories – some apocryphal, some true – about Japanese soldiers still hiding out in the jungle.

Most Melanesians were initially militarily neutral in the conflict, although they were used extensively on both sides as labourers, guides, carriers and informers – sometimes press-ganged by the Japanese and Australians. But some were heavily involved with the Allies, operating behind enemy lines as 'coastwatchers'. A number of Papua New Guineans were decorated for their bravery. It is estimated that almost a third of Tolais from northern New Britain were killed.

On 2 July 1937 aviator Amelia Earhart and her navigator Fred Noonan left Lae on PNG's north coast and flew off into oblivion.

Postwar Experience

The Melanesian experience of WWII caused a sharp resurgence in cargo cultism. The war's sudden arrival and its massive impact could not have been more profound. US soldiers – many of them black – treated locals as equals and shared food with them. This was something that locals had never experienced from their colonial overlords. The postwar profligacy of the massive US war machine – where boats were scuttled and guns and jeeps were dumped in the sea before the soldiers disappeared in

1963–69	1975	1989	1994
The Dutch pull out of western New Guinea, transferring control to Indonesia subject to a UN-administered plebiscite – the sham 'Act of Free Choice' legitimises brutality towards independence-seeking Papuans.	Papua New Guinea gains full independence from Australia on 16 September. Michael Somare, who helped lead the nation towards self-government, becomes the first prime minister.	The first PNG Defence Force (PNGDF) soldiers are killed as civil war breaks out in Bougainville; the following year PNGDF troops are withdrawn from Bougainville and the island is blockaded.	Two of Rabaul's volcanoes – Vulcan and Tavurvur – erupt, burying the prettiest town in the Pacific in volcanic ash; nearby Kokopo becomes the new capital of East New Britain.

giant transport planes – sent very strange messages to people who were living subsistence lifestyles.

Every year, 23 July is commemorated as Remembrance Day for the Papua New Guineans who died in WWII. It's also the anniversary of the 1942 battle between the Papuan Infantry Battalion and the Japanese invaders that took place near the Kumusi River in Oro Province.

Towards Independence

Masses of abandoned war equipment was put to use in developing New Guinea. Even today you can see how Marsden matting is used for fencing and building material, and many WWII-era Quonset huts are still standing. However, the war's main impact proved to be social and political.

An influx of expatriates to Papua and New Guinea, mainly Australians, fuelled rapid economic growth. The expat population grew from about 6000 to more than 50,000 in 1971. (Today it's around 20,000.)

Colonialism wasn't popular in the 1950s and '60s and Australia was urged to prepare Papua and New Guinea for independence. A visiting UN mission in 1962 stressed that if the people weren't pushing for independence, then it was Australia's responsibility to do so. Australia's policy of reinforcing literacy and education was part of a concerted effort to create an educated social group that could run government.

In 1964 a House of Assembly with 64 members was formed. Internal self-government came into effect in 1973, followed by full independence on 16 September 1975.

Barely recovered from the devastation of WWII, in 1951 the district headquarters of Central Province, Higaturu, was flattened when Mt Lamington erupted, killing more than 3000 people. The new capital, Popondetta, was built further from the volcano.

Troubled Young Nation

Law and order became a more serious issue in the 1990s, when mineral-rich PNG began to develop large-scale mining operations. These fast became the greatest contributors to the economy, but also social, environmental and political burdens that, in the 1980s and '90s, took a heavy toll. First the giant Ok Tedi gold-and-copper mine poisoned much of the Ok Tedi and Fly Rivers, and then conflict over profits from the Panguna copper mine in Bougainville led to war. Rebel leader Francis Ona and the Bougainville Revolutionary Army (BRA) fought for independence from PNG.

The Bougainville war drained resources and divided PNG along tribal lines for years; it also strained relations with the Solomons. In 1997 the government of Sir Julius Chan hired mercenaries to try to crush the separatists. What became known as the Sandline Affair was a disaster, but ironically the fall-out brought world attention to the conflict and forced the protagonists to find peaceful solutions.

The 1980s and '90s saw PNG face a series of challenges: a volcanic eruption in 1994 buried much of Rabaul; ongoing border problems

1997	1998	1999	June 2005
The Sandline Affair makes headlines worldwide, as PM Julius Chan hires South African mercenaries to put down Bougainville rebels; Chan resigns but the affair hastens negotiation of a peace agreement.	On 17 July, a 10m tsunami hits the coastal region west of Aitape in Sandaun Province, killing more than 2200 people and injuring another 1000.	Australian mining giant BHP admits to causing major environmental damage in the operation of the gold-and-copper Ok Tedi mine. Deforestation and decimated fish stocks lead to various class-action lawsuits.	Peace at last returns to troubled Bougainville. The Autonomous Bougainville Government is sworn into office on 15 June 2005 with Joseph Kabui as its president.

CARGO CULTS

To many New Guineans, it seems the strange ways and mysterious powers of the Europeans could only have derived from supernatural sources. Cult leaders theorised that Europeans had intercepted cargo that was really intended for the New Guineans, sent to them by their ancestors in the spirit world. One cultist even suggested that the white people had torn the first page out of their bibles – the page that revealed that God was actually a Papuan.

If the right rituals were followed, the cult leaders said, the goods would be redirected to their rightful owners. Accordingly, docks were prepared and crude 'airstrips' laid out for when the cargo arrived. Other leaders felt that if they mimicked European ways, they would soon have European goods – 'offices' were established in which people passed bits of paper back and forth. But when locals started to kill their own pigs and destroy their gardens, the colonial government took a firm stand. Some leaders were imprisoned while others were taken down to Australia to see with their own eyes that the goods did not arrive from the spirit world.

Seeing black American troops during WWII with access to desirable goods had a particularly strong impact. In Manus Province in 1946, a movement started by Paliau Moloat called the New Way, or Paliau Church, was initially put down as just another cargo cult. But Paliau's quasi-religious following was one of PNG's first independence movements and a force for modernisation. He opposed bride prices, for example, and sought to dissuade the local populace's belief in the arrival of actual cargo from the sea.

Paliau was imprisoned in the early days, but in 1964 and 1968 he was elected to the PNG House of Assembly. He was seen by his followers as the last prophet of the world. He died on 1 November 1991.

involving the Organisasi Papua Merdeka (Free West Papua Movement) strained relations with Indonesia and saw thousands moved to refugee camps in PNG; and a growing level of corruption and government misspending sucked money away from where it was needed most – education and health. All this served as a backdrop to the revolving door of prime ministers and no-confidence motions that characterised politics in PNG.

The New Millennium

In March 2002 the PNG government passed legislation that brought into effect autonomy arrangements of the Bougainville Peace Agreement (BPA), which guarantees a referendum for Bougainvillean independence by 2020. The Autonomous Bougainville Government was sworn into office on 15 June 2005 with Joseph Kabui as its president.

2007	August 2011	October 2011	February 2012
Michael Somare (whose face appears on the K50 note) assumes the role of prime minister for the fourth time, capping nearly four decades in politics.	After spending months away on medical leave, Prime Minister Michael Somare is replaced by Peter O'Neill. Somare's return causes a power struggle, leading to a failed pro-Somare coup in 2012.	Following discoveries of enormous gas fields, work commences on an 850km-long pipeline – part of the US$19 billion LNG (liquefied natural gas) project, which could potentially double the country's GDP.	The *Rabaul Queen* sinks in rough seas between Kimbe and Lae with over 100 passengers missing presumed dead. It's PNG's worst maritime disaster.

Francis Ona, leader of the BRA and staunch opponent of the BPA, died of malaria barely a month later on 24 July 2005. Ona's supporters continued to defend the so-called No-Go Zone around the abandoned Panguna mine. The proliferation of weapons in the No-Go Zone remains a concern.

The area around Tuno in the No-Go Zone is also where Noah Musingku maintains his own fiefdom. Musingku operated an illegal pyramid fast-money scheme called U-Vastrict that left investors all over PNG empty-handed. He fled to Bougainville in 2005 where he feted Francis Ona, proclaiming him King of Papala and then assumed this bogus title himself when Ona died. Musingku hired eight Fijian mercenaries as bodyguards and to train his private army, offering them US$1 million each. In November 2006 there was armed confrontation between the Fijian ex-soldiers and their trainees on one side, and pro-government Bougainville Freedom Fighters on the other. To date, all but one have either returned to Fiji or turned themselves over to the PNG police – none received the money promised to them. These bizarre circumstances aside, the UN regards the negotiated peace agreement on Bougainville as one of the most successful anywhere in the world in modern times.

> The 10-year secessionist war in Bougainville claimed an estimated 20,000 lives.

'Grand Chief' Sir Michael Somare, PNG's 'father of independence', returned in 2002 for a third stint as prime minister and introduced electoral reforms to create a more stable political climate, and in turn to help the economy. Somare was the first prime minister in the country's history to avoid the familiar no-confidence motion and then be re-elected in July 2007 as an incumbent prime minister. However, Somare returned to the prime ministership under strained relations with Australia.

When Prime Minister Michael Somare took leave from the country in 2011 to receive medical care abroad, he unexpectedly remained away for nearly five months. During his absence, MPs officially removed Somare from his post and installed Peter O'Neill as prime minister. When Somare returned to PNG, he tried to reclaim his position, which led to a ruling by the Supreme Court in his favour. O'Neill and MPs refused to recognise the court order, resulting in a deadlock until January 2012, when 'a mutiny' was carried out. Soldiers loyal to Somare seized key military barracks and placed military chief Brigadier-General Francis Agwi under house arrest. The whole affair greatly discredited Somare in the eyes of many Papuans, who felt that after his 43 years in parliament, including 18 as prime minister, it was time to move on.

June–July 2012	September 2013	May 2014	July 2015
The election of 2012 is marred with violence and accusations of corruption; even a bizarre cannibal cult interrupts proceedings. Peter O'Neill is returned as prime minister.	A party of trekkers and their guides and porters is attacked by machete-wielding men on the challenging Black Cat Trail in Morobe Province. Three porters are killed and the trail is closed.	The first natural gas flows from the Hides project in the Southern Highlands for processing near Port Moresby. Exports of LNG to Asia start soon after.	Papua new Guinea celebrates 40 years of independence and is host country to the 15th Pacific Games (where it is the major medal winner) and the Pacific Islands Forum.

Environment

By Tim Flannery

The island of New Guinea, of which Papua New Guinea is the eastern part, is only one-ninth as big as Australia, yet it has just as many mammal species, and more kinds of birds and frogs. PNG is Australia's biological mirror-world. Both places share a common history going back tens of millions of years, but Australia is flat and has dried out, while PNG is wet and has become mountainous. As a result, Australian kangaroos bound across the plains, while in PNG they climb in the rainforest canopy.

PNG – A Megadiverse Region

Tim Flannery is a naturalist, ecologist, environmental activist, author and Australian of the year in 2007. He has been director of the South Australian Museum, adjunct professor at Macquarie University and is currently a professorial fellow at Melbourne University and chair of the Climate Council.

PNG has the third largest, and some of the most diverse forests on earth, and it owes much of its diversity to its topography. The mountainous terrain has spawned diversity in two ways: isolated mountain ranges are often home to fauna and flora found nowhere else, while within any one mountain range you will find different species as you go higher. In the lowlands are jungles whose trees are not that different from those of Southeast Asia. Yet the animals are often startlingly different – cassowaries instead of tapirs, and marsupial cuscus instead of monkeys.

The greatest diversity of animal life occurs at around 1500m above sea level. The ancestors of many of the marsupials found in these forests were derived from Australia some five million years ago. As Australia dried out they vanished from that continent, but they continued to thrive and evolve in New Guinea, producing a highly distinctive fauna. Birds of paradise and bowerbirds also abound there, and the forest has many trees typical of the forests of ancient Gondwana.

As you go higher the forests get mossier and the air colder. By the time you have reached 3000m above sea level the forests are stunted and wreathed in epiphytes. It's a formation known as elfin woodland, and in it one finds many bright honeyeaters, native rodents and some unique relics of prehistory, such as the giant long-beaked echidna. Above the elfin woodland the trees drop out, and a wonderland of alpine grassland and herbfield dominates, where wallabies and tiny birds, like the alpine robin, can often be seen.

Papua New Guinea is still very much a biological frontier, so it's worth recording carefully any unusual animal you see. In little-visited regions, there's a chance that it will be an undescribed species. There are still hundreds of species – especially frogs, reptiles and insects – waiting to be discovered.

Lowlands

Flying into Port Moresby you'll encounter grassland – a far cry from the eternally wet forests that beckon from the distant ranges. Such habitats exist in a band of highly seasonal rainfall that stretches across southern New Guinea, and the fauna you'll see there is much like that of northern Australia. Magpie geese, brolgas and jabirus occupy the floodplains, as do sandy-coloured agile wallabies, Rusa deer (which were introduced a century ago) and saltwater crocodiles.

Where the dry season is shorter, however, the savannah gives way to lowland jungles, where the largest native land animal you'll encounter is not a mammal or a reptile but a bird – New Guinea's southern cassowary.

It's the nature of rainforests that their inhabitants form intimate relationships, and the cassowary stands at the centre of an intricate web. It eats the fruit of rainforest trees, its stomach strips the pulp from the fruit but passes the seeds unharmed, and from them new forest trees can grow – unless a sinister-looking parrot is nearby. The vulturine parrot is a cockatoo-sized bird with the colours of an Edwardian gentleman's morning suit – a sombre black on the outside, but with rich vermilion linings. Its head is naked and bears a long, hooked beak, hence its common name. Until recently no one knew quite why its head was so odd – then one was seen neck-deep in cassowary faeces. The bird specialises, it seems, in picking apart reeking cassowary droppings in search of the seeds, and for such an occupation a bald head (which prevents the faeces from sticking) and a long pincer-like beak are essential requirements.

New Guinea's snake fauna includes some extremely venomous species, such as the taipan and king brown snake, which are limited to the savannahs. Generally speaking the higher up the mountains you go, the fewer venomous snakes there are.

Mountain Forests

In the forests of New Guinea's mountains, including its high-mountain elfin woodland, there is often a distinct chill in the air at dawn. Out of the mist you might hear the pure tones of the New Guinea whipbird, or the harsher calls of any one of a dozen birds of paradise. Just why New Guinea is home to such an astonishing variety of spectacular birds has long puzzled biologists. Part of the answer lies in the lack of mammalian predators on the island. The largest – a marsupial known as the New Guinea quoll – is only kitten-sized. Thus there are no foxes, leopards or similar creatures to prey on the birds, which as a consequence have

Top Wildlife Reads

Throwim Way Leg, by Tim Flannery

Birds of Northern Melanesia, by Jared Diamond and Ernst Mayr

Birds of New Guinea, by Thane K Pratt & Bruce Beehler

Mammals of New Guinea, by Tim Flannery

A Handbook of New Guinea's Marsupials and Monotremes, by James Menzies

ENVIRONMENT PNG – A MEGADIVERSE REGION

WILDLIFE SPOTTING

Ambua Lodge Comfortable spot in the Tari Gap, Southern Highlands.

Kumul Lodge Specialist birders' lodge 40 minutes from Mt Hagen.

Crater Mountain Wildlife Management Area For the more adventurous; in the Southern Highlands area.

Karawari Lodge In pristine lowland rainforest in the foothills of East Sepik Province.

Walindi Plantation Resort Famous among divers, Walindi also offers superb birdwatching.

Kamiali Wildlife Management Area Huge hawksbill and leatherback turtles nest along the Huon Gulf Coast of Madang between November and March.

Sibonai Guesthouse An excellent place to see Goldie's Bird of Paradise and other unique avian species on Normanby Island.

Jais Aben Resort Easy access for divers and snorkellers to a stunning variety of marine wildlife near Madang.

Lake Murray Lodge New, luxurious birding and fishing lodge on Lake Murray in the Western Province, home to over 50% of PNG's bird species.

Panasesa Resort Dive the world's most extensive and pristine reefs in the remote Conflict Islands.

developed such astonishing colours and spectacular mating rituals as to beggar belief.

If you can get well away from the villages, perhaps by accompanying experienced bushmen on a two- or three-day walk to distant hunting grounds, you might get to see a tree kangaroo. These creatures are relatives of Australia's rock wallabies which, five million years ago, took to the treetops. There are eight species in New Guinea, but in the central ranges you are likely to see just two. Goodfellow's tree kangaroo is a chestnut-coloured creature the size of a Labrador. Higher up you may encounter the bearlike Doria's tree kangaroo. It is shaggy, brown and immensely powerful, and lives in family groups.

Alpine Regions

Where the woodland gives way to the alpine regions, the tiger parrot calls from stunted umbrella plants, rhododendron bushes and tufted orchids are covered with flowers, and any woody plants are festooned with ant plants. In a perfect example of the intimate ecological relationships that abound in the forest, the ant protects the plant, while the plant provides shelter for its tiny defenders.

> Australia and New Guinea have the world's only macropods and monotremes. The agile wallaby is found in New Guinea and Australia, but most of New Guinea's macropods are endemic tree kangaroos that are quite distinct from Australia's species of kangaroos and wallabies.

ENVIRONMENTAL CHALLENGES

The biggest environmental challenges faced by Papua New Guinea's natural world are pollution and the destruction of rainforest habitats caused by the mining and logging industries, and the conversion of land to oil palm plantations. Nepotism and corruption have been widely recognised as impediments to implementing and policing policies that effectively manage the way the country's natural resources are accessed and exploited.

PNG has environmental laws in place and gives some rights to traditional land owners, but the state owns all buried mineral deposits and water resources and has the right to determine their use. Environment groups claim the government has allowed a number of profitable mines to operate in ways that are detrimental to natural and social environments.The Ok Tedi gold and copper mine, located along the upper Fly River, is government owned, makes a significant contribution to the country's GDP and provides employment and investment in the region. However, the mine's operations, in particular the discharge of mining waste materials into the river system, has adversely affected the environment downstream from the site, impacting upon the livelihoods of of tens of thousands of people living in 120 villages near the river. PNG also has several other large mines that have been strongly criticised by environmental groups for the way they discharge waste into river systems or the sea, including the Ramu mine located in the Sepik, the Pogera mine in the Highlands and the Lihir mine on Lihir Island.

The export of raw logs plays a similarly important role in PNG's economy. The World Bank cites estimates that claim 70% of all logging in PNG is conducted illegally, with primary forest being destroyed at an rapid rate. Most logging companies operating in PNG are foreign-owned operations. One way logging companies obtain access to hardwood resources is via Special Agriculture and Business Leases (SABLs), which grant 99-year rights to some 12% of the country's land area. A commission of inquiry backed by the national government has determined the vast majority of SABLs were corruptly obtained and there are ongoing legal proceedings around the revoking of the leases.

A number of the palm-oil companies, most of which are Malaysian, operate in PNG and produce sustainable palm oil that's certified by the Roundtable on Sustainable Palm Oil (RSPO; www.rspo.org). However, there are also numerous other oil palm plantations whose operations do meet these global standards. Companies regularly come into conflict with local communities opposed to the conversion of community forest to oil palm plantations. In a landmark case in 2014, Malaysian palm-oil giant KLK had two leases in Collingwood Bay declared illegal and cancelled at the order of PNG's National Court.

Well-worn tracks wind through the alpine tussocks. Some are made by diminutive wallabies, others by giant rats. New Guinea is home to a spectacular diversity of rats, which comprise fully one-third of the mammal fauna. These distant relatives of the laboratory rat are spectacularly varied: some look like miniature otters and cavort in mountain streams, others resemble small, tree-climbing possums, while still others look, and smell, like rats from elsewhere.

In two of the highest mountain regions in PNG – the Star Mountains in the far west and Mt Albert Edward near Port Moresby – one of the country's most enigmatic birds can be seen. Known as McGregor's bird of paradise, it is a velvet-black bird the size of a large crow that makes a distinctive rattling sound as it flies. Under each wing is a large orange spot, and behind each eye a fleshy, flapping orange wattle of skin.

There are 41 species of birds of paradise, of which 36 are unique to New Guinea. Two species are found in both New Guinea and northern Australia. The male Raggiana decorates the flag of PNG. Birds of paradise first appeared in European literature in 1522.

The Kokoda Story *By Peter FitzSimons*

Each year around 5000 Australians walk the Kokoda Track. For them it is part pilgrimage, part opportunity to pay homage to the soldiers of WWII and part extraordinary challenge. For it is not for the faint-hearted. It's 96km of steep terrain: humid, slippery and potentially dangerous. Local guides are needed to ensure safety and to provide stories and a connection to the environment.

A Historical Synopsis

Written on your thumbnail, the story of the Kokoda Track goes like this...

Peter FitzSimons is a journalist, former Australian rugby player and author of *Kokoda*.

The Japanese bombed Pearl Harbor on 7 December 1941, and were at war with the Allies, including Australia, almost immediately thereafter. From there, Japan's superbly trained army swept through Southeast Asia knocking over country after country, stronghold after stronghold, including most notably Singapore on 15 February 1942. By late July '42, the first of an initial wave of 13,000 Japanese soldiers landed on the north coast of New Guinea and set off south along a jungle track that passed through the tiny outpost of Kokoda before coming out near Port Moresby – which it was their intention to occupy. The Australian military and political leadership was alarmed at the possibility that, if successful, the Japanese would be able to use Port Moresby as a base from which to launch southwards, perhaps landing in Queensland, Australia. However, in the first instance only 400 inexperienced militia soldiers of the 39th Battalion could be mustered to stop the Japanese invaders, or at least hold them up long enough for the more experienced veterans of the Australian Imperial Force (AIF) – who were being rushed forward – to get there.

TOP KOKODA READS

There is a reasonable choice of publications about Kokoda available. Here are some of our recommendations:

➡ *Kokoda* by Paul Ham (2004) – War history told from both the Japanese and Australian perspective.

➡ *Those Ragged Bloody Heroes* by Peter Brune (1992) – The Kokoda battle through the eyes of the soldiers who fought there, raising questions about the leadership.

➡ *The Kokoda Trail: a History* by Stuart Hawthorne (2003) – A 130-year history of Kokoda: colonial, missionary and adventurer presence along the trail.

➡ *Kokoda* by Peter FitzSimons (2004) – Gripping account of the WWII battle.

➡ *Blood and Iron* by Lex McAuley (1991) – The battle tale researched by an ex-Australian Army serviceman.

➡ *The Path of Infinite Sorrow: The Japanese on the Kokoda Track* by Craig Collie and Hajime Marutani (2012) – The Kokoda story told through the eyes of Japanese soldiers.

➡ *The Kokoda Campaign 1942: Myth and Reality* by Dr Peter Williams (2012) – Dispels some of the more popular myths to get to the facts.

The legend of the Kokoda Track, thus, concerns firstly the story of what happened when those two forces met in the middle, at a place called Isurava, and then the subsequent actions up and down the length of the track, with the 'front line' – such as it was – often being judged by where the pointy end of the bayonet of the most forward troops of each army could be found.

The fighting at Isurava was savage and without mercy from either side. And, while through sheer weight of numbers and an almost suicidal courage the Japanese finally prevailed at Isurava, in so doing they used up much of their fighting force. Certainly, the Japanese soldiers nevertheless pressed on, down the track – being ambushed all the way by the Australians, who now set out to weaken them further – but ultimately the invaders were all but exhausted by the time those that remained could get to within rough sight of Moresby.

It was there, at Ioribaiwa Ridge, that the Japanese military leadership (having no word for 'retreat') ordered their soldiers to 'advance to the rear'. The Australians were able to chase the Japanese back down the same track whence they came, all the way back to where they had first landed. More bitter fighting ensued as the Japanese dug in with fresh reinforcements, but at last, with the help of newly arrived American forces, it was all over on 22 January 1943. That was the day that the last Japanese resistance was wiped out at the head of the track, and the Australian flag was raised in those parts once more.

In the course of the previous six months in New Guinea, Australia had lost 2165 troops, with 3533 wounded. The US, which had only come into action very late in the piece, had lost 671 troops, with 2172 wounded. It was the Japanese, operating so far from their homeland, with military officers perhaps less concerned with the sanctity of their soldiers' lives, who suffered most. Some 20,000 Japanese troops landed in Papua, of which it is estimated the Japanese lost 13,000.

Recent Interest

In recent times interest in Kokoda has surged, as Australians have learned more about what occurred. It is a compelling story, an extraordinary story, and it makes Australians proud. And it was for a very good reason that Australian Prime Minister Paul Keating kissed the ground when he arrived at Kokoda in 1992 to pay tribute. It was a symbol of the fact that Australia was finally recognising what had been achieved in this place. Here, Mr Keating said, the Australian soldiers were not fighting for Empire; they were fighting 'not in defence of the Old World but the New World. Their world. They fought for their own values.' Which was why, he explained, 'for Australians, the battles in Papua New Guinea were the most important ever fought.'

KOKODA TIMELINE

7 December 1941
The Japanese bomb Pearl Harbor.

15 February 1942
Singapore falls to the invading Japanese forces.

4–8 May 1942
In the Battle of the Coral Sea, around the eastern tip of New Guinea, the US Navy and Imperial Japanese Navy savage each other to such an extent that the only way left for the Japanese to take Port Moresby is overland, via the Kokoda Track.

21 July 1942
Japanese forces land on the north coast of New Guinea, at the top of the Kokoda Track.

28 July 1942
The Japanese take the small outpost of Kokoda – significant because its airstrip is the only one in the area – and in the process kill the commander of Australia's 39th Battalion, the key force opposing them.

26 August 1942
The Battle of Isurava begins. It ends on 30 August, as the Australians, bloodied but unbowed, pull back.

8 September 1942
The Battle of Brigade Hill. Again, the Japanese eventually prevail, but are severely weakened. Before the month is out, the Japanese at Ioribaiwa Ridge, overlooking Port Moresby, receive orders from Tokyo to 'advance to the rear'.

22 January 1943
The last Japanese at the head of the track surrender; the Kokoda campaign is finally over.

The People of PNG

PNG people are closely related to people from other parts of the Pacific. There are Papuans, the first arrivals; Melanesians, who represent 95% of people and are related to people from the Solomon Islands, Vanuatu, Fiji and New Caledonia; Polynesians, related to New Zealand Maori, Tongans, Samoans and Hawaiian islanders; and Micronesians, related to people in the Marshall Islands, Kiribati and Nauru.

Population

The total population of PNG is 7.74 million, of which only 13% live in urban areas – most of the rest are subsistence farmers. Nearly two million people live in the Highlands, the most densely populated part of the country. Many Highlanders migrate to Port Moresby and elsewhere, but few coastal people move into the Highlands. Melanesian people still identify more strongly with their clan links and their origins than with the people they come to live with, so enclaves exist in the settlement areas of the big cities, and there is a traditional distrust between Highlanders and coastal people.

PNG is the most linguistically complex country in the world with more than 12% of the world's living languages – 820 living languages – but many have less than 1000 speakers. In the Solomon Islands alone, more than 70 languages are spoken.

Lifestyle

There is a great chasm between PNG's small minority of university-educated urbanites, who lead sophisticated middle-class lives, and the illiterate subsistence farmers and hunters in the remotest reaches of the country, who live entirely off the land and who may never have seen a town. Everybody else falls somewhere in between.

The majority of PNG's population is rural; 40% lives below the poverty line and in many rural communities people live completely outside the cash economy, with no electricity or sanitation and very few possessions, bartering for what they need. They build their houses out of sago palm, grow tubers and betel nut, and supplement their diet with what they can catch in the jungle or fish in the rivers and along the coast. Rural dwellers' daily rhythms tend to be dictated by the sun and the seasons, and their livelihood is particularly vulnerable to droughts and other plagues of nature.

Change is afoot. People marry more outside their traditional clans and homelands, and *tok ples* is becoming replaced in some villages with Tok Pisin. Isolated communities are being confronted with foreign mining and logging operations and associated changes. More and more rural dwellers move to the capital and find themselves living in squalor in city-fringe settlements, and tribal life finds itself in conflict with an urban existence.

Yet urban or rural, most PNG dwellers chew *buai* (betel nut), go to church, revere dead ancestors and fear *masalais* (malevolent spirits).

After the great American military machine left at the end of WWII, cargo cults began to sprout. People built runways for imaginary planes to land on and deliver *kago* (material wealth from the skies).

Traditional Lifestyle

Ownership in the Western sense didn't exist in traditional PNG societies; instead ownership was a concept tied up in family and clan rights, controlled by elders.

In traditional Melanesian culture there are three main areas of everyday importance – prestige, pigs and gardening. A village chief shows wealth by owning and displaying certain traditional valuables, or by hosting lavish feasts where dozens of pigs are slaughtered. *Bigmen* (important men or leaders) don't inherit their titles, although being the son of a chief has advantages. *Bigmen* must earn their titles by accolades in war, wisdom in councils, magic-practice skills and the secret arts that are *tambu* (taboo) for women. Particularly in the Highlands, people have to be made aware how wealthy *bigmen* are, so ceremonial life in this region focuses on ostentatious displays and in giving things away.

There are various ways in which this is formalised; it's part of a wide circle of exchange and interclan relationships. Wealth isn't given away in the Western sense. Your gifts cement a relationship with the receiver, who then has obligations to you. Obligation and payback are deadly serious in Highlands culture; Melanesia has no privileged classes, but individuals still inherit land through their parents. Land ownership is extremely important in PNG and the Solomons, and every single scrap of land belongs to someone. Disputes over land ownership today arise from the clash between collective (clan) ownership and Western-style personal ownership.

Pigs are extremely valuable; they're sometimes regarded as family members and you may see them being walked on leads in the Highlands.

Animism, Christianity & Spirit Houses

People in both countries still maintain animist beliefs. Despite the inroads of Christianity, ancestor worship is still important. The netherworld is also inhabited by spirits, both protective and malevolent, and there are creation myths that involve animal totems. This is stronger in certain areas: islanders from Malaita in the Solomons worship sharks while some Sepik River people revere crocodiles. Jesus coexists with traditional beliefs without supplanting them.

Men's cults are widespread throughout Melanesia and involve the ritualised practice of 'the arts' and ancestor worship in men's houses and *haus tambarans* (spirit houses). This can involve the building and display of certain ceremonial objects, song and dance, and the initiation of boys into manhood. It manifests in different ways in different societies, but it is very secretive and deadly serious – in the Sepik boys are cut with crocodile markings as part of their initiation, while Tolais boys are visited by *dukduks* (masked forest spirits) to perform their initiation rites.

Top Albums

Tangio Tumas, by Narasirato

Serious Tam, by George Telek

Diriman, by Hausboi

Faya, by O-Shen

Hem Stret, by Sharzy

Dollar Man, by Litol Rastas

Maiae, by Tipa

Ninalik Ndawi, by Lani Singers

Naka Blood, by Naka Blood

Brand Niu Day, by Akay47

THE PEOPLE OF PNG ANIMISM, CHRISTIANITY & SPIRIT HOUSES

THE WANTOK SYSTEM

Fundamental to Melanesian culture is the idea of *wantoks* (meaning 'one talk' in Tok Pisin) and your *wantoks* are your clan or kinfolk. Every Melanesian is born with duties to their family, extended family, friends and finally *wantoks* (in that order), but they also have privileges. Within the clan and village, each person can expect to be housed and fed, and to share in the community's assets.

The *wantok* system is an essential support system in the poor communities all over PNG and the Solomon Islands. For villagers, it is an egalitarian way for the community to share its spoils and a means of survival in a country with no other 'safety nets'. In rapidly changing circumstances, the village and the clan provide basic economic support as well as a sense of belonging.

However, when these ideas are transposed to politics and social affairs, it becomes nepotism and, at worst, corruption. Candidates don't get to run without the support of their fellow *bigmen* (important men or leaders), who expect that when 'their' candidate is elected, their generosity will be repaid. The *wantok* system is also the greatest disincentive to enterprise.

The *wantok* system is a microcosm of the battle being waged between the modern and the traditional in PNG and the Solomons. It is so deeply entrenched that some educated youngsters choose to move away from their families to avoid the calls for handouts. And without it, life would be much harder for many others. Just saying 'no' to a *wantok* is rarely an option.

While men's business and *haus tambarans* are *tambu* for women, men's cults and their initiation rites are all about rebirth.

Many PNG Christians feel a profound connection to Israel, hence the Israeli flags on some people's cars and houses, and some Gogodala tribes view themselves as a Lost Tribe of Israel.

Since Saudi Arabia began offering higher education scholarships to young men in PNG, the Sunni religious movement of Wahhabism has taken root in some places in the Highlands since some find Islam to be close to their own Melanesian culture, especially regarding gender roles.

Women's Roles

Sexual politics are complicated in traditional Melanesian society. In some places in the Highlands husband and wife don't live together at all, and sexual relations are not to be taken lightly. Some Melanesian men have two or more wives. In many belief systems men consider women dangerous, especially during menstruation. In many places land rights pass through the mother, and older women can wield great power in the villages.

Women carry *kago* (cargo) in *bilums* (string bags) home from the market while the man walks unburdened. Women do most of the food gardening, and in some parts of the Sepik, they do the fishing also. Traditionally, men practise arts that are exclusively their domain and, although these can sometimes be shown to women travellers, they are still *tambu* for local women.

According to reports by Human Rights Watch and other NGOs, Papua New Guinea has one of the world's highest rates of domestic violence and violence against women in general (at its worst in the Highlands), with an estimated 70% of women experiencing assault or rape during their lifetime. Domestic violence has long been criminalised, but perpetrators are seldom held accountable. UNICEF reports that nearly half of rape victims are under 15 years old and 13% are under seven years old.

Sorcery

In recent years, PNG has been brought to international attention for the most unwholesome of reasons: the lynchings or torture-murders of those accused of practising sorcery. Belief in sorcery is widespread throughout PNG, particularly in the Highlands, and unexplained deaths tend to be attributed to the practice of dark magic. Those accused of sorcery are almost invariably women, particularly those who tend to stand out somehow. It wasn't until 2013 that the 1971 Act that made sorcery illegal was abolished; it was previously seen as a valid legal defence for those accused of murdering 'sorcerers'.

Arts

PNG's arts are regarded as the most striking and varied in the Pacific, and Solomon Islanders, being great carvers, are part of the same cultural tradition. The lack of contact between different villages and groups of people has led to a potent array of indigenous art.

In traditional societies, dance, song, music, sculpture and body adornment were related to ceremonies. Art was either utilitarian (such as bowls or canoes) or religious. Since European contact, art has become objectified. There have always been master carvers and mask-makers, but their role in traditional cultures was to enable the ceremonies and rituals to be performed correctly, and to serve the clan and chief.

The production of artefacts is itself often ceremonial and ritualistic. On some of the islands, secret men's societies build *dukduks* or carve *malangan* masks (totemic figures honouring the dead). Women are forbidden to look upon a *dukduk* or *malangan* until it is brought to life in a ceremony by a fierce anonymous character.

Bride price is the formalised gift-giving of money and traditional valuables to the father of a would-be bride. It might include shell money, cash, pigs and even SP Lager. Part of becoming a man and commanding respect is working hard to raise a bride price so you can marry.

Bill Bennett's *In a Savage Land* (1999), filmed in the Trobriands, is about a couple of anthropologists in the 1930s and their take on the 'Islands of Love'. Australian musician David Bridie's soundtrack won a host of awards.

Survival Guide

Directory A–Z

Accommodation

Papua New Guinea offers poor value in terms of accommodation. When compared with the cheap-as-chips places of nearby Indonesia, or even with the developed-world prices of neighbouring Australia, hotel rates make for grim reading.

Booking well ahead is imperative during festival times when tour groups descend en masse. Apart from festival weekends and national holidays, tourists make up such a small percentage of hotel guests that there is no clearly defined high or low season.

Camping

➡ Camping is not a traditional part of Melanesian culture. Travellers are usually welcomed into whatever dwelling is available.

➡ All land has a traditional owner somewhere and you need to seek permission to camp – finding the landowner could take a while.

➡ Unless you're planning on doing some seriously off-the-beaten-track trekking, don't bother bringing a tent.

Hotels & Resorts

➡ The vast majority of hotels fall into the midrange and top-end categories in terms of price if not quality. They principally cater to the large mining consortiums and their notoriously deep pockets.

➡ In major towns, hotels are equipped with a bathroom, cable TV, phone and air-con, and might include a fridge, tea- and coffee-making facilities, breakfast, and free transport to and from the airport. Despite their hefty five-star price tags, don't expect much beyond three-star quality.

➡ Truly top-end resorts are few and far between. Tariffs may include some activities as most tourist-oriented resorts revolve around diving, birdwatching, trekking, fishing or cultural visits. **Trans Niugini Tours** (www.pngtours.com) is the largest such operator with seven luxury lodges scattered throughout the mainland.

➡ Wherever you head, don't forget to ask about specials, and corporate and weekend rates.

Missions, Hostels & Guesthouses

➡ The cheapest accommodation options are usually the region's many mission guesthouses, community-run hostels and private guesthouses. Mission guesthouses are mainly for church types, but the lodgings are generally clean, homey and open to travellers.

➡ Quality varies and the cheaper ones have no air-con and shared bathrooms.

➡ You'll have to put up with a few rules – drinking and smoking are discouraged (or banned) and you can expect to hear grace before meals.

➡ Managers are usually interesting people and great sources of information – best described as Bible-handlers rather than -bashers.

➡ Among the missions, the Lutheran guesthouses are consistently good.

Rental Accommodation

Large numbers of expats come and go, and there is no shortage of long-term rental accommodation. Much of it is attached to midrange and top-end hotels, but there are some less expensive alternatives. Check www.pngbd.com/forum/f74s.html in the Papua New Guinea Business Directory.

BOOK YOUR STAY ONLINE

For more accommodation reviews by Lonely Planet authors, check out http://lonelyplanet.com/papua-new-guinea/hotels. You'll find independent reviews, as well as recommendations on the best places to stay. Best of all, you can book online.

Village Accommodation

One of the great experiences of travelling in PNG is taking the opportunity to stay in a village. Village accommodation comes in all manner of guises. It might be a basic hut in a highland village; a tiny thatched stilt house in the Trobriand Islands; or one of the simple village guesthouses on the Huon Gulf coast, or around Tufi, Milne Bay, the Sepik or New Ireland. It might not be a village house at all, but a spare room in a school or space in a police station, in a church house or just about any building you see. Just ask.

Payment Village accommodation can be pretty rough, but it's the cheapest way to see the country, and in most villages you'll find a local who'll put you up. You must pay; K30 to K50 is a fair amount to offer a family providing you a roof and *kai* (food). Ask locals, before you head out of town, what might be appropriate compensation – a live *kakaruk* (chicken) could be the go. But a live *kakaruk* can be a hassle to lug around, so maybe a sack of rice, or some canned beef, salt, tea or sugar might be better.

Men and women In some villages couples might be asked to sleep in separate buildings to observe local custom. Most rural villages have a men's house and these spaces often function as domiciles for elderly or widowed men and young male initiates, as resthouses for male guests and as places where men practise 'the arts'. Men's houses are *tambu* (forbidden) to women – female travellers will be enthusiastically 'adopted' by the village women and quickly engaged with the womanly affairs of the community.

Haus kiaps In some villages there's a *haus kiap* – a village house set aside for travellers to stay in. These were originally erected for accommodating visiting *kiaps* (government patrol officers) and some remain today.

Children

People who bring their *pikininis* (children) to PNG are often overwhelmed by the response of local people, who will spoil them mercilessly given half a chance. Child-rearing in Melanesian culture is a communal activity and just when you're starting to fret about your missing two year old he/she will turn up being carried on the hip of a six-year-old girl.

There are few really child-friendly sights – no theme parks or carousels – but the practicalities of travelling with children aren't too bad.

➜ Top-end and midrange hotels should have cots, and most restaurants have high chairs. You'll be lucky, however, to find dedicated nappy-changing facilities anywhere, and forget about safety seats in taxis – working safety belts are a novelty.

➜ As you'd expect in a country where you'll see bared breasts everywhere you go, breastfeeding in public is no problem.

➜ A limited range of nappies and baby formula is available in larger towns.

➜ There are no daycare centres catering to travellers, though top-end hotels may recommend a babysitter.

Customs Regulations

Visitors to PNG are permitted the following:

➜ 200 cigarettes (or 50 cigars or 250g of tobacco)

➜ 2L of alcohol

➜ 1L or 500g of perfume

➜ New goods to the value of K1000. Exceed this K1000 threshold and things get ugly. One way to get around this is to ditch the packaging before you board the PNG-bound plane.

Since most people fly into and out of PNG from Australia, the customs and quarantine restrictions that apply in Australia are particularly pertinent. If anything you are carrying is deemed a quarantine risk, you'll have to pay to have it fumigated, a process that can take several days, and if you have a same-day onward connecting flight, you can kiss your artefacts goodbye. Post can be a good alternative.

Items that will see you starring in an Aussie border-security reality TV show include the following:

➜ Animal parts, such as skin (often used on Kundu drums), teeth or feathers. Clean feathers are OK, but cassowary feathers are illegal.

➡ Polished wood won't cause much alarm, but anything with bark is deemed risky.

➡ Woodcarvings must not have the telltale holes of burrowing insects, or else they will be fumigated at the owner's expense.

➡ No grass or seeds, but shells are fine.

➡ *Bukaware* (basketry) itself is fine, but small bugs love to hide in the weaving, so this sometimes raises alarms.

➡ Betel nuts, fruit and other plant material.

Finally, anything created before 1960, including traditional stone tools, WWII relics, certain shell valuables, and any item incorporating human remains or bird of paradise plumes cannot be exported.

If you are uncertain of what your purchases are made of, get them checked at the National Museum in Port Moresby.

Electricity

PNG's supply is 240V. Plugs have three flat prongs, as used in Australia and NZ.

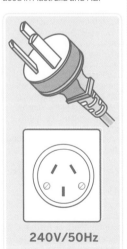

240V/50Hz

TRANSPORTING INDIGENOUS ARTEFACTS

If you're bringing some of PNG's wonderful indigenous art home, make sure you know the regulations of your home country. Australia in particular has very strict guidelines and all items must be declared. Woodcarvings must not have the telltale holes of burrowing insects, or else they will be fumigated at the owner's expense; cassowary feathers are illegal; no grass or seeds, but shells are fine.

Embassies & Consulates

All embassies are in Port Moresby.

Australian High Commission (Map p56; ☑325 9333; http://png. highcommission.gov.au/pmsb/ home.html; Godwit Rd, Waigani) There's an honorary consulate (Map p86; ☑472 2340; Lae Chamber of Commerce, Professionals bldg, 5th St) in Lae.

French Embassy (Map p53; ☑321 5550; www.amba france-pg.org; Defens Haus, cnr Champion Pde & Hunter St, Town)

Indonesian Embassy (Map p56; ☑325 3544; www.kemlu. go.id/portmoresby; Kiroki St, Waigani) There's a **consulate** (☑457 1372; vanimo.kenlu. go.id; ⊙9am-noon & 2-4pm Mon-Fri) in Vanimo.

Japanese Embassy (Map p53; ☑321 1800; www.png. emb-japan.go.jp; 1st fl, Cuthbertson House, Cuthbertson St, Town)

New Zealand High Commission (Map p56; ☑325 9444; www.nzembassy. com/papua-new-guinea; Magani Cres, Waigani)

Solomon Islands High Commission (Map p56; ☑323 4333; sihicomm@daltron.com. pg; unit 1, GB House, Kunai St, Hohola) Poreporena Fwy.

UK High Commission (Map p56; ☑325 1677; www. gov.uk/government/world/ papua-new-guinea; Kiroki St, Waigani; ⊙8am-4pm Mon-Thu; to noon Fri)

US Embassy (Map p53; ☑321 1455; portmoresby.usem bassy.gov; Douglas St, Town; ⊙7.45am-4.30pm Mon-Fri)

Food

Although the restaurant scene has improved markedly in recent years, PNG is probably not going to excite the gourmet traveller.

Seafood If you like seafood you won't be disappointed. Most coastal resorts, and even some Highlands hotels (where the fresh reef fish are flown in), can put on a great seafood buffet.

Staples The traditional village diet consists largely of starchy vegetables. Which starchy vegetable is served depends on where you are. In the Highlands it will probably be tasty *kaukau* (sweet potato); on the islands it's taro or yam; and in the Sepik and other swampy areas of PNG *saksak* (sago) is all the rage. *Rais* (rice) is universally popular.

Meat Pigs are the main source of meat protein, although they are generally saved for feasts. Chicken (*kakaruk*) is also quite popular. A legacy of WWII is the prevalence and popularity of canned meat and fish. Locals often prefer tinned fish (*tinpis*) to fresh fish, and whole supermarket aisles are devoted to bully beef (*buli*).

Vegetables Produce available at markets is varied and excellent. You'll see capsicums (bell peppers), tomatoes, peanuts, avocados and spectacular fresh tropical fruit. In the Highlands you can sometimes get strawberries, cauliflower and broccoli.

Where to Eat & Drink

Where you eat will depend on your budget. In towns and cities the ubiquitous *kai* bar will probably lure you in for a snack at least once. *Kai* bars look and taste like a greasy spoon; that is, they sell chips (fries), meat pies, sausage rolls, deep-fried dough balls and even crispy chicken heads. They're easy to find – just follow you nose and look for people milling around.

Outside of Port Moresby there are few stand-alone eateries; your best bets are usually the restaurants associated with hotels, which serve pizza, hearty meat-and-three-veg pub-style meals or decent Chinese dishes. A few good Indian and Korean restaurants are recent and welcome additions to the PNG dining scene.

Gay & Lesbian Travellers

It's quite noticeable that recently gay men are more prepared to express themselves. These days you do see effeminate Melanesian men, and while they may not be strident or provocative about it, there's nothing ambiguous about their sexual orientation. And that's pretty gutsy – homosexuality is illegal and homophobia is quite palpable (unlike in Polynesia where there are strong traditions of transgenderism and homosexuality). Local women, on the other hand, don't seem so prepared to 'fly the flag' in public.

➡ Any local 'gay scene' that exists is closeted and underground. This is not surprising given that the churches have been reinforcing for years the idea that homosexuality is morally reprehensible.

➡ Because of the legal status LGBT travellers should be cautious.

➡ You'll see many local people hold hands as they walk down the street – women with women and men with men. But don't misunderstand – this is simply an expression of friendliness and affection that's common in Melanesian societies.

Health

With sensible precautions and behaviour, the health risks to travellers in PNG are low. Mosquito-transmitted disease is the main problem.

Recommended Vaccinations

The World Health Organization (WHO) recommends that all travellers be covered for diphtheria, tetanus, measles, mumps, rubella and polio, regardless of their destination.

Vaccination for yellow fever (and the certificate to prove it) is required if you are entering from a yellow fever–endemic country. Vaccinations are also recommended for hepatitis A, hepatitis B, typhoid fever and Japanese B encephalitis.

Malaria

Malaria, both malignant (falciparum) and the less threatening but relapsing forms, are found in all areas of PNG below 1000m. Since no vaccine is available you'll have to rely on mosquito-bite prevention (including exposing as little skin as possible, applying topical insect repellents, knockdown insecticides and, where necessary, bed nets impregnated with permethrin) and taking antimalarial drugs before, during and after risk exposure.

Availability of Health Care

In Port Moresby and Lae you can expect primary care of a high standard but limited by the lack of access to sophisticated medical equipment. Specialists in internal medicine, surgery and obstetrics/gynaecology are also available in these centres, while in Port Moresby there are also paediatric, orthopaedic, dental and psychiatric specialists.

In secondary centres (eg Madang), the quality of service can be lower – often because of lower-quality diagnostic and treatment facilities. Small hospitals, health centres and clinics are well placed throughout these centres but staffing and facilities will vary.

Drinking Water

The municipal water supply in the capital and in the majority of major towns can be trusted. If you're trekking, drink only from streams at a higher altitude than nearby villages. It's always a sensible precaution to boil, filter or chemically disinfect water.

Insurance

In a country where help is often a helicopter ride away, a travel insurance policy to cover theft, loss and an emergency flight (medivac) home is essential. Read the small print to check it covers 'potentially dangerous' activities such as diving and trekking.

Internet Access

➡ There is usually at least one (and often only one) internet cafe in major towns.

→ Rates are often laughably high – anything from K15 to K30 per hour.

→ If you need to stay in regular contact with the online world or plan to spend a lot of time in small villages, it is worth buying a local SIM card for your smartphone or modem data stick for your laptop from either of the countries' mobile phone providers, Digicel (www.digicelpng. com) or B-Mobile (www. bmobile.com.pg).

Legal Matters

Most police are courteous enough (even friendly!) but don't expect them to do much about any crime perpetrated against you. For years police have been outnumbered, out-gunned and out-motivated by gangs of *raskols* (bandits), and the number of crimes solved is piteously low. Police frustration is common, and don't be surprised to hear of swift justice being applied when a *raskol* is caught.

Maps

For the most up-to-date maps of PNG towns you need look no further than the nearest telephone book. It features a colour map section that covers all the major centres and it's free.

Country Maps

There are two country maps of PNG that should be available to purchase online, if not necessarily at your local bookshop. Hema Maps' *Papua New Guinea* (1:2,167,000) 3rd Edition (2004) is the most common, and is readily available in PNG as well. More recent is ITMB's *New Guinea* (1:2,000,000), published in 2010, which has Indonesia's Papua Province on the reverse side. This is probably the pick of the two.

Trekking Maps

If you're trekking, or just want more detailed maps, contact the **National Mapping Bureau** (NMB; Map p56; ☑327 6222; www.lands.gov.pg/ Services/NMB/index.html; Eda Tano Haus, Waigani Dr, Boroko), order the maps you want and then collect them from the office in Port Moresby when you arrive. The topographic maps range in scale from 1:2000 through 1:50,000, 1:100,000 or 1:250,000. They have the whole country covered, though they're often out of stock, out of paper or out of date.

Kokoda Maps

If you're walking the Kokoda Track, the NMB's *Longitudinal Cross Section of the Kokoda Trail* (1998) is very useful, though not to scale. Available at the **Kokoda Track Authority** (KTA; Map p54; ☑323 6165; www.kokodatrackauthority.org; 2nd fl, Brian Bell Bldg, Boroko; ◷9am-4pm Mon-Fri).

Money

The kina has risen in value against major currencies thanks to the massive investment pouring in to the country for oil and LNG projects.

ATMs

ATMs are fairly common in cities, and those at the following banks allow you to withdraw cash against your Visa or MasterCard on the Cirrus, Maestro and Plus networks. If the machines are broken, head inside and you should be able to get a cash advance against your credit card over the counter.

ANZ (www.anz.com/png/importantinfo/atmlocations.asp)

Bank South Pacific (www.bsp.com.pg)

Westpac (www.westpac.com.au)

Cash

→ PNG's currency is the kina (*kee*-nah), which is divided into 100 toea

(*toy*-ah). Both are the names of traditional shell money and this connection to traditional forms of wealth is emphasised on the notes – the K20 note features an illustration of that most valuable of village animals, the pig.

→ You don't need to go too far off the track before you're fully reliant on cash. In remote areas, having enough small bills is important. People are cash poor and won't have change for K50.

→ Traditional currencies, such as shell money and leaf money, are still occasionally used. You'll see women in the Trobriand Islands carrying *doba* (leaf money), which is dried banana leaves with patterns incised on them.

Credit Cards

Credit cards are only accepted in top-end hotels and by a few restaurants and shops in the larger cities and towns. Visa and MasterCard are the favourites, with Amex, JCB and Diners Club not so widely accepted. Credit card payments often incur an additional charge.

Travellers Cheques

Travellers cheques are accepted at banks throughout PNG, though commission rates vary from bank to bank and also from branch to branch. The biggest drawback with using travellers cheques is that you'll most likely be forced to join insanely long queues that snake through the bank and, on occasion, clear out the door.

Opening Hours

Opening and closing times can be erratic, but you can rely on most businesses closing at noon on Saturday and remaining closed all day Sunday.

Banks 8.45am to 3pm Monday to Thursday, to 4pm on Friday

Government offices 7.45am to 12.30pm and 1.45pm to 4pm weekdays

Post offices 8am to 4pm Monday to Friday, 1am to 11.30am Saturday

Restaurants 11.30am to 2.30pm and 6pm or 7pm to 10pm, or whenever the last diner leaves

Shops 9am to 5pm or 6pm Monday to Friday, 9am to noon Saturday

Photography

PNG is pretty close to a photographer's nirvana. The stunning natural colours and locations are just the start, and shooting a cultural show could be the holiday highlight. A few points to consider when shooting in PNG:

➡ Bring plenty of memory cards or a storage device – you're going to shoot many more shots than you're expecting.

➡ Bring spare (charged) batteries – many places in PNG are off the grid and charging batteries may be difficult.

➡ You'll find people are generally happy to be photographed, even going out of their way to pose for you, particularly at *singsings* (celebratory festivals/dances). But ask permission

before shoving a camera in someone's face, especially around the markets of the bigger cities – Port Moresby, Lae and Mt Hagen – as people can get a little testy about this.

➡ Some people, usually men dressed in traditional style, might request payment if they are photographed – K10 is a popular price. If you've gone ahead and taken a photo without getting permission and establishing a price, you may well find yourself facing an angry, heavily armed Highlander demanding K20 or more in payment. It would take some nerve to argue.

➡ *Never* take a photograph of, or even point a camera in or at, a *haus tambaran* (spirit house) without asking permission from a male elder.

For more tips, see *Lonely Planet's Guide to Travel Photography*.

Post

PNG has an efficient postal service and you can usually rely on your mail or parcels getting home, even if it takes quite a while. Note that there is no postal delivery in PNG, so everyone and every business has a PO box.

International aerograms Cost K2.50.

Letters or postcards Up to 50g cost K6 to Australia and the Pacific, K8 everywhere else.

Package (5kg) Costs K170 to Australia and K308 to the USA or Europe. You might've been feeling impetuous when you bought that 20kg skull rack, but you'll be thinking long and hard about the cost of posting it home – K318 to Australia, and K570 to either the UK or USA. All parcels are shipped via airmail.

Public Holidays

In addition to the following national holidays, each province has its own provincial government day (usually a Friday or Monday) and there is usually a *singsing* to mark the occasion.

New Year's Day 1 January

Good Friday March/April, variable dates

Easter Monday March/April

National Remembrance Day 23 April

Queen's Birthday Second Friday of June

PNG Independence Day 16 September

Christmas Day 25 December

Boxing Day 26 December

PRACTICALITIES

Newspapers PNG has two daily English-language newspapers: the *Post-Courier* (www.postcourier.com.pg) and the *National* (www.thenational.com.pg) . The weekly *Wantok Niuspepa* is written entirely in Tok Pisin, while the weekend *Sunday Chronicle* (www.thenational.com.pg) is PNG's only locally owned newspaper.

Radio PNG has two government-funded national radio stations: Karai on the AM band and Kalang on FM. National commercial stations include NauFM (96.5FM) broadcasting in English and YumiFM (93FM) broadcasting in Tok Pisin. BBC World Service can be heard in Port Moresby on 106.7FM. There are numerous regional radio stations mostly devoted to local pop music. For a full list of stations and frequencies see radiostation-world.com.

TV EMTV and Kundu 2 are the only free-to-air stations in PNG. There are seven 'cable' (actually satellite) channels plus a range of stations from rural Australia that can also be picked up by those with the capabilities.

Weights and measures PNG uses the metric system.

Safe Travel

It's difficult to get the balance right about the dangers of travelling in PNG. As with any destination, if you read about violent crimes, you may exaggerate the danger and not visit and so never understand that Melanesians are by nature among the most gentle, hospitable and generous people in the world. While urban drift has undoubtedly caused 'law and order' issues, it's not like the Wild West where gun-law rules and stepping outside is to put your life in danger.

If you use your common sense, especially in larger towns, the chance of encountering the notorious *raskols* is small. Violent crime is not unusual, but the victims are rarely tourists.

So what does this mean for the traveller? Most importantly, don't be paranoid. Those who have travelled to developing countries probably won't be overly concerned, but inexperienced travellers may find the lack of obvious civil structure in the cities intimidating.

Bear in mind that everything is much more relaxed outside Port Moresby, Lae and Mt Hagen. Tribal fighting is still common deep in the Highlands, and while this can make things unpredictable it rarely embroils outsiders. Expats may tell you not to ride the buses and PMVs, but that's an overreaction as long as sensible precautions are taken. It would be silly to flaunt the obvious discrepancy in wealth, for example.

It would be highly unusual to encounter any trouble in the areas that travellers are likely to frequent in the daytime with people around. The mantra is common sense.

Here are some tips:

➡ Don't flaunt your wealth – wear unremarkable clothes and keep your camera hidden.

➡ Always keep at least K50 '*raskol* money' in your pocket to appease any would-be thief. Hide the rest of your money in a money belt or your shoe.

➡ Speak to people rather than being aloof.

➡ Be especially careful on the fortnightly Friday pay nights when things can get pretty wild.

➡ If you get held up, as in this situation anywhere, stay calm. Most robberies are fairly unsophisticated affairs.

GOVERNMENT TRAVEL ADVICE

For the latest travel warnings and advice log onto the following (overly cautious) websites:

Australian Department of Foreign Affairs & Trade (www.smartraveller.gov.au)

Canadian Department of Foreign Affairs (www.dfait-maeci.gc.ca)

Japanese Ministry of Foreign Affairs (www.anzen.mofa.go.jp)

New Zealand Ministry of Foreign Affairs & Trade (www.safetravel.govt.nz)

UK Foreign & Commonwealth Office (www.fco.gov.uk/en/travel-and-living-abroad)

USA Department of State/Bureau of Consular Affairs (www.travel.state.gov)

Shopping

➡ There is no shortage of wonderful artefacts and craft objects to take home: ebony carvings from the Trobriand Islands, masks and animal carvings from the Sepik, Madang and New Ireland provinces, and even penis gourds from the upper Sepik and possum-bone necklaces from the Highlands.

➡ The best advice to shoppers is to buy one good piece you really like, rather than armfuls of small inferior carvings and artefacts. If you're heading to the Sepik, or any other remote area for a serious shopping spree, bring your own bubble wrap to protect your purchase.

➡ Be aware of Australia's strict regulations if you're thinking of bringing PNG and Solomons artefacts through Australian customs (p232).

Bargaining

There is no tradition of bargaining in Melanesian culture, so don't expect to be able to cut your costs much by haggling. Bargaining is, however, starting to creep into some aspects of society, souvenir shopping being one. For example, artists who are used to dealing with Westerners (eg at Port Moresby's markets or at the Goroka Show) will have experienced bargaining, so probably won't be too offended if you make a lower bid for their work. But forget about the old 'offer one-third and work up to a half' maxim; it's more like they ask K300, you offer K200 and you get the piece for K250. Maybe. Some artists are used to being asked for a 'second price' but few will appreciate being asked for a 'third price'.

Telephone

Telecommunications can be very unreliable and in the more remote parts of the country a working telephone line is pretty rare. Dialling out of PNG can also be problematic as the limited number of international lines fill quickly.

PNG has different police emergency numbers for each city. They're all listed on the inside cover of the phone book. There are no area codes in PNG.

Some useful numbers:

Ambulance ☑111

Country code ☑675

Dialling outside PNG ☑00

International directory assistance ☑345 6789

PNG directory assistance ☑345 6789

Mobile Phones

➡ Almost everyone in PNG has a mobile phone, and often one from each of the two mobile phone companies Digicel (www.digicelpng.com) and B-Mobile-Vodaphone (www.bmobile.com.pg). SIM cards (K7 to K25) and prepay top-up cards (from K2) are readily available and basic handsets start at K49.

➡ Off-peak calls cost K0.25 per minute and peak time (6am to 7pm) calls cost K0.50 per minute.

➡ Considering the mountainous terrain, mobile phone coverage is fairly good and continuously improving.

Phonecards & Telikad

Most PNG cities have phonecard public phones, but people rarely buy a phonecard that needs to be inserted into a phone. More useful is the Telikad, which is available in K5, K10, K20 and K50 denominations.

Telikads are widely available and easy to use. Just dial ☑123 from any fixed-line phone, including any public phone, then '☑1' for English, and follow the voice prompts to enter your 12-digit code and the number you're calling.

Satellite Phones

There are two functioning networks: Iridium (www.iridium.

com), which is worldwide and uses a Motorola phone; and Aces (www.acesinternational.com), which only covers parts of Asia and uses Ericsson phones. Aces is a fair bit cheaper, but less reliable.

Time

➡ The time in PNG (excluding the Autonomous Region of Bougainville) is 10 hours ahead of UTC (GMT).

➡ When it's noon in PNG it will be noon in Sydney, 9am in Jakarta, 2am in London, 9pm the previous day in New York and 6pm the previous day in Los Angeles.

➡ There is no daylight saving (summer time) in PNG.

➡ The Autonomous Region of Bougainville is on Solomon Islands time, 11 hours ahead of UTC (GMT).

Toilets

In villages you might find a long-drop consisting of a pit with a hollow palm trunk on top, and a toilet seat on top of that. And that's relatively extravagant. If you're in a village and can't spy a loo, be sure to ask someone.

Tourist Information

There is little in the way of organised tourist offices that hand out maps and brochures, and a lack of funding has seen some of the best offices closed in recent years. Your first stop should be the web page for the PNG Tourism Promotion Authority (www.papuanewguinea.travel), which has boatloads of links.

There are three remaining regional tourism offices.

East Highlands Province Tourism Bureau (Map p106; Elizabeth St, Goroka) This office presumably springs into action during the Goroka Show, but it is usually closed and it looks

doubtful it would have much in the way of information.

Madang Visitors & Cultural Bureau (Map p94; ☑422 3302; www.facebook.com/TourismMadang; Modilon Rd, Madang) This is one of the best resourced information centres in the country. The friendly staff has up-to-date information on accommodation and attractions throughout the province, including hard-to-reach destinations such as Simbai and Karkar Island.

Milne Bay Tourism Bureau (Map p70;☑641 1503; www.milnebaytourism.gov.pg; Charles Abel Hwy, Alotau; ☺9am-4pm Mon-Fri, 10am-noon Sat) A hopelessly under-resourced centre, but if you're lucky you can get a map of town here, and the friendly staff do their best in pointing travellers in the right direction; seek out Modakula, as he's particularly helpful. They can advise on accommodation on the D'Entrecasteaux Islands, help arrange village stays and provide transport tips.

Travellers with Disabilities

Unfortunately there is little infrastructure that caters for the needs of disabled travellers. Access ramps are virtually nonexistent and only the most upmarket hotels are likely to have lifts (elevators).

Visas

All nationalities require a visa to visit PNG and must have a valid passport or internationally recognised travel document valid for at least six months beyond the date of entry. There are heavy penalties for overstaying any visa.

For the latest details on regulations pertaining to tourist, working and business visas visit the Immigration & Citizenship Service Authority (www.immigration.gov.pg).

Tourist visas

There are two ways to get a tourist visa.

ON ARRIVAL

Western Europeans, Americans, New Zealanders and citizens of most Pacific countries (except Australia) can obtain a 60-day tourist visa on arrival for free. The diplomatic stoush that resulted in Australia being dropped from the visa-on-arrival list may well be resolved by the time you read this. At the time of research there were plans to allow visa on arrival for Australians arriving at Alotau (Gurney airport), Mt Hagen, Kokopo and Madang on yet-to-be-scheduled direct flights. The process is simple enough: once inside the terminal, fill out a form, and take one passport photo to the immigration desk. This process can be fraught, however, if you have a same-day connecting flight out of Port Moresby into the provinces – the queues can be *very* long and the process can take hours.

IN ADVANCE

Australians are among those who must get a visa in advance. A 60-day tourist visa can also be obtained (again no fee) at any PNG diplomatic mission.

Visa Extensions

Tourist visas can be extended once only, for one month, for a K400 fee. To do it yourself, go to the **Department of Foreign Affairs' immigration section** (Map p56; ☑323 1500; ground fl, Moale Haus, Wards Strip, Waigani; ☺9am-noon Mon-Fri), where you'll battle hordes of agents who are on first-name terms with the staff. Extending a

visa takes one to two weeks, though occasionally travellers do it faster.

If money is not too tight, using an agent will save you a lot of grief. Agents can be found in the *Yellow Pages* under 'Visa Services'.

Volunteering

There are several organisations operating volunteer projects. These projects are often in remote communities, so this sort of work is not for those who will faint at the sight of a spider.

Activities range from teaching and medical assistance to advisory roles with local area councils. Most are either associated with the churches or with international volunteer organisations.

Most of the following organisations have projects in PNG:

Australian Business Volunteers (www.abv.org.au)

Australian Volunteers International (AVA; www.australianvolunteers.com)

Canadian University Service Overseas (CUSO; www.cuso international.org)

Japan International Co-Operation Agency (JICA; www.jica.go.jp/png)

Voluntary Service Overseas (British VSO; www.vso.org.uk)

Volunteer Service Abroad (NZ VSA; www.vsa.org.nz)

Useful Websites

Two other useful websites that have details for those interested in volunteering:

Global Volunteers (www.globalvolunteers.org)

Volunteer Abroad (www.volunteerabroad.com)

Women Travellers

Plenty of women travel to PNG with a travel companion of either gender. It is possibly safer in a pair or group, than doing so alone, but quite a few solo women have written to us with glowing reports of their trips. It is recommended that women remain aware of where they go, what they wear and how they act to avoid unwanted attention.

➡ As showing your thighs is considered sexually provocative, shorts and revealing skirts are best avoided, as are skimpy tops and other revealing clothing.

➡ You won't see local women wearing Western-style swimwear. Unless you're at a resort it's best to wear a *laplap* (sarong) while swimming.

➡ At night, it's better to take a taxi (in Moresby, Alotau, Wewak...), even if you have a male companion.

➡ Avoid secluded spots at all times. Rapes and muggings are not uncommon, especially in urban centres. Avoid any situation where you're alone with someone you don't know well.

➡ In some parts of PNG tribal beliefs about women and their menstrual cycles persist. If you're menstruating, it's better not to mention it. In the Sepik, for example, women are thought to have powerful energies that can be harmful to men. It is *tambu* in many places for a woman to pass over a man – to step over a seated man's outstretched legs or even over his possessions – and a man mustn't swim under a woman in a canoe.

Transport

GETTING THERE & AWAY

Entering the Country

The vast majority of visitors to Papua New Guinea (PNG) arrive by air at Port Moresby's Jacksons Airport with nothing more than a passport with six months' validity, an onward ticket and enough money to support themselves for the length of their stay. Visas are currently free of charge, but this could change, so check www.immigration.gov.pg before you leave. Another option is to cross PNG's only land border from Jayapura (Papua Province, Indonesia) to Vanimo in the Sandaun Province.

Flights and tours can be booked online through www.lonelyplanet.com/bookings.

Air

Airports & Airlines

The good thing about flying into PNG is that you don't have to shop around too much looking for a ticket. The major international airport is Port Moresby's **Jacksons Airport** (☑324 4704). In late 2015, recently instigated direct flights from Cairns to Rabaul/Kokopo had been suspended, and there were reports that flights linking Brisbane with Mt Hagen and Alotau (Gurney airport) would commence.

At the time of research only three companies offer international connections to PNG, but it's likely that this will change.

Air Niugini (☑Australia 1300 361 380, in PNG 180 3444; www.airniugini.com.pg) PNG's national airline flies to Australia (Cairns, Brisbane and Sydney), Indonesia (Bali), Japan (Tokyo), Philippines (Manila), Singapore, Fiji (Nadi), China (Hong Kong) and Solomon Islands (Honiara).

Qantas (QantasLink; www.qantas.com) A code-share agreement with Air Niugini means that even though you book your ticket with Qantas, or QantasLink (the regional arm of Qantas), and are issued with a Qantas boarding pass, the aircraft may actually be run by Air Niugini. Regardless, Qantas Frequent Flyer points are awarded and can be redeemed for any flight with a Qantas flight number.

Virgin Australia (www.virginaustralia.com) Virgin Australia flies between Brisbane (Australia) and Port Moresby six days a week.

Tickets

ASIA

Air Niugini flies Between Bali (Denpasar) and Port Moresby one day each week. Garuda Indonesia and a couple of Indonesia's new budget airlines fly to Jayapura

---

CLIMATE CHANGE & TRAVEL

Every form of transport that relies on carbon-based fuel generates CO_2, the main cause of human-induced climate change. Modern travel is dependent on aeroplanes, which might use less fuel per kilometre per person than most cars but travel much greater distances. The altitude at which aircraft emit gases (including CO_2) and particles also contributes to their climate change impact. Many websites offer 'carbon calculators' that allow people to estimate the carbon emissions generated by their journey and, for those who wish to do so, to offset the impact of the greenhouse gases emitted with contributions to portfolios of climate-friendly initiatives throughout the world. Lonely Planet offsets the carbon footprint of all staff and author travel.

(Papua), just across the border from PNG.

Air Niugini has weekly flights between Port Moresby and Manila (four days each week), Singapore (five days), Hong Kong (three days) and Tokyo (Saturday only). Philippine Airlines is expected to join Air Niugini on the Manila–Port Moresby route in 2016.

AUSTRALIA & NEW ZEALAND

Papua New Guinea is well connected to three Australian cities: Cairns, Brisbane and Sydney. Australians and New Zealanders will need to make their way to one of these cities for an onward flight to Port Moresby.

THE PACIFIC

Air Niugini flies to Nadi (Fiji) via Honiara (Solomon Islands). The only other way of flying to PNG from the Pacific is via Australia.

EUROPE

Flying via Asia or Australia is the obvious way to get to PNG from the UK, Ireland or continental Europe. The Singapore option is shorter, but coming via Australia gives you a bit more flexibility with onward connections. Some European airlines allow baggage to be checked through to Port Moresby.

USA & CANADA

There are a couple of options from North America: fly to Australia, then on to Port Moresby; or fly to Narita (Tokyo), Hong Kong, Manila or Singapore, then on to Port Moresby.

Land

Border Crossings

The only land **border crossing** (☻PNG 9am-5pm, Indonesia 8am-4pm) is between Vanimo in Sandaun Province and Jayapura in Papua Province (West Papua Region), Indonesia. Leaving PNG

for Indonesia is relatively straightforward.

INDONESIA VISAS

If you haven't already got an Indonesian visa in Port Moresby you'll need to get one at the **Indonesian Consulate** (☎457 1372; http://vanimo.kemlu.go.id; ☻9am-noon & 2-4pm Mon-Fri) in Vanimo. It takes 24 hours to issue a 30-day visa (single/multiple entry K120/300). You'll need two photos, a completed application form (which you get there), a passport valid for at least six months and, occasionally, proof of onward travel. It's best to say you're heading for Bali or Manado as they are less controversial destinations than anywhere in Papua.

TRANSPORT TO THE BORDER

On Tuesday and Thursday locals travel by PMV (K10, 1½ hours) to the Batas Market on the Indonesian side of the border to stock up on cheaply made goods. Immigration officials turn a blind eye to shopping day-trippers, although this courtesy is seldom extended to foreigners. Tuesdays and Thursdays aside, only occasional PMVs travel all the way to the border from Vanimo's main market. If you are desperate and PMVs are conspicuously absent, **Sandaun Surf Hotel** (☎457 1000; vanimosandaunsurfhotel@gmail.com; s/d K370/400; ❀) will drive you there for K200. To get from the border to Jayapura catch a shared taxi (400,000Rp for the whole car) or hitch.

PNG VISAS

To enter PNG requires a visa ,which (in theory) can be obtained from the **PNG Jayapura Consulate** (☎967-531 250; Blok 6 & 7, Ruko Matoa, Jl Kelapa Dua, Entrop; ☻9am-noon & 1-2pm Mon-Fri). To apply for a free-of-charge, 60-day tourist visa fill out the application form and write a cover letter

requesting a visa and stating where you want to go to in PNG. You will also need two colour passport photos (6cmx 4cm) with your signature on the back; a photocopy of an onward air ticket out of PNG; and a photocopy of the information page of your passport. A far more convenient ploy is to obtain your visa from another PNG mission in advance.

PAPUA PERMIT

Remember: foreigners are required to obtain a travel permit known as a *surat keterangan jalan* (or more commonly, *surat jalan*) to travel to most places outside of Jayapura (though this is rarely enforced except for very remote regions). This is easily obtained at the **police station** (Polresta; Jl Yani 11; ☻9am-3pm, Mon-Fri) in Jayapura. Take your passport, two passport photos, a photocopy of your passport pages showing your personal details and Indonesian visa, and a list of every place you intend to visit in Papua.

Sea

There are plenty of boats plying the waters around PNG, but very few are scheduled services to other countries.

Unless you are a Torres Strait Islander, it is illegal to island-hop across the string of Torres Strait Islands in Australian territory between Thursday Island (TI to locals) and PNG. You can exit Australia from TI, but you must go directly to PNG, usually Daru, where you can pass through immigration if you already have a visa.

Private Boats

PNG and the Solomons are popular stopping points for cruising yachts, either heading through Asia or the Pacific. Ports where you can clear immigration include Alotau, Daru, Kavieng, Kimbe, Lae, Lorengau, Madang, Misima Island, Port Moresby, Rabaul,

Samarai and Vanimo. You must get a visa before you arrive. See Noonsite (www.noonsite.com) for a full rundown.

Cruise Ships

The following companies offer luxury cruises that incorporate some of the PNG islands – usually those in the Milne Bay Province.

Aurora Expeditions (www.auroraexpeditions.com.au)

North Star Cruises (www.northstarcruises.com.au)

Coral Princess (www.coralexpeditions.com)

Tours

The major PNG-based inbound tour operators offer a wide variety of tours but prices are usually disconcertingly high. Smaller operators such as those based in Goroka (p107) are also worth checking out.

Eco-Tourism Melanesia (www.em.com.pg) Focuses on village-based tours and cultural, wildlife, birdwatching and trekking trips.

Melanesian Tourist Services (www.mtspng.com) Operates the high-end Madang Resort (incorporating Niugini Diving Adventures) and Kaliboboi Village, plus the live-aboard *Kalibobo Spirit*.

Niugini Holidays (www.nghols.com) Probably the biggest range of tours, from specialised family tours to surfing, fishing, diving, trekking, war-veterans tours and more.

Trans Niugini Tours (www.pngtours.com) Based in Mt Hagen, Trans Niugini operates several luxury lodges. There are general tours, wildlife tours, treks, cruises and tours of the cultural shows. The lodges are Tari's Ambua Lodge; the Sepik's Karawari Lodge and its boat the *Sepik Spirit*; Malolo Plantation Lodge north of Madang; Bensbach Wildlife Lodge and Lake Murray Lodge, both in the Western Province; and Mt Hagen's Rondon Ridge.

GETTING AROUND

Air

About 2000 airstrips have been cut out of the bush or into hill tops and coral islands during the last 80 years or so. Although less than a quarter of these airstrips are regularly used today, PNG is heavily reliant on air transport to connect its isolated and scattered population. It is worth remembering the following points when travelling by air around PNG:

➡ For lighter aircraft, the baggage limit is 16kg (but 20kg is usually accepted). Excess-baggage charges are reasonable but can add up.

➡ Some remote strips have no facilities, just a guy with a two-way radio who meets the flights, and at many of these remote strips you'll have to buy your ticket direct from the pilot – cash only.

➡ Outside the main centres (or when the phones lines are down) don't rely on being able to pay for anything by credit card.

➡ Unpredictable weather combined with mechanical problems and complex schedules can frequently lead to delays or cancellations.

Airlines in the Region

Local offices are listed on airline websites.

Air Niugini (☑327 3663; www.airniugini.com.pg) The major carrier in PNG operating larger planes to the larger centres.

PNG Air (☑7373 7100; www.pngair.com.pg) Formerly known as Airlines PNG, this is the main secondary airline in PNG with an extensive route map to major and minor airports across the country.

North Coast Aviation (☑472 1755; www.nca.com.pg) Covers remote destinations out of Lae.

Travel Air (☑7090 3887; www.travelairpng.com) The country's newest airline, with a rapidly expanding network.

Fares

Nobody pays the full fare for Air Niugini or PNG Air domestic flights. Both airlines have a number of different pricing tiers and each flight usually has a limited number of seats at discounted rates. Obviously the cheap seats are the first to go so book as early as possible to get the cheapest rate.

It's worth remembering that the cheaper fares are usually subject to all manner of restrictions (including nonrefundable cancellations or penalties for date changes). Take the time to read the fine print.

Boat

Boat Charter

Many dive operators charter their boats, some for extended cruises. Melanesian Travel Services (www.mtspng.com), owners of the Madang Resort Hotel, operates charters to the Sepik River and throughout the islands on the supersmart, 30m *Kalibobo Spirit*. Walindi Plantation Resort (www.walindi.com) operates the excellent MV *FeBrina* to access remote dive sites along the New Britain coast.

Cargo Boats

Sailing from one exotic locale to the next – via who-knows-where – on a slowly rolling freighter has a certain Joseph Conrad–style romance to it. While cargo boats generally don't take travellers, it's worth trying your luck. Lae on the north coast is the main shipping hub in PNG, and it's the best place to look; ask around the port to see what's going where. You'll almost always have more luck getting on a freighter by talking directly to the ship's captain (and perhaps investing in a few SP Lagers) rather than the office staff.

Passenger Boats

There are no passenger vessels linking the north and south coasts or any running along the south coast. Things are a little better on the northern coast and from the mainland to the island provinces with scheduled services offered by two companies. Chebu Shipping offers a dedicated ferry service (plus cargo), whereas Star Ships (aka Rabaul Shipping) vessels now carry primarily cargo and some passengers. Students are sometimes entitled to discounts.

Chebu Shipping (☑Lae 7198 7869) The MV *Chebu* is a dedicated passenger ferry with three classes of fare that plies the Solomon and Bismark seas from Lae (departing every Sunday at 11am) to Buka (arrives Wednesday), via Kimbe (arrives Monday) and Rabaul (arrives Tuesday). The return voyage departs Buka on Wednesday, Rabaul on Thursday and Kimbe on Friday.

At the time of writing, the Buka service was only fortnightly, with the ferry turning back from Rabaul to Kimbe and Lae, but keeping to the above schedule. Expect the schedule to change.

Star Ships (Rabaul Shipping; ☑in Lae 472 5699, in Rabaul 982 1071, in Wewak 856 1160; rabship@starships.com.pg) At the time of research, Star Ships connected Lae with Bialla in New Britain, occasionally stopping at Kimbe on the way, and occasionally going on to Rabaul, depending on cargo and passengers. The *Carlvados Queen* operated between Madang and Wewak (Sepik) or Madang and Wasu (Morobe), on a highly variable timetable. Star Ships only offered deck class (air-vented seats and berths) at the time of writing.

There are sometimes simple snack bars on board that might just be someone with soft drinks in a cooler and a carton of *kundu* (beef) crackers.

Small Boats

TRADE BOATS

Trade boats – small, wooden boats with thumping diesel engines – ply the coast, supplying trade stores and acting as ferries. They are irregular but if you're prepared to wait, they can get you to some off-the-track places. Don't expect comfort, bring your own food and make sure the operator is trustworthy before you commit yourself to a day or two aboard. If you're in a major centre, such as Alotau, ask around the port and at the big stores, which might have a set schedule for delivering supplies to the area's trade stores. Negotiate the fee before you leave.

BANANA BOATS

For shorter distances, there are dinghies with outboard motors, often known as speedies or banana boats. These are usually long fibreglass boats that leap through the waves and are bonejarringly uncomfortable. They operate in much the same way as regular PMVs, only leaving when full. Travellers are increasingly using these boats to get from Angoram (on the Sepik River) to Bogia (from where you can travel to Madang) and between Aitape and Vanimo.

Warning

Note, banana boats are no fun at all when the wind picks up, and the wind can pick up with little warning. People die reasonably frequently in open-sea banana-boat crossings and you will need to exercise common sense before boarding one. Don't contemplate a trip in rough weather or if the boat is dangerously overloaded. Remember that these boats usually do not carry life jackets or any kind of safety equipment.

Car & Motorcycle

Driving yourself around PNG is not really a viable way of travelling because the country has only a few roads – the Highlands (Okuk), Ramu and Sepik Hwys – that connect two or more places you might want to visit.

Driving Licence

Any valid overseas licence is OK for the first three months you're in PNG.

Hire

Four-wheel drives can be hired in most PNG cities, including on the islands, and in Lae and Port Moresby you can hire a plain old car. You must be 25 to hire a car and

---

THE 2012 FERRY DISASTER

On 2 February 2012, Rabaul Shipping's MV *Rabaul Queen* capsized and sank in rough seas as it travelled between Kimbe (New Britain) and Lae. Of the 350 passengers and 12 crew on board only 246 survived, although some passengers maintain the true fatality rate is far higher, and that the boat was carrying in excess of 500 people that day. Whatever the case, it is becoming clear that in addition to the bad weather and giant waves, overcrowding played a part in the tragedy.

Sea transport is a major communication lifeline in the PNG archipelago, and it is clear that there were many lessons to be learned through this tragedy. The national government and the new operators of the MV *Chebu*, which include the Autonomous Government of Bougainville, appear to have heeded the call for a safe replacement service.

have either a credit card or K2500 cash as a deposit.

Hiring anything will cost you an arm and probably both legs, and the rates are even higher when you add the per-kilometre charges, insurance and tax. For example, a compact car (the cheapest option) costs from K300 per day, plus K1 per kilometre, plus 10% VAT, plus any fee for personal insurance.

One-way rentals are available at locations along the Highlands (Okuk) Hwy but may be subject to one-way drop-off fees. The bigger companies have offices around PNG but you will also find a number of smaller agencies based at the major airports.

Avis (☑324 9400; www.avis. com.pg)

Budget (☑323 6244; www. budget.com.pg)

Hertz (☑325 4999; www. hertz.com.au/p/hire-a-car/ papua-new-guinea)

Travel-Car (☑Jacksons Airport 7091 3888)

Road Conditions

➡ Perhaps the most pertinent point about the roads in PNG is that there aren't many. Port Moresby, for example, is not linked by road to any other provincial capital except Kerema, and that road is subject to seasonal difficulties.

➡ The most important road is the Highlands (Okuk) Hwy, which runs from Lae to Lake Kopiago, via Goroka, Mt Hagen and Tari. Madang is also connected to it via the Ramu Hwy.

➡ Road conditions are variable, to say the least. Many are full of potholes and only passable by 4WD, and only then in the dry. Others are recently sealed, all-weather affairs. If you're planning on getting out of the towns, a 4WD is almost a necessity.

Road Hazards

Roads in PNG come with a range of hazards. There is the deterioration factor: many suffer from lack of maintenance. There's the wet-season factor: it rains, you get bogged. And then there's that one you can't do much about: the *raskol* (bandit) factor. Your chances of being held up are admittedly quite slim, but it's worth reading up on what to do if it happens to you (p236).

If you are involved in an accident in a crowded environment, don't stop, keep driving and report the accident at the nearest police station. This applies regardless of who was at fault or how serious the accident (whether you've run over a pig or hit a person). Tribal concepts of payback apply to car accidents. You may have insurance and you may be willing to pay, but the local citizenry may well prefer to take more immediate and satisfying action.

Road Rules

➡ Cars drive on the left side of the road.

➡ The speed limit is 60km/h in towns and 75km/h in the country.

➡ Seat belts must be worn by the driver and passengers.

Hitching

Hitching is an important mode of travelling in the region. The lack of scheduled transport means jumping onto a van, truck, canoe, freighter, plane – or whatever else is going your way – is a time-honoured way of getting around. You'll often be expected to pay the equivalent of a PMV fare. If your bag is light, it's also sometimes possible to hitch flights at small airports.

Keep in mind that hitching is never entirely safe in any country. Travellers who decide to hitch are taking a small but potentially serious

risk, and solo women should be extra careful. People who choose to hitch will be safer if they travel in pairs and let someone know where they are planning to go.

Taxi

Considering PNG's reputation for nocturnal danger, it's surprising there are not more taxis. Port Moresby and Alotau have plenty and there are two in Madang and another two Vanimo. That's it.

If you do manage to get a taxi you'll find most of them are complete clunkers – windscreens that look like road maps, broken seats and no radios or meters – you'll have to negotiate the fare before you get in.

PMV

PMV (public motor vehicle) is the generic term for any type of public transport, and wherever there are roads, there will be PMVs. Whether it's a dilapidated minibus, a truck with two facing wooden benches, a pick-up with no seats whatsoever but space in the tray, or any other means of transport (boats are also referred to as PMVs), the PMV is one of the keys to travelling cheaply in PNG. It's also one of the best ways to meet local people.

There's no real science to using PMVs; just turn up at the designated departure point and wait for it to fill up, although the following tips are worth keeping in mind.

➡ Many rural routes have only one service a day so ask around a day ahead for when and where it leaves (usually the local market).

➡ From small towns, PMVs often start out very early in the morning, drive to another (usually larger) town, then wait a couple of hours while the morning's passengers go to market before returning.

➡ Out of town you can assume that anything with lots of people in it is a rural PMV. If you want to get off before the end, just yell 'stop driver!'

➡ In most urban areas PMVs travel along a network of established routes. Stops are predetermined and are often indicated by a yellow pole or a crowd of waiting people; you can't just ask to be let off anywhere. The destination will be indicated by a sign inside the windscreen or called out by the driver's assistant in a machine-gun-style staccato.

➡ Market days (usually Friday and Saturday) are the best days for finding a ride.

➡ Most of the time, travelling in a PMV is perfectly safe; your fellow passengers will be most impressed you're with them and not in some expensive 4WD. There is, of course, a risk of robbery, especially on the Highlands (Okuk) Hwy. Lone women travellers are also at greater risk and should think twice about travelling by PMV. If you do, find a vehicle with women passengers and get a seat nearby.

➡ PMVs have a crew of two: the driver, who usually maintains an aloof distance from the passengers; and the conductor, who takes fares and copes with the rabble.

➡ Don't be surprised if you have to wait for your change; it'll come when the conductor gets the change sorted.

➡ For PMVs travelling along the Highlands (Okuk) Hwy and in other potentially bandit-prone areas, the driver may decide to delay departure to avoid night-time travel or to join a convoy if there has been recent *raskol* activity.

Language

After the national pidgins of Papua New Guinea and the Solomon Islands, English is the most widely understood language, but while it's quite common in the cities and large towns, in rural areas you'll need some basic pidgin in order to communicate. Luckily pidgins are fairly straightforward for English speakers to get a handle on.

TOK PISIN (PAPUA NEW GUINEA)

More than 800 languages are spoken in Papua New Guinea – a whopping 12% of the world's indigenous languages. Linguists divide these languages into 14 major groups. Austronesian languages are spoken by a sixth of the population and dominate the islands and the coastal areas. Enga is spoken by about 165,000 speakers in the Highlands region, and is the predominant spoken native language in Papua New Guinea. Kuanua has about 60,000 speakers.

In the early days of British New Guinea and then Australian Papua, the local language of the Port Moresby coastal area, Motu, evolved into Police Motu, and was spread through Papua by the native constabulary. It's still widely spoken in the southern Papuan part of Papua New Guinea.

Tok Pisin (or as it has also been called, New Guinea Pidgin English, Tok Boi, Neo-Melanesian) has its origins in the Pacific labour trade and shows influences of German.

WANT MORE?

For in-depth language information and handy phrases, check out Lonely Planet's *Pidgin Phrasebook*. You'll find it at **shop.lonelyplanet.com**, or you can buy Lonely Planet's iPhone phrasebooks at the Apple App Store.

It is now learned as a second language in most villages, while in the big towns it is becoming creolised (adopted as the first language). As the national language of independent Papua New Guinea, it is used regularly by more than two million speakers.

Tok Pisin is used in all areas of daily life, including the administration, education, churches and the media. It has been a written language since the 1920s, and although an official writing system exists, nonstandard spellings still abound.

Most Tok Pisin words are of English origin, but many words referring to local phenomena originate in local languages. Second-language Tok Pisin speakers are often influenced in their pronunciation and grammar by the conventions of their mother tongue.

Pronunciation

Note that *p* and *f* are virtually interchangeable in both spelling and pronunciation, as are *d* and *t*, *j* and *z*. The combination *kw* represents the English 'qu'. Vowels and vowel combinations are pronounced clearly, even when unstressed and at the end of a word, as follows: *a* as in 'art', *e* as in 'set', *i* as in 'sit', *o* as in 'lot', *u* as in 'put', *ai* as in 'aisle', *au* as the 'ou' in 'house' and *oi* as in 'boil'.

Basics

Hello.	*Gude.*
Goodbye.	*Lukim yu.*
Yes.	*Yes.*
No.	*Nogat.*
Please.	*Plis.*
Excuse me./Sorry.	*Sori.*
Thank you (very much).	*Tenkyu (tru).*
How are you?	*Yu stap gut?*
I'm well.	*Mi stap gut.*

What's your name?	Wanem nem bilong yu?
My name is ...	Nem bilong mi ...
Where are you from?	Ples bilong yu we?
I'm from ...	Ples bilong mi ...
What's your job?	Wanim kain wok bilong yu?
I'm (a/an) ...	Mi ...
I (don't) understand.	Mi (no) save.
More slowly, please.	Yu tok isi isi plis.
I need help.	Mi laikim sampela halp.

a little	liklik
big	bikpela
brother	brata
child	pikinini
man/woman	man/meri
relative	wantok
sister	susa

Accommodation

Do you have a single/double room?	Yu gat rum slip long wanpela/tupela man?
How much is it per night?	Em i kostim hamas long wanpela de?
Can I see the room?	Inap mi lukim rum pastaim?
I like this room.	Mi laikim (tru) dispela rum.
Is there a mosquito net?	I gat moskita net i stap?
Is there a bath /shower?	I gat rum waswas i stap?
Is there a laundry?	I gat rum bilong wasim (ol) klos?
Where's the toilet?	Haus pekpek i stap we?
I want to stay ... days.	Mi laik stap ... de.
I'd like to check out today/tomorrow.	Mi laik bai mi lusim hotel tede/tumora.

Food & Drink

Is the restaurant open/closed?	Haus kaikai i op/pas?
Do you have an English menu?	Yu got menyu long Tok Inglis?
Does this dish have meat?	I gat abus long dispela kaikai?

NUMBERS – TOK PISIN

1	wan
2	tu
3	tri
4	foa
5	faiv
6	sikis
7	seven
8	et
9	nain
10	ten
20	tupela ten
30	tripela ten
40	fopela ten
50	faivpela ten
60	sikispela ten
70	sevenpela ten
80	etpela ten
90	nainpela ten
100	wan handet

I don't eat beef/ pork/chicken/ dairy products.	Mi tambu long bulmakau/ pik/kakaruk/ susu samting.
I'd like...	Mi laikim...
The bill, please.	Mi laik peim kaikai bilong mi.
I enjoyed the meal.	Mi laikim tumas dispela kaikai.

Shopping & Services

I'd like to buy ...	Mi laik baim ...
How much is it?	Hamas long dispela?
What's that?	Wanem dispela?
I'm just looking.	Mi lukluk tasol.
That's very cheap.	Pe/Prais i daun (tru).
Is that your lowest price?	I gat seken prais?
I'll take it.	Bai mi kisim.

I'm looking for ...	Mi painim ...
a bank	haus mani/benk
the church	haus lotu
the hospital	haus sik
the market	maket/bung
the police	polis stesin

Time & Dates

What time is it?	*Wanem taim nau?*
It's (eight) o'clock.	*Em i (et) klok.*
morning	*moningtaim*
afternoon	*apinun*
evening (7pm–11pm)	*nait*
night (11pm–4am)	*biknait*
yesterday	*asde*
today	*tede*
tomorrow	*tumora*
Monday	*Mande*
Tuesday	*Tunde*
Wednesday	*Trinde*
Thursday	*Fonde*
Friday	*Fraide*
Saturday	*Sarere*
Sunday	*Sande*

Transport & Directions

Is transport available?	*I gat bas, teksi samting?*
How much is it to ... ?	*Em i hamas long ... ?*
How long is the journey?	*Hamas taim long go long ... ?*
I'd like a ... ticket.	*Mi laik baim tiket long ...*
one-way	*i go long tasol*
return	*go na i kambek*
What time does the ... arrive?	*Wanem taim ... i kamap?*
What time does the next ... leave?	*Long wanem taim neks ... i go?*
boat	*bot*
bus	*bas*
plane	*balus*
Where is ...?	*... i stap we?*
Can you draw a map?	*Inap yu wokim/droim map?*
Straight ahead.	*Stret.*
Turn left/right.	*Tanim lep/rait.*
How far is it?	*Em i longwe o nogat?*
behind	*bihain long*
in front of	*ai bilong*
near	*klostu*
far	*longwe*

PIJIN (SOLOMON ISLANDS)

Officially, there are 67 indigenous languages and about 30 dialects in the Solomon Islands. It is quite common for people from villages separated by only a few kilometres to speak mutually incomprehensible languages. As a result, the national language of the Solomons is Solomon Islands Pijin, or Pijin for short.

Early 19th-century sailors stimulated the evolution of Pijin. The recruitment of labour (including Solomon Islanders) from the 1860s to 1900s to work in mines, and in Oceanic canefields and plantations, spread the language all over the Pacific. By the 1930s Pijin was being spoken by missionaries in many areas, helping to spread it further. While English is now the official language of the administration, many government staff use Pijin in everyday conversation.

Pijin speakers use two versions. One is a simplified form used by islanders for the purpose of communication with their English-speaking employers. The second is the 'true' Pijin, which they use among themselves.

Pronunciation

Pijin pronunciation varies a lot because most speakers are influenced by the sounds of their own native languages. Pijin has five vowels, pronounced as follows: *a* as the 'a' in 'father', *e* as the 'e' in 'bet', *i* as the 'ee' in 'deet', *o* as the 'o' in 'gone' and *u* as the 'oo' in 'soon'. When two different vowels are joined, both vowels are pronounced. Doubled vowels have a longer vowel sound than single ones.

Basics

Hello.	*Halo.*
How are you?	*Hao?/Oraet nomoa?*
Fine.	*Oraet nomoa.*
Goodbye.	*Bae-bae.*
See you later.	*Lukim iu (bihaen).*
Yes./No.	*Ia./Nomoa.*
Excuse me.	*Ekskius plis.*
Thank you.	*Tanggio tumas.*
What's your name?	*Hu nao nem blong iu?*
My name is ...	*Nem blong mi ...*
Where are you from?	*Iu kam from wea?*
I'm from ...	*Mi kam from ...*
Say it again.	*Talem kam moa.*
Where's the toilet?	*Wea nao toelet?*
Help me!	*Iu mas helpem mi!*

NUMBERS – PIJIN

1	wanfala
2	tufala
3	trifala
4	fofala
5	faefala
6	sikisfala
7	sevenfala
8	eitfala
9	naenfala
10	tenfala
20	tuenti/tuande
30	teti/toti
40	foti
50	fifti
60	sikisti
70	seventi
80	eiti
90	naenti
100	handred

Food & Drink

I want to book a table (for four).	Mi laek fo bukim wanfala tebol (fo fofala).
What do you have on your menu for today?	Wanem nao iufala garem long lis fo kaikai tude?
What do you have to drink?	Watkaen dring nao iufala garem?
I want ...	Mi laekem ...
Do you have beer?	Waswe, iu eni bia?

Shopping & Services

Do you sell ...?	Waswe, iufala salem ...?
What's this?	Wanem nao diswan?
How much is this?	Hao mas nao diswan?
I want to buy this/that.	Mi laek baem diswan/datwan.
I don't want this/that.	Mi no wandem diswan/datwan.

Time & Dates

| What time is it? | Hemi wataem nao ia? |
| It's (one) o'clock. | Hemi (wan) klok. |

this morning	tude moning
this evening	tude ivining
yesterday	iestade/astade
today	tude
tomorrow	tumoro
Monday	Mande
Tuesday	Tiusde
Wednesday	Wenesde
Thursday	Tosde
Friday	Fraede
Saturday	Satade/Sarere
Sunday	Sande

Transport & Directions

I want to go to ...	Mi laek go long ...
How long will it take to get to ...?	Hao long nao bae hemi tekem fo kasem ...?
What does it cost to go to ...?	Hao mas nao fo go long ...?
Where can I buy a ticket for ...?	Wea nao mi save peim tiket fo tekem go long ...?
When does the ... leave?	Wataem nao ... hemi aot?
When will we arrive at ...?	Wataem nao bae iumi kasem ...?
Where is a/the ...?	Wea nao ...?
bus stop	bas stop
hospital	hospitol
market	maket
pharmacy	famasi
post office	pos ofis
Is it near/far?	Waswe, hemi kolsap/farawe?
How long would it take to walk?	Hao long nao bae hemi tekem fo wakabaot go?
It's near the ...	Hemi kolsap long ...
It's on the opposite/right/left side.	Hemi long narasaet/raetsaet/lefsaet.
Turn left/right here.	Tane lef/raet long hia.